COCKNEY REDS

COCKNEY REDS

The Story of
MANCHESTER UNITED'S
Southern Army

Robert Cleur
with Steve Little

Milo Books

Published in May 2019 by Milo Books

ISBN 978-1-908479-93-8

Typeset by e-type

Printed and bound in Great Britain by
Clays Ltd, Elcograf S.p.A.

www.milobooks.com

WHO ARE THE COCKNEY REDS?

'The Cockney Reds not only had numbers, they had some cracking lads who were as game as any. They were fighting before they set off, fighting at the game and fighting again when they got back'

Tony O'Neill, *Red Army General*

'Make no mistake, the Cockney Reds were not a secondhand firm, they also had numbers and for a long time they were the ones doing the business for United in London'

Paul Brittle and Danny Brown, *Villains*

'As a United fan, I am aware that a significant portion of our support comes from the London area and that over the years, the Cockney Reds have provided the boys with no end of intelligence and physical support in their quest for empire'

Ian Hough, *Perry Boys*

'The Cockney Reds were just as hardcore as any Manc'

Colin Blaney, author of *Grafter*s

'They are a game mob, but I don't understand why they don't just go down Millwall or West Ham'

Andy Nicholls, *Scally*

CONTENTS

PROLOGUE

Banana Bob. It could be the name of a children's TV character. It is a tag I have lived with for well over forty years, and came about in the early Seventies on a journey to a game in the north of England. I was travelling with a drunken load of United fans on one of the football special trains of the day. I made some lewd comment about the practical use of a banana, having seen us pass a Fyffes banana lorry on the adjacent M1 motorway. Someone shouted, 'Shut up, Banana Bob,' and that's how the moniker was born – or so I recall. But the memory plays many tricks. Throughout this book many of my fellow Cockney Reds will contribute their own comments and stories, and you will see that they don't always dovetail. That's the problem when you rely on fading memories – plus we did drink a fair bit in those days.

One good mate, Jimmy, known to all as 'The Ghost', has a different recollection. He has a far better memory than me, so I will stand corrected:

THE GHOST *I first met Bob during the 1969/70 season and we have been mates ever since. The Fyffes banana lorry travelling on the M1 alongside the train is a total myth. I remember very well what happened. It's true we were on a train and there was a lot of banter going on between Bob, me, and some other blokes. Bob was eating a banana while*

9

giving us all some serious lip, so one of the lads said, 'Shut up and eat your banana, Bob.' Everyone laughed and from that point on he was called Banana Bob.

So there we are. To be honest it's not been easy venturing off down this memory lane and dredging up facts from almost a lifetime ago, especially now that I qualify for a state pension. I am indebted to The Ghost and all those others who've helped me out – even when they contradict me!

This is not just my story. It is as much about the Cockney Reds as a group, and how they became the southern version of United's core Mancunian support. Yet it is impossible to write anything close to the whole story of the Cockneys and all the different firms. Many Mancs think any United fan with a southern accent is a Cockney Red, and even fans down south might think that too, but I know what a real Cockney Red is: one with a past, a reputation. Some who have, in recent years, joined me and my old mates from way back might think they are genuine Cockney Reds, but in my book they are not.

The southern United support stretches from as far as Northampton to Brighton, from Cheltenham to Southend, yet the core is from the suburbs of London: tough areas of the capital that produced numerous hard lads, many of them forming their own gangs, both in the football world and outside it. I can speak only as I find, and mainly about my own firm, which rose up in South London, but there are so many more, especially those in North London and the East End, who are as much part of the Cockney Reds as we are. I respect them for what they have done over the years. On match days we would all come together, with perhaps as many as a hundred that I knew personally from my area and hundreds more from elsewhere.

As a South London kid I was brought up alongside youths who supported Chelsea, Arsenal, Tottenham and Millwall, but by the autumn of the 1965, when I was fifteen and first went to watch them, Manchester United were once again the rising stars of British football. They had just won the First Division title, having already finished runners-up the season before. It just so happened that my first visit to a professional game involved United and I was sold on them from then on, mainly due to the fanatical support they had and the buzz from being in amongst their fans. My football journey had begun.

Up to that point in my life I had been a difficult child. My mother once said she thought I turned out the way I did because she must have dropped me on my head when I was a baby. As soon as I entered my teens I was hanging around with a biker gang and was never far from trouble. This was to set me up for the football violence to follow. I was also often at odds with the law away from the terraces. With the 1960s in full swing, life for us baby-boomer teenagers was changing. There was no war to fight and no more National Service, and rationing was a distant memory. Discipline in schools and outside was no longer as harsh as it had once been, and liberalism spread through society. People began to test and break the old barriers of behaviour, conformity and of social class. I am convinced this influenced crowd behaviour on the football terraces too. As the 1970s approached, violence in and around grounds became a national concern. I was to be a leader in this: a hooligan, a thug, a criminal even, and not just at football matches.

I became a leading figure in the Cockney Reds as we grew in number and influence, a 'face' other clubs' firms came to respect. I am not glorifying what we did back in the day, but what happened off the pitch in football is as big a story as what happened on it. The 'English disease' of football hooliganism was to become front-page news, and eventually stirred Her Majesty's Government to get tough in the Thatcher years, when tragedies on the terraces and beyond added to the stigma surrounding our national game. This story will reflect on that and the many unsavoury incidents many of us perhaps should not now be proud of, yet in some ways still are. It is as much a reflection of what society was like in those dark days, when the conduct of the police at games was often as brutal and arbitrary as that of the fans, and added to the general air of tension and violence. It was a world away from the well-controlled and professionally monitored policing of big games today.

Many of us Cockney Reds come from similar backgrounds, and some of those old mates of mine have gone on to become very successful, with thriving careers, driving quality cars and staying in five-star hotels when they follow the team. It has not been so easy for me, and remains tough as I approach my seventieth birthday with a dodgy back and type-two diabetes, though I still enjoy work and will continue with it. Whatever our changes in circumstance, I am proud that I still have all those mates I made through following the Reds, and we remain close.

Looking back over a misspent life raises some awkward emotions. I have been arrested countless times, served several spells at Her Majesty's pleasure and even spent a period in a Spanish jail. Sometimes I wonder how different my time could have been. But once you are seen by your peers as a 'somebody', in whatever you do, you tend to play up to that image, especially when you are young and impressionable. Perhaps I should repent now that I am an old boy. Yet I have to say honestly that the fire still burns inside, just below the surface. Even in recent times that bile and aggression has occasionally spilled over. Perhaps I am still trying to live up to the so-called legend. This book might even add to that, although I hope that the humour and friendship comes through too. I have had to change some names to protect the guilty and even the innocent – and myself, on occasion. Anyway, here it is, warts and all: the story of Banana Bob and my part in the Cockney Reds.

CHAPTER 1

THE MAKING OF A HOOLIGAN

I was born in Calcutta, India, of all places. Dad had been posted overseas with the army, and remained there after demob to become a civil servant, working for His Majesty's Customs in what up until 1948 was a colony of the British Empire. By the time I arrived, in 1950, we had returned the country to the Indian people to govern themselves, but there was a handover period and Dad had to stay on, so we didn't come home for a few years, by which time I had a sister. Dad had a French connection way back – hence my unusual surname – and Mum was British, with Scottish blood and a little Portuguese. So you might say I'm a bit of a mongrel. But Indian? No.

Mum, a nurse, met Dad whilst working in India. She was a kindly soul and I remained quite close to her, as kids do. Dad was always working and so a bit aloof and took little active interest in my upbringing, at least not until I got myself into serious trouble, when he really did help me out and showed a different side to his character. Mum was staunch Catholic, although Dad was not, and my sister and I were brought up in that religion. Dad was a fine tennis player, winning many cups and trophies, and he did take me along to watch and give the game a go, but I never took to it. On returning to the UK, he worked for London Transport. That connection came in handy later when I was old enough to go off on my own to watch football games, as I could use the family pass for free travel into London from our Surrey home, although trips to places further afield like Manchester remained too costly for a long time.

I grew up in a nice terraced house in a pleasant, middle-class part of Wimbledon; no inner-city slum and deprived background for me. In the early Sixties we moved to the small town of New Malden, which was historically part of Surrey but latterly became South-west London. With Mum being a nurse, we started taking in some elderly lodgers, whom she looked after, and this set her off into a different sort of health care as years went by.

From the time I started school, at the age of five, I was defiant and unmanageable. I had no attention span and must have been a pain to the teachers. Discipline at home was strict, no-nonsense and based on religious principles, and my unruliness was clamped down upon quite severely. Exactly where my wild streak came from, Lord only knows – it certainly wasn't from my parents, and my sister was as pleasant and obedient a child as you could wish to meet. I once read somewhere that the life characteristics of a person are mainly formed in their first five years of life. In me that is very true: I was a rebel with a hint of nastiness, even then. I went on to think school a total waste of time.

When I was eight, I was packed off to a Catholic school, St Joseph's College, in Beulah Hill, Upper Norwood, where I was to mainly stay until I was sixteen. At thirteen, I was made to board there for a term, then had to repeat the experience for another term in a later year. I see now my parents thought it might improve my behaviour. It didn't – it actually made me worse. The school was not some place at the other end of the country, being only a short distance from where

I lived, but it was horrible. It was all boys and very strict. No doubt my parents wanted the rebelliousness knocked out of me. Certainly the priests and the lay teachers were not averse to beating our bare arses for relatively minor offences and some boys were possibly abused in other ways. I felt picked on by the staff, which did not bring the best out of me. I enjoyed art and woodwork but couldn't see the point of subjects like chemistry and Latin, although I heard the latter every week as an altar boy at church. I did have a chance to relieve my frustrations through sport, playing rugby for the school and trying cross-country and gymnastics, which I enjoyed.

I went through my teens in the 'C' stream. We were an unruly lot. The teachers eventually gave up on me and I was told by the head of discipline, Brother Solomon, that I would end up in prison. Like his biblical namesake, he was wise enough to see that. I was at constant war with the staff and against strictness in all its forms, from lessons and homework to the uniform rules that decreed that we had to wear caps up until the fifth senior year. Most boys just knuckled down and gained from the excellence this top school had to offer, but I believed then that it had failed me. Now I see that I was the one at fault.

I would take issue then with anyone who wanted it. I had running battles with boys in the year above me and clashed with one in particular several times. Suspension and expulsion were constantly threatened, and in truth my behaviour was appalling, but slowly I began to feel I was somebody. I developed a reputation, and other boys sort of looked up to me. The more the staff at school abused me, one way or another, the worse I became. It is not surprising I later ended up a football hooligan and in constant trouble with the Law. Strangely enough, I never played football.

* * *

Saturday, September 25, 1965. My first match. A mate had invited me along to Highbury to see Arsenal play Manchester United, and from the moment two excited fifteen-years-olds emerged from the tube station near to the ground, I was overwhelmed by the intensity and excitement. We joined a massed crowd of 57,000 queuing at the turnstiles and ended up behind one of the goals, squashed, swaying and tumbling in a chanting, baying mob of United supporters, interspersed with a few Arsenal. The home fans begrudgingly moved to one side of the terrace for their own safety and the police formed a line between the two, but sometimes that line was broken and fighting broke out. It hooked me like a drug. United lost 4–2 (Johnny Aston and Bobby Charlton scored) but the result was irrelevant. I was caught up in this atmosphere of pride, hope, hate, anger and excitement – everything about the afternoon made an impression on me and no doubt appealed to my rejection of authority. I knew this was for me. United were my team from that day on, and whenever they were in London, I would be there.

The early Sixties was also the time of the Mods and rockers. I was firmly in the rocker camp, with a quiff like Elvis, wearing leathers and hanging around older blokes with motorbikes. I would have loved to experience those pitched battles between the two groups in 1964 at resorts like Clacton, Margate, Broadstairs and Brighton, but was a bit too young to attend. Perhaps it was just as well, as I would almost certainly have got into trouble. In fact by 1966 my parents had all but given up on me. I was about to leave school with one O-level, in art, and was out of control. I allowed myself to be sucked into the biker group, which was to lead me into all sorts of confrontations, not just with Mods but also with other biker gangs.

We were part of a fledgling Hells Angels crowd from the Sutton/Carshalton/ Mitcham locality and got involved with others from the area who were older and into biking, although they did not have a name for their group. We were excited to be accepted by them even though I was not old enough to have a motorbike myself, although I desperately wanted one. Fortunately getting a lift around was easy enough. By sixteen I was an accepted member of the Sutton bikers, who regularly met up with other groups at a café in Morden, near what is now an industrial estate. At weekends certain parts of Surrey became focal points for the bikers, not least Box Hill, a favourite haunt overlooking the North Downs. We also met at another coffee shop in Morden, rather than in pubs, as we were not yet into alcohol. Various like-minded groups would congregate, and we might be anything up to two hundred-strong at times. We would all head off down to Margate or somewhere similar on a weekend, which often ended up in a fight. The Ace café on the North Circular Road, in London, the famous home of teddy boys, greasers and rockers, was another popular meeting spot. Everyone respected its history and I saw little trouble there. The same can't be said of another café near Chelsea Bridge, where some sort of row was always brewing, amid a constant atmosphere of simmering tension and intimidation, usually resulting in a standoff or full-blown brawl.

British motorbikes were our first choice and by the time I was eighteen I had a 650 Triumph. By then we were an established and recognised Hells Angel chapter, based in Kent. Violence was never far away and could occur at any time, unlike at the football, which was just once a week at best. We hated the Mods, their music, their hair, their attitude, and took them on whenever we came across them. Inevitably, the coppers took an interest in us. The country had been shaken by those riots of 1964 and the police were under pressure to do something about it. They became intent on clamping down on any gathering of Mods or rockers. Yet the more they got involved, the more dangerous we seemed to become, and this, I'm convinced, set off the gang culture that was eventually to spread into football. As the Sixties wore on the Mods and rockers waned and football became the outlet for those who craved the excitement we got from our gangs. Violence moved to football grounds, and the police failed to grasp what was happening or to control it. Gangs began to form around the bigger clubs in particular. I saw this first hand watching United towards the end of the decade: the police adopted a lightweight approach, and it was not until the Eighties that they became more heavy-handed. It also seemed that the changes the Swinging Sixties brought to society were spreading to all areas, including the national game.

Away from the football, I encountered what we then called 'aggro' on a daily basis. People today may find it hard to believe but there was trouble all the time. While Saturday was for football, with perhaps a midweek game as well, other days saw just as much fighting and petty crime. There was a boom in nightclubs around this time, rarely fashionable places but often just a room above a pub, or a tarted-up civic hall. This meant more places to hang out – and for trouble to start. I was drawn into another group of mates, away from the football and biker scene, who were involved nicking motorbikes and cars. It did not take much to get us into a fight, mostly over 'protecting' our territory, which was the Sutton area. We were known as 'the Old Sutton' even though most were barely into their twenties.

I became a name, with a reputation. Just like at school, I thought I was someone others could look up to: an out-of-control youth who commanded respect and could dish out a hiding. If something, or more likely someone, needed sorting, I would go to any lengths to do so. I could also rely on mates in both the Hells Angels and Old Sutton to back me, and they became like family. By my late teens I was on a slippery slope. Put bluntly, I was a thug, aggressive and nasty, reacting even if someone just looked at me the wrong way. Usually I would be the first into a fight and certainly I would be in there to finish it. Perhaps that Catholic upbringing left some morality in me, as I was hardly ever tooled-up, relying on my feet, fists and head. I was also never seriously into drugs, nor a heavy drinker at first. Thankfully we never went *too* far.

Nevertheless, in 1970 I appeared at the Central Criminal Court in the City of London, the historic Old Bailey. Twelve of us from the biker gang were up on a series of related charges. Mine was causing an affray, then considered a more serious charge than today. One of our blokes, a nutter, had whacked a copper and broken his leg, and Old Bill were not impressed, which was perhaps why we were sent to such an imposing court.

It had all started this Friday night in 1969 in Rose Hill, Sutton, not far from where I was living. The Rose pub was a regular flashpoint, a place where rival groups of lads would often mix. On this particular evening we had met up in another pub nearby before moving on and parking in a side road up from the Rose. It was a smart avenue with trees along a central reservation, dimly lit by two lampposts. We wanted to check if some people we had previously clashed with were in the vicinity of the pub, and sent out some scouts to look for them while the rest of us milled about in the road next to the cars. It was quiet, with only an occasional vehicle passing by. Just as our lads returned to give us an update, several unmarked vans arrived and pulled up beside us. Out poured a number of blokes, wielding sticks, coshes and other weapons.

They weren't the mob we had been expecting and I didn't recognise any of them, but anyway they set about us.

The din seemed to wake the neighbourhood. Front doors opened and outside lights went on as the locals came out to investigate the commotion. Some hurriedly went back indoors, but others stayed in small groups to watch the unfolding scene. I hesitated on the edge of it all, not sure what was really going on. I later learned that our recent exploits had alerted the coppers and they were watching the first pub we had been in. They had seen us leave there and allowed us five minutes to get to the Rose and perhaps start something before making their arrival. Our attackers were plain-clothes coppers, tooled up and mob-handed.

My mates fought back and a few from both sides were put on the floor. I remained on the fringes, and once I realised our assailants were coppers, I knew this was one we couldn't win, and walked off down the road to make my way home. Some ten minutes later, two cops in a van caught up with me and grabbed me. They started claiming, falsely, that I had done all kinds of things. In the end they settled on claiming that my studded leather belt was an offensive weapon and that I had used it during the fight, which was totally untrue. I have been guilty of a few things in my life but this time I was innocent.

I was granted bail and the case took nearly a year to reach court. Dad hired a costly lawyer, who argued my case skilfully at trial, which was just as well, as the Old Bill told lie after lie. They even produced the pickaxe handles they had used and claimed they were *our* weapons. Even my dad agreed that we were all being fitted up, despite being at first appalled about my involvement. The bloke who broke the copper's leg did get put away for three years, and a couple of others got a few months. I was also found guilty, but came away with a conditional discharge. The old judge clearly had some inkling that whilst we were hardly innocents, this was something of a fit-up by Old Bill. In those days juries believed whatever coppers said, and this one largely ignored our defence, but the judge treated most of us leniently with his sentencing.

This was my first major run-in with the cops but by no means the last. By the late Sixties I had become a bit of a face to the local police, following a few minor offences like driving while disqualified and supposedly not giving way to a pedestrian on a crossing along the Embankment in London. Plenty had gone on in the twelve months between my arrest and appearing at the Bailey. One of our regular outings to the seaside had led to a set-to with some skinheads at Brighton, with us on the stony beach and them on the promenade. They outnumbered us and surprised us by running down a ramp we hadn't seen and stoning us, so we took flight. Some time later, the leader of our gang said to me, 'You say you're a hard case, but you chickened out in Brighton.' I was sorely tempted to chin him, but instead just told him to, 'Fuck off.' That was it for me; I left the bikers behind and joined a gang of local lads instead. They were up for anything.

I also became involved in the social scene around where I lived. Sutton was a lively place at night, with the Red Lion and Whistle Stop pubs crowded even during the week. Gang fights often broke out, although these were rarely football-related: terrace rivalries between the locals were set aside except on match days. I was good mates with plenty of Palace and Chelsea lads, which was how their firms came to know me at matches. Gangs from the local estates were into all sorts of petty crime. Apart from the inevitable brawls, we would break into shops to nick and sell stuff, steal from cars and sometimes hot-wire them. When I didn't have any work on, I would sign on the dole.

By my early twenties I was also more heavily into drink. Almost every night there was something going on around Sutton, Carshalton and, in particular, Croydon, and driving while drunk was commonplace. After the pubs closed, Scamps in Sutton was a popular nightclub where lots of naughty people gathered. Quite a few top-notch villains frequented the place and if you wanted to move up a league into big-time crime, this was where you could. I did not, but that's not to say I was not involved in plenty of illegality. I knocked around with Dave T, a very well-known face from Mitcham and one of my early heroes (and a bad influence, some might say). We were constantly in scrapes, often ordering drinks and not paying or leaning over the bar and nicking bottles when the staff had their backs turned.

One night at the venue's sister club – also called Scamps – in Croydon, we found that the owners had hired a new group of bouncers, who took it upon themselves to try to sort us out. In the past we had barged our way in, never paying and generally taking liberties. This time the bouncers grabbed me and Dave and threw us out of the door so quickly that our friends inside did not see it, otherwise all hell would have broken loose. In the process I was glassed on the back of the head, which bled heavily. I ended up driving to the Roundshaw estate in Wallington to a mate's house. People there tried to persuade me to get treatment but all I wanted was to return for revenge. They could see I was losing a lot of blood and eventually dragged me off to hospital, saying they would sort out matters at the club – and when they said that, they meant it. Later I learnt they did go back that night and it was indeed 'sorted': I ended up with a load of stitches but the bouncers ended up in intensive care, my mates using baseball bats and carpet knives to attack them as they left the club for home.

The St Helier Arms was another tasty local pub frequented by many hardcases. It saw regular glassings and stabbings, which in turn led to serious injuries and arrests and prison sentences for those responsible. Years later, in the Nineties, it gained infamy when some punter was shot, decapitated and had his hands cut off in a gang-related attack. I wasn't there that night, although some of my mates were; to a man they told Old Bill they were in the toilet at the time and saw nothing – it must have been bloody crowded in there. So this was not quite the tranquil Surrey some might imagine.

We would go anywhere if we heard of a lively night on offer. The Croydon Suite (later Sinatras) nightclub was another favourite haunt, as was the Orchid in Purley. We would arrive mob-handed by car or train, usually in our various groups from Sutton, Carshalton and elsewhere, some-times up to two hundred-strong in total. Often we came up against another tough group from Croydon, a mix of white and black lads, who were known for some reason as 'the Bangholes'. Once 'The Liquidator' reggae song started up there would be a few football chants and then it would kick off. Old Bill would often come into the club with German Shepherd dogs to stop the trouble and escort us outside, but the fighting would continue in the road between the club and West Croydon station. It was like being at a game, with skir-mishes breaking out among various groups before we were rounded up, escorted to the station and put on a train. On some nights there would be hundreds of us out in these clubs, and the mayhem would spread far and wide. In December 1971 the police pulled me in after the latest in a series of such incidents and told me in no uncertain terms that I was persona non grata, and if seen anywhere near Croydon centre, my mates and I would be unceremoniously nicked – on whatever charge they could find.

Gate-crashing parties was another favourite pastime, whenever we heard about one on the grapevine. Sometimes six or seven carloads of us would turn up. If we got in, great; if turned away, it led to a mass punch-up with whoever was there that we didn't like. After being barred from one such party, we ended up around midnight at a hot dog stall by the clock tower in Epsom High Street. I exchanged words with a guy I knew, but nothing came of it, and as there were not many hostile locals about to pick a row with, we decided to head back in cars to the Sutton area. I was in the back of one with a girlfriend while my two mates were in the front. As we drove through Carshalton two cars started chasing us. We thought it might be someone from Epsom who had followed us, so I told the driver to go to the St Helier Arms, where I knew we would find backup. But the driver heard a bell ringing, which cop cars had at that time, and insisted we stop.

It was indeed Old Bill. They arrested us and took us to Sutton nick, where they asked where we had been that evening. Around the time I had first left the biker group, there had been an ongoing local war between different factions from Sutton/ Carshalton and the Epsom area. It transpired that someone had been glassed in an Epsom pub called the Drift Bridge and had subsequently died. Being well known to the police, and having been in Epsom that evening, I was a suspect. They questioned me for hours. I denied everything and was eventually released in the morning when it was clear I had not been at the scene. It was an example of how a fight could turn into a fatality in the blink of an eye, but I didn't heed the warning.

While I was sometimes in work and sometimes not, I went out most nights, and needed money to pay for it. To earn some cash on the side, I helped some mates who had a contract to renovate a posh house up West London. They had a key to get in, and came up with the idea of robbing the place while the family was out and making it look like a break-in. There was a short window of opportunity when the wife took the kids to school around nine in the morning, with her old man at work. There was no nanny or grandparents living there, so it would be a doddle. My mates needed a driver to look after their car in what was a busy area with limited parking, so they asked me and I agreed. Twice we went to do the job but were held up in traffic and missed the time slot. When we finally did arrive on time, one of the lads phoned the house to check if anyone was in and got no reply. I dropped the two lads off and parked up to wait.

They got into the house, only to find an old man up a ladder painting the wall. They didn't know what to do, and considered simply tying him up and carrying on, but that would have been an altogether more serious offence. Instead they turned around, crept out without him knowing and legged it back to the car for me to drive them home. Weeks later they went back without me and did the necessary. One of these lads went on to do an awful lot of bird but made a huge amount out of his thieving. He is now dead, but I still see his brother occasionally.

My night-time life was just as likely to get me into bother. One night in Scamps I was with my best-man-to-be, John, and his brother, Tommy – two hard lads who had been brought up in a children's home in Banstead – when we chased four blokes who had given us some lip. The blokes ran down the stairs and out into the street, where they went to a car around the corner and opened the boot. They pulled out a variety of weapons, including those kung fu sticks attached with a chain. I backed off while John and Tommy ran back through the club doorway to an office where they knew the bouncers kept some baseball bats. Returning tooled-up, they advanced towards the four blokes, who turned and jumped into their car. It wouldn't start. I picked up a rock and hurled it through the windscreen, showering them with glass. Luckily for them the ignition fired up and they sped off, leaving us to return to the club. They never came back to bother us again.

Such fights rarely had anything to do with football, although occasionally we would come across some mouthy fan who would piss us off and need sorting out. One was a Chelsea gobshite we met in the Red Lion in Sutton. There was pool table in the back room and me and this Chelsea twat got into an argument during which he threatened me with his cue. I held back and told the bloke to wise up, but only because I was in my best white trousers and trainers and didn't want to mess them up. Instead I went home, changed into my jeans and Doc Martens, returned to the pub and called for the bloke to come outside. He refused, so some of my mates dragged him into the street. Before I could get at him, he managed to break free and run off to a cab office over the road, where the people locked him in. I shouted threats and banged on the door, and was close to smashing it down when I heard wailing sirens heading my way. I called it off and went home – he could wait until another day.

Similar events happened all the time. Violence was a drug to me, and I was also out drinking most nights. It got to the stage where I decided to cut back on the booze and even started to avoid fights, partly because I was finding plenty of female company to occupy me and partly to avoid driving whilst drunk. I was also banned from quite a few venues, including Scamps – although perversely they would hire me to work there when they were short of doormen, as they knew I could handle myself. I moved through a succession of girlfriends, all attractive and fun to be with. I would like to think I treated them well. They might have known what I was up to but made no attempt to change me, and I was a different person when with them – just as I am today with my wife and family.

Looking back I do regret some of the nonsense, but it was my life, the way I was – and things were to get far worse through the Seventies, the golden age of football hooliganism. I already had this grounding in non-football violence, and it was to boil over into something even worse. Was it my experience at that boarding school that set me on the wrong path, or was it a home life with very little fatherly advice or encouragement? Or was it in me even before I started school? Did I want to be the exact opposite of my Dad? Was that visit to Highbury in 1965 my first hit of an exciting, addictive drug? A mind doctor would have a field day with all this. Whatever the cause, I was about to be at the forefront of an era of violence and mayhem.

CHAPTER 2

THE RISE OF THE COCKNEY REDS

How far do we have to go back to find the start of the modern hooligan age? I have mentioned my first experience at Highbury, when the atmosphere was threatening rather than outright violent. Some Cockney Reds who go back even further than me recall a gentler, less tribal era. One of them was at the 1964 FA Cup semi-final between Man United and West Ham:

I was only fifteen and badly wanted to go to this game. Just to show how different things were then, I managed to get a ticket and a place on the West Ham train special taking thousands up to the game. It was all very well behaved. I was with a group of West Ham who were all in their thirties and they sort of protected me and made sure I was OK. I even stood amongst the West Ham, and celebrated with a few other Man United nearby when Denis Law scored for us. No-one around us seemed to be at all bothered. Mind you we were 2–0 down at the time, and went on to lose 3–1.

Compare that experience, where rival fans mixed without trouble, to the enforced segregation by the end of the decade.

London boys were by then flocking to Manchester United games, but the name 'Cockney Reds' did not stick until the early Seventies. We would often rock up at games that did not involve United, particularly if they involved teams we didn't like, just for the trouble. One was in January 1970, when my local club, non-league Sutton United, were drawn at home to Leeds United in the FA Cup. Leeds were in their pomp, the reigning First Division champions, and before the game all the local hooligans, football and non-football, were up for having a pop at them.

The little Gander Green Lane ground was filled to the rafters to see the mighty Leeds, under Don Revie, strut their stuff and run out 6–0 winners. But for me and my mates, including my pal 'The Ghost', the football was a sideshow. We thought Leeds United were an arrogant lot, dirty and sly, with take-no-prisoners thugs like Norman Hunter. The poor reputation of their players was matched by their supporters; Leeds were disliked by all and sundry. We regarded them as cocky northern bastards who thought they owned everywhere they went. Well, we saw to them that day.

It was easy to get into the Leeds end at little Sutton, with or without a ticket, especially as we wore no colours and our London accents confused everyone. Their fans seemed confused by us and not quite so cocky when they found us mingling with them. At the end my little firm headed straight out of the ground to ambush any Leeds walking back to either West Sutton station nearby or Sutton's main station. It turned out they had all come by coach and were parked in a different direction, at the top of Collingwood Park, to the north. It didn't matter, as other local groups lay in wait and attacked them around the fringes of the park. Pitched battles broke out and missiles were hurled at the coaches as the Leeds fans hurried on board. They left a few injured behind, to be carted away by ambulance to St Helier Hospital. By the time I had made my way to the scene of the fighting, it was all over. We saw it as a total victory: Leeds might have won 6–0 but they met their match off the field, and not for the last time.

This was the first time I had seen such a mix of yobs looking for the opposition. It was not just Man United fans but gangs off the estates, from various pubs and from other clubs: Crystal Palace, Chelsea, Brighton and more. The reputation Leeds were building made them a target and, in hindsight, I feel this game was a watershed moment in the growing hooliganism at football. Many lads were so excited by their day at Sutton that they went on to join our ranks as time went on, strengthening the violent 'firm' we had become.

As a large and growing group, we London-based Reds began to play a major role in the violence now attached to football, and within that group I began to make my name as someone who was handy in a fight. At that time our unlikely leader was a bloke called Snowy, a huge man-mountain from Ewell, near Epsom, who looked like a hillbilly and turned up for every game in the same donkey jacket. He was a loner, older than us but still not much more than mid-twenties. He always had two big bottles of pop and a bag of sandwiches his mum had given him, and looked very little like a hero – but he was to us. He stood out in a crowd, and despite his appearance he was a proper hardcase. I call him our leader, but he didn't really stand at the front of us and carry the fight, like I and others were to do later. Instead he would simply always be there, a formidable presence, and we would scurry to join him because the opposition would not want to mess with him when a fight broke out. Whether on the train to matches, or at Euston concourse surrounded by rival fans, he just stood out. Over time he eventually drifted away – perhaps he found a woman, but we never found out. Rumour was that he died a few years later.

THE GHOST *Snowy was the main man by 1970 but Bob soon took over as our top player. It was I suppose a natural progression for Bob, especially as the violence became more widespread and heavy. If Tony O'Neill was to become the Red Army General, then Bob was in time his equal in the Cockney Reds.*

I did not see myself as a natural leader, but I became a face other firms began to recognise and respect. If I was the leader, then The Ghost was always at my shoulder. An imposing figure – tall, tough, uncompromising, violent – he frightened even some of our own boys at times, and if he told you to do something you bloody well did. He would pick a fight with anyone. To this day he remains the same and is not someone you would want to cross. He started supporting United in the late Sixties, and one of his first games was a Watney Cup match at Reading's old Elm Park ground. It became his baptism, and a welcome to the group that was to become the Cockney Reds:

THE GHOST *We won 3–2 and this was when the famous hooligan chant started: 'A-G, A-G-R, A-G-R-O, AGGRO!' It became a sign to pile in, like a war cry. I was outside the ground, with thousands trying to get in, when a milk float came by. Now how stupid can you be to drive into us lot! Both full and empty bottles flew everywhere and the poor old milkman just ran off. People were hit and windows to the surrounding houses were smashed, with glass all over the road. In the ground we were surprised to find a strong-looking Reading mob. We soon found out that they were actually a hundred or more Chelsea on a day out. I* *had not seen anything like it before as the whole of one end charged towards the pitch and spilled onto it, shouting 'A-G, A-G-R ... ' As a teenager caught up in all of this, I was sold from then on.*

We soon started travelling to games in a large group, normally after meeting first at Euston Station. I quickly teamed up with two South London hardcases, Tooting Steve and Griff from Mitcham. Tooting Steve would always stand by you, and would steam into anyone. Snowy, once our unofficial leader, continued to tag along but was seen at fewer and fewer games. For a while two handy lads called Clank and Choc, from Dartford, Kent, were also prominent. Add in The Ghost and we became a team feared by all and fearful of none, causing countless incidents of violence.

Griff, unlike the rest of us, always had a knife and was not afraid to use it. He was stocky in build, strong and aggressive – some said evil – and in the Eighties would serve a three-stretch for stabbing his partner's bit-on-the-side. He was known for thrusting his knife into the arses of his victims – painful but not life-threatening – and it became a kind of trademark. We accepted him then for what he was, but in more recent times he was sent to prison for a crime that even we couldn't stomach, and we haven't seen him since.

Later my great mate Joe was to come along as a major face, by which time the Cockney Reds were a recognised force. He would be as much a lieutenant alongside me as The Ghost was. Joe lived on the Totterdown Fields Estate in Tooting, built before World War One as a 'cottage' estate of council-owned properties to provide rented homes for those who previously had lived in run-down areas of inner London. Where he lived were nice houses, but by the Seventies other parts of the estate were plagued by flourishing street gangs. Petty crime, such as stealing, breaking and entering and even knife fights, was commonplace and particular gangs controlled certain areas. Joe was sucked into this. I was raised in, I suppose, a more middle-class area of privately-owned houses, yet I would actually have loved to be a part of what Joe had, a taste of that American ghetto style we saw in films such as *West Side Story*. As the years have passed Joe has prospered and runs a thriving family business, lives in a fine home, drives top-of-the-range motors and holidays all round the world – he even has membership access to the posh enclosure at Royal Ascot. But when he was younger his firm was quite a force, felt even in the West End of London.

JOE *Our young mob out of Tooting sort of ran parts of the West End in the early Seventies, when I was about sixteen. We would travel up from Tooting Broadway on the Underground and get off at Leicester Square or Charing Cross – never paid – and then terrorise the streets around Soho. The Maltese ran that area then; controlling the pimps and prostitutes. We would loiter in doorways and at street corners, sometimes as many as twenty-five of us, a threat to punters looking for girls. This upset the Maltese but they didn't want to take us on so instead would pay us off. I could pick up more in one evening that way than my normal week's wage, although in return the Maltese would expect us to stay away completely. But we would return after a few weeks and start over again.*

We didn't always get our own way, as other gangs tried to muscle in on our little scheme. One in particular were the Mile End crew, from the East End, who already ran something similar to us nearby and wanted to expand onto our turf. It was the culture of that time. Many were West Ham fans, although later, when I knew their main football faces, I didn't spot any from that time. We ended up having a big fight with Mile End just off Trafalgar Square. Knives were pulled and there were a couple of stabbings. We were outnumbered and were eventually forced to retreat back down the tube. They then sent a message to us saying that, as we had stabbed one of them, they were coming down to Tooting to wipe us out.

They kept their word, arriving in force some weeks later at Tooting Broadway station; there must have been over two hundred of them. They looked like something from a war film as they lined up across the road from an amusement arcade called Lots of Fun, where about fifty of us were hanging out. It should have put the fear of God into us, but we had been warned they were coming that night by a Tooting girl who was going out with one of them. As a result we were able to tool up with our usual knives. We also had an old Luger stashed away behind the cistern in the toilet of the arcade. We would occasionally bring this out as a threat in extreme circumstances, although I can never recall it being fired and I'm not sure it actually worked, or if we had any ammunition.

Only a few of us were what you would call football hooligans, the rest were local troublemakers. Also with us inside the arcade were a large group of local black lads, who asked what was going on. We told them this crew was down to serve us up. 'That ain't happening,' our West Indian mates said. There were another fifty of them, and together we gave the Mile End mob the shock of their lives – they thought they would meet only token resistance. They had also brought a lot of what I would call dead wood, lads who just wanted to make a show and were no use in a proper ruck. We tore into them and they quickly ran. We caught some and stripped them of their clothes, and *they were well-turned-out bunch, with sheepskin coats, Crombies and the like.*

That was the culture of the time. The tear-ups were as bad outside of football as in it. After all, football was only for that one day of the week. It simply gave me the opportunity to continue the sort of mayhem I was involved in for the other six days. The difference at football was that there you were in a much larger mob and it was easier to lose yourself in the crowd, hence there was less chance of the police spotting you.

So it was not just me who was involved with this sort of thing, we all were in our different ways and in different circumstances. The point is that many of our mob were not just football hooligans – they were much more.

There were some real characters within our growing number, none more so than Tony. A little older than me, he had supported United from the days of the Munich air tragedy. He came from Chislehurst, in South-east London, and has, from the Sixties onwards, sported the look and hairstyle of the late Rick Parfitt, which he has more than once used to his advantage. We dubbed him 'Status Quo Tony' as a result. He once famously paid £800 for a Wembley final ticket only to be thrown out, pissed, for swearing and shouting about how noisy and irritating the band was before the game. He is United through and through, and witnessed the birth of the Cockney Reds.

STATUS QUO TONY *As we moved into the very early Seventies, I became aware of Bob and his little group emerging. They were some way below others in the hooligan pecking order at United, and of course the Mancs held sway. That was to change, however, as the Mancs* *pulled the London mob into their world, and the Cockney Reds were born. The leading lights at United then included this hardnut from Wythenshawe, south Manchester, called Geoff Lewis, who had put a Man City fan's eye out in the Sixties and got two years for it. On the day of his release, he was re-arrested at a game against Middlesbrough and was put back in the nick. While he wasn't a Cockney Red he would often stay with one of us when he was down for London games. Many of those who went on to lead the hooligan side learnt from him.*

I came across Geoff some time later, at a game at St James' Park, Newcastle, in October 1971. It was the day the IRA announced they were out to kill George Best, and he responded by scoring the winner. We had been in the pub since 10am, having caught the overnight train from London. A load of Mancs turned up and joined us – then Newcastle arrived. What followed was the biggest pub fight I had ever seen: there were bottles, glasses, chairs, pot plants and pictures off the wall flying around the pub, and I swear fans were even swinging on the chandeliers, a sight not seen before or since. I got out of it pretty smartish with my mates before the police arrived, and we headed for the Gallowgate End, well tanked up. We had no tickets but I got in by diving over the turnstiles. We found ourselves near Geoff Lewis. He promptly attacked some Newcastle fan who, I recall, received a boot print on his face as a result.

By the start of the Seventies hundreds of young lads from London and the South-east were joining the regular trek north to watch United's home games or to attend more local away grounds when the Reds visited. They witnessed the mayhem that often accompanied our travelling army, and the Cockneys played a full part in this as we fought to establish ourselves. Many of those young lads chose to join in, though many more were there for the football and avoided the more dangerous stuff. Alan, a quiet lad from Brentford, opted for the latter but, like many others, would sometimes get caught up in events. Such a day came when, as a sixteen-year-old, he latched onto our group to travel to Newcastle.

ALAN *I was travelling on my own, but on these trips you would look for protection from the hardcases and this was one when I really needed them. As we tried to leave Newcastle Station incognito, with no scarves or colours on display, we met a welcoming committee of local skinheads in Dr Marten boots and braces. I had not seen skinheads for a few years at games, but Newcastle was the land that time forgot. I managed to walk past them quickly, keeping my head down. I looked back and saw one of our lads try to remain inconspicuous by stepping in between an old couple and talking to them as if he had known them for years. Whether it was his Crombie overcoat that gave him away, I don't know, but as he and the old couple walked down some steps he was tripped from behind. The couple kept walking and he got a kicking. The rest of us legged it into the town, and several of the United fans from the train had to take refuge in a shop until the police arrived.*

Even when we got inside the sanctuary of the ground, at the Gallowgate end, bricks were being launched at us from outside. I saw plenty of bloody noses before the game had even started. However, thinking that we were now relatively safe we got our scarves out and started singing. Ten minutes before kick-off, two Geordies ran from the home end, got to the halfway line, turned and, on their knees, begged for more to join them. It was a bizarre sight, but more and more did indeed invade the pitch and move towards our end. I looked as though we were in trouble again but fortunately, whilst a few did reach our end, there was enough resistance to keep them at bay. Nevertheless we were thankful that the police formed a cordon to send them, now about 750-strong, back to the Leazes End.

We had an escort of sorts back to the station, but the police buggered off when the trains to Manchester departed, leaving those of us going to London unprotected. A few of us got a kicking and I had to take refuge in a café as Geordies marauded around the station. When the London train arrived, some made a dash towards the platform and you had the almost comical sight of the ticket collectors taking the ticket and trying to pull the fans through, with the Geordies trying to pull them back into the station. I had noticed there was a wall by the platform and as the melee was going on I climbed over and got on the train seconds before it left. It was traumatic, yet exhilarating in many ways – as it would continue to be as the years went by.

This type of experience was common for many fans, who would not necessarily look for trouble but would get caught up in it through no fault of their own. They would often need our protection. Some would later boast of having steamed in themselves, even when they hadn't. Quite a few were all mouth, looking to take some glory but never earning it. To me that sort would never be true Cockney Reds.

Newcastle was one of the few places I rarely went to, for whatever reason, but trips there helped forge the Cockneys into a recognisable force. Even before the trip that Alan recalls, The Ghost had been up there in 1970 to experience a typical Geordie welcome, and just about lived to tell the tale.

THE GHOST *We went up on the overnight train to see United lose 1–0 to a ninetieth-minute Wyn Davies goal. The journey took over six hours and we arrived at Newcastle Station at about seven in the morning, about fifty of us, mostly teenagers. We had been drinking McEwan's and Tartan bitter all night. We walked through the two big arches at the station entrance and across the road, where up to eighty Newcastle sat waiting. They were nearly all in white coats like those that butchers wore, a common sight at games back then, and some were wearing bowler hats. Some also had their eyes painted, like Alice Cooper. The whole thing was weird and surreal.*

It soon kicked off. We had hoped we could hang on and stand our ground until the Manchester trains arrived with reinforcements, which would have been an achievement to be proud of against overwhelming numbers, but in the end the Old Bill came and saved us. Trouble continued around the various bars, and when hundreds of us moved on to the ground we were bricked and bottled. This continued when we broke into their Leazes End. The Geordies had a song at the time: 'One, two, three, four, five – if you wanna stay alive – keep out the Leazes End.' The Leazes was their home end, with away teams normally given the Gallowgate. Some of our mob were black, a rare sight in Newcastle in those days, and had to put up with monkey chants and other abuse. It didn't help our mood.

Much has been written about that day and I was gutted to have missed it. When the game ended, United apparently steamed out into the street, only to be met by literally thousands of Newcastle and forced to retreat back to the ground. United then attacked again and came in for a bit of a hiding but this time no-one ran, they just took it. Even the coppers waded into United with truncheons drawn. Our mob eventually reached the railway station, where they reformed and charged back outside, clobbering the coppers and diving into the Newcastle. Many of the Geordies had already gone home, thinking they had won the day, but this was United, and we don't take that sort of thing lightly. Once the Manchester trains had left for home, the Cockney boys were again left alone and held their own on the platform as Newcastle came on. It was best described as 'mental' by someone who was there, and the boys even made the main TV news that night – not for the first time, nor the last.

Many of us, it has to be said, were happy to live up to the reputation forged on trips like this: 'the scum of the earth', as one politician called us. But it was another game that immortalised our firm. We made the front page of *The Sun* in August 1973 after playing at Highbury, where the police tried to segregate fans properly for the first time. They failed and it all kicked off. The newspaper dubbed us the 'Cockney Reds' the following Monday. While we had already called ourselves that for some time, the name was now etched forever.

CHAPTER 3

MORE THAN A FOOTBALL HOOLIGAN

I was very much the proverbial loose cannon in my mid-teen years. I spent hours out on the streets, hanging around with mates and getting up to no good. I did, however, find a Saturday job when I was fifteen, working for a fruit and veg chain at various shops in Sutton, Cheam and Putney, and was as good as gold there – I never nicked a thing, as the owners were very decent to me. The cash I earned gave me some freedom. I was desperate for a motorbike but Dad was adamant I wait until I was at least sixteen and legally old enough to ride one, so I saved as much of my earnings as I could, to that end. I also began to spread my wings with the boys, and our Sutton group grew in numbers. One of our favourite haunts was a nightclub that opened just outside Sutton on the Croydon road. It was actually a village hall, but that was all that was available locally at the time, and it was cheap enough to get in – although we rarely paid. Some of these 'nightclubs' had bouncers on the door, but they found it hard to stop a dozen or so determined gate-crashers. All sorts of lads would mix at venues like these dotted around South London: Mods, rockers, smoothies and suedeheads, and a large number of local criminals.

Despite being constantly in some sort of trouble – and having only O–level Art as a qualification – I managed to hold

down a succession of jobs after leaving school. Ahead of my
Old Bailey trial I was taken on by a firm handling the conver-
sion of homes to North Sea gas in the Morden/Wimbledon
area. They knew about my criminal charge and threatened to
sack me if I was found guilty. In the event, whilst I was convicted – albeit with only a conditional discharge – I neglected
to tell them the verdict, and they never bothered to check. I
was able to finish my training course and went out to houses
to convert them to the new gas supply. We had a mobile work-
shop and travelled from one job to another. They were good
times, but after six months I had had enough and left.

I was continually drawn into one criminal incident after
another. By the end of 1970 I had bought a Ford Cortina off
a mate, which I knew he had stolen. The logbook had been
left in the glove compartment, so it was a tidy little deal for
him to sell it, and a result for me too: I swapped it soon after
for a Mark 2 Jaguar. I felt like the bollocks, swanning around
in my Jag, and it helped to pull the birds. Unfortunately it all
went belly-up when the original owner of the Cortina spotted
someone cleaning it one day on a driveway and contacted
Old Bill, who eventually traced it back to my mate and me. I
was arrested, held on remand for three weeks, and received a
suspended sentence in January 1971, just before my twenty-
first birthday.

By then I had been given the moniker of Banana Bob on
that train journey and was stuck with it. Hardly any of the
United crew actually knew my real name, and many still
don't. It was also during this time the Cockney Reds really
came together. The 1971/1972 season was probably the one
when I went to the most matches – more than forty – and
the one when I started regularly attending home games,
usually in the Stretford End. But for me most of the action
was outside or away from the ground, with us mustering in

places where there was likely to be few police and, better still, near where opposing fans might arrive, like stations or coach drop-off points.

By the end of 1971 we were a recognised and respected group, and even the Mancs had begun to look up to us. We weren't just South London: there were blokes like Clarkey, Mick the Con, Frank and many others who made up a very tidy firm from Finchley, and other notable contingents from East London, St Albans and elsewhere. United's army grew bigger and bigger as our antics, particularly on away trips, began to attract widespread publicity, helping to draw in more like-minded youths, rebels and trouble-causers from all over the country. That December, thousands of United infiltrated the home end at Stoke City's old Victoria Ground and took it over. A huge ruck resulted and I was grabbed by the police. Fortunately, Denis Law scored for United at that very moment, the crowd erupted, and in the confusion I broke free. It was a lucky escape, but life now seemed to consist of one arrest after another.

A few Saturdays later I was on my way back from another game and parked up in Sutton to get a burger from a stall outside the train station. Some police officers came over and asked to see my driving licence, then searched the car. A mate on the back seat had some pills on him and, like an idiot, dropped them in the ashtray. I was done for the pills and got a fine. For another non-football offence I received an extended suspended sentence in early 1972. I also had to report to a probation officer every week or so. Sometime later, I nicked a bundle of records from a shop, only to be stopped in a street nearby by a couple of coppers. Instead of ditching the records and running off, I tried to blag my way out of it, without success. My face was now known to the local plod and that didn't help.

Things took an even worse turn one weekend in the summer of 1972 when, at the same burger stall by Sutton Station, a mate I was with became involved in an argument. It led to a fight and I joined in. Someone called the police and they arrived just as my mate hit this fella with an iron bar. We were both arrested and were eventually prosecuted for malicious wounding. I was guilty by association, I guess, and the injury to the bloke was considerable, so I received six months, plus an add-on of the three months suspended from earlier.

Having been held on remand at Ashford Middlesex (now HMP Bronzefield) before the trial, I was afterwards shipped to Wormwood Scrubs for two months, then transferred to Pentonville, where I was due to serve the other seven months (I was released after four). The Scrubs was particularly unpleasant. Sporadic riots broke out, and we were kept in our cells all day and fed just once, as the staff were either dealing with the riots or kept away for their own safety. There were some heavy criminals in there, many on remand for the most serious crimes. I kept my nose clean and had a chance to chat a few times to a screw who was a Millwall fan, but not many others were into football.

Pentonville was a little easier and I managed to blag work in the clothing shop, where there was a separate toilet and shower and I could wear different clothes each day. I met John Parrott, a fellow bricklayer and the older brother of a biker mate, and we got on well together, along with Alan Chadwick, a friend from the Rose Hill days. There were still some tough gangster types on my wing, many of whom I knew from South London. The time soon passed. I earned an extra £2 or £3 a week in the shop, allowing me to buy 'luxuries' like butter and extra tobacco, which as a non-smoker I could trade for chocolate, sweets, soap and toothpaste. I was also able to keep up with goings-on at United by having my own copy of the *Manchester Evening News* delivered using my extra cash. Only a few inmates or screws were interested in football but there was a rush every Thursday night to get in front of the small TV in the recreation area to lust over the dancers of Pan's People on *Top of the Pops*, the blonde one in particular!

I was released in January 1973 and was soon back at United games, where I found that the reputation of 'Banana Bob' had grown. Perhaps word had got around about my time inside, and I had become a sort of cult figure, despite being barely in my twenties. A lot of lads in their mid-teens had started following United, and seemed to need some older Reds to look up to. I did not seek to be any sort of leader but I suppose I was – although others might say differently. Certainly, any notoriety I had was due to action rather than words.

With plenty of travelling north for games, home and away, the Cockney Reds continued to enlarge. My local group would usually meet up at Tooting Broadway underground, never pay, and get off at Euston Square station, just short of Euston, where there was no ticket check and few police. We would then walk up to Euston Station to meet others arriving at the concourse from all over the south-east. There would almost always be other clubs' fans at Euston too, either setting off or arriving. Trouble usually flared, although on many occasions all we seemed to end up doing was fighting with Old Bill. Once we were on our way, other Reds from places like Northampton and Corby (a hard lot) would join us up the line.

* * *

My career ambitions went no further than a job that paid decent money without pushing me too hard. What I really desired was sufficient cash-in-hand to get around the pubs and clubs, run a motorbike and a car, find some birds who were up for it, and most of all, have the time to get around the country to watch United and enjoy the feeling of being part of those huge crowds. To be able to attend midweek games, I would also need a job where I could get time off or could bunk off without much trouble. Hence I had a succession of posts, including working for a couple of years at British Rail in an office at East Croydon, which had the advantage of giving me discounted train travel, although I rarely paid on match days anyway. After a succession of other, short-lived jobs, I started labouring on building sites. I enjoyed the outdoor life and eventually, working alongside a bricklayer and learning that trade, I realised this was something that suited me – building something from scratch and being creative. This was no doubt the artist in me coming out, plus it paid well, and even better as I got on. I became flush compared to some of my mates.

The country itself seemed spent. Strikes were breaking out everywhere, especially on the railways and at power stations, and we saw three-day working weeks, with inflation running at over twenty per cent. English football had nosedived after the glory of 1966 and was pretty rubbish, and the only things that kept me going were girls, the Cockney Reds and a good strong dose of ultra-violence.

Unfortunately the way I behaved at games continued to seep into my life away from football. My building-site work gang included the odd fellow Cockney Red, and in late December 1975 we knocked off at midday to finish for Christmas, and headed to the nearest pub. We were joined by a gang from another building firm working the same site, including a couple more mates. They were due to go back to work after lunch, but decided to stay for a few more pints with us instead. Eventually they thought it best to show their faces back on the site, but when they got there the foreman told them in no uncertain terms that they were sacked. They were ordered to pick up their tools, leave and not bother coming back.

They returned to the pub and told us what had happened. Pissed up as we were, someone said, 'We ain't having that, let's go back and sort him out.'

We arrived mob-handed at the site as the foreman was loading his van. He backed off with his arms held up, saying, 'Look, I was only doing my job. You were out of order taking the mick like that.'

'It's fucking Christmas, what do you expect?' a mate said. 'You can't put us out of work at this time of year just for that.'

'I can and I have,' answered the foreman, opening the van door to get in. He was yanked out, and my mate hit him with a hammer. The bloke went down with blood spurting from his head and looked in a bad way. Some other workers on the site came over, saw his injuries and pitched into us. One came at me with a large chunk of wood. I drew a work knife from my pocket, pointed it at him and said something like, 'Come on, then.' He stopped in his tracks, and he and his mates backed off. I left before they had second thoughts, throwing away the knife when I got back to my flat.

Someone reported the incident to Old Bill and, with me having a reputation, I was grassed up. I was arrested and charged with threatening behaviour, GBH and carrying an offensive weapon. For this I received six months jail time at Dorking Magistrates in January 1976 – not my finest hour. At first I was sent to Wandsworth Prison; wrongly, as it happened, as it is only supposed to take prisoners serving more than a year. It is known as the toughest prison to be in, so I protested strongly on arrival and was transferred to Pentonville for the second time in three years, although not before the pantomime of the screws not being able to undo the locks on my cuffs. As before, Pentonville was an easier regime compared to the harshness of the Scrubs or what I had heard about Wandsworth, and I blagged a job in the works department, as I was now a proficient bricklayer. Again, there were very few football people there, although I became friends with a Millwall hooligan and we swapped a few stories and vowed to meet one day on the terraces (we never did). I was banged up in D wing, which was the best in terms of comfort and where we had longer hours out of our cells. I read loads of books and had a radio to listen to music and the sport. I also had regular family visits and also a good number of Cockney Reds would turn up from time to time.

It was never too unpleasant inside and I felt it some sort of badge of honour to have had the experience, like so many of my friends inside and outside of the Cockney Reds. It was something to add to my hooligan c.v.

CHAPTER 4

THE EARLY SEVENTIES

'What I look for is a good game, a good piss-up, and a good punch-up.' So said a Millwall fan interviewed in the late Seventies for a *Panorama* documentary on hooliganism. All around the country, fellow football yobs nodded their heads in agreement. I could not disagree either. My Cockney Reds journey had led me to the same conclusion. My biker days had ended after the Brighton beach incident and instead I was regularly following the Reds, as well as getting involved in some dodgy dealings away from football. Although I was still living at home with the family – when I wasn't banged up inside – I was now 'someone' and felt I could take on the world.

My little firm were a handy mob. We would meet around Euston to go off to games, and to travel north would usually catch the inter-city, although for a couple of years 'football specials' were provided. These were old rolling stock, often consisting of former cargo carriages with barred windows and broken toilets, and were little better than cattle trucks. No wonder the blokes cooped up in there for a few hours would burst out like animals and run amok. We never paid a fare, as the sheer number of fans meant the rail people just gave up trying to inspect tickets. We gave the 'Hectors', a general name for any ticket inspector, a bad time. All sorts of jibbing went on, with fans sometimes pretending to be foreign and incapable of understanding what Hector wanted. Some locked themselves in the toilets and pretended to be puking non-stop to avoid a ticket inspection; others claimed their ticket had been inspected elsewhere on the train. It was usually mayhem.

The Reds from London were getting a reputation beyond the city boundaries and were always looking for likely targets – anyone, really. We rarely came off worst. We often avoided the mainstream mass of United fans, who tended to be accompanied by large contingents of police, rarely or never wore club colours, and began to plan and execute ambushes of our rivals, giving us the upper hand. Soon to be dubbed the 'Cockney Reds' by the Mancs, we did all we could to live up to the reputation of a firm with form and attitude, and were about to embark on our journey as a formidable force – a group to be reckoned with. Today I am not so proud of some of the things we did, but at the time it was all exciting, and right up my street.

One formative Cockney outing was a trip to Halifax Town in July 1971, in the old Watney Cup, a sort of pre-season friendly knockout with a selected group of teams. Four of us went in a car, with my mate Brucie from Wallington driving overnight all the way up, so that we could be there early, have a few beers and not miss any action. Hordes of Reds poured over from Manchester, some of them even walking the thirty miles from the city. They then proceeded to set about the town. One United group loitered around a large war memorial, abusing shoppers as they passed by; another sat in the town garden, drinking and tossing empty beer cans at random strangers. Numerous shops were robbed and even the Boots and Woolworths stores were looted. No one much cared about scaring the locals; it was all part of the fun. As the morning wore on a few lads from Leeds turned up looking for a fight but they were soon seen off. Any local opposition from Halifax also quickly dissolved, and the worst fighting was between different sets of United. It must have felt an invading army was sweeping through, pillaging as they went.

The Shay was such a small ground that tickets were at a premium but we managed to buy some off a tout. We need not have bothered, as hundreds of our fans smashed down a gate and swarmed inside, throwing bricks over the police cordon into the home fans and onto the pitch. The ground itself was a shithole and, even though it was summer and the season had not started, the pitch already looked crap. United put out a strong side, despite Halifax being in the Third Division. Willie Morgan missed a penalty, Halifax scored twice, then we got one back from George Best from the spot – cue fans invading the pitch to celebrate, me included. I'm sure the encroachment was as much to do with the game being on TV as anything else, to show the world we were uncontrollable, even at such a low-key game. At the final whistle we returned to the streets, and surged into a small supermarket to ransack the shelves. The staff were terrified but to us it was all just a laugh. I managed to pick up some bottles of wine, some posh choco-lates and even a few joints of meat, and took it all to the car to sell when I got home. Robbing and looting would become a common feature of such away trips.

Visiting tough cities like Liverpool was, of course, a very different proposition to sleepy old mill towns like Halifax. We despised Liverpool FC more than any other team, and the enmity was entirely mutual – if anything, they seemed to hate us even more. Weirdly, this meant that we developed an odd sort of affinity with their local rivals Everton, at least in the early days. That is not to deny that we also had trouble with them, as one of the Cockneys, Alan from Brentford, found when he made the trip to Goodison Park in the 1972/73 season, at the age of seventeen.

ALAN *I met with my mate, 'Hairy', who had a mass of black hair and a beard and was a few years older than me. With United struggling in the league at the time, the numbers on the train, run by travel organiser Dobbin, were well down, and there were few United fans about when we arrived at Lime Street Station, so we proceeded to get something to eat at a Wimpy bar. Waiting to cross the road at the lights, I heard the shout of 'E for B and Docherty', a popular United chant in the early Seventies [it was based on a TV advert, featuring George Best claiming that eggs for breakfast were good for you, and had the catchphrase 'E for B and Georgie Best', which was adopted when Tommy Docherty became manager – RC]. Just as I went to join the group singing it, Hairy grabbed me and said, 'When did you last see skinhead United fans with plain red-and-white scarves?' I instantly knew I'd had a lucky escape, as they were Liverpool hooligans waiting for numpties like me to show themselves.*

We proceeded to a crowded bar. Two enormous Scousers in their mid-thirties managed to push into the seats next to us. We nodded and grunted, not wishing to give our southern accents away, and sat in silence while they openly boasted about beating up a copper the night before. They then moved on to discuss plans to ambush United fans, both in the town and at the train station. Hairy and I both finished our drinks at the same time and made a sort of grunt to show we were getting up to go. The two were so engrossed in their ambushing plans they ignored us. I'm sure we would have been battered if they had suspected we were Reds.

We got separated on the way back to Lime Street after the game, meaning I had to go alone on a bus back to the station. It was filled with Everton fans, and I prayed no one would ask me the time or who I supported. There was a full-scale battle when I approached the station. The Evertonians, even though their team had won 2–0, had gathered there to attack any departing United. The police managed to get the Manchester train away, albeit with bottles and stones being thrown as it departed, but the London train wasn't due to leave for another thirty minutes and so we became the focal point of their attention. There were probably only thirty to forty of us, consisting of the depleted Cockney Red firm and some scarfers and ordinary fans from London. Bottles and bricks were thrown at us and the police had a hard time stopping Everton getting into the station.

The guy next to me was a regular traveller, the double of Rick Parfitt and always dressed in denim. He was about twenty-five but I rarely saw him with the main London firm. Imagine my surprise when he pulled out a knife at least six inches long from his jacket and said, 'Don't worry, if the bastards come in I'll take a few down with me.' I had never seen such a knife at close quarters and I'm sure he would have used it if he had to, although I was later told he was not known as one of the violent Cockney crowd. After what seemed like an eternity the police managed to get us on the train under a barrage of missiles. Merseyside in the Seventies was not for faint hearts if you were a United fan.

For me the 1972/73 season was a non-starter, as I spent most of it idling my time in the Scrubs or Pentonville. Once I was back it was all but over, and United were on the slippery slope that would lead to relegation the following season. By

May 1973 Bobby Charlton had retired – I was thrown out of the ground for fighting at his last match, against Chelsea at Stamford Bridge – while Denis Law had been released and Tommy Docherty had been brought in to replace Frank O'Farrell as manager. The 'Doc' reinstated George Best, whom O'Farrell had sacked, but Besty was a shadow of the superstar he had been. The glory days were over, and the fans' discontent was increasingly to show itself on the terraces and out on the streets.

I was geared up for the start of the following season and in August 1973 a visit to Arsenal's Highbury ground would see the Cockney Reds' reputation well and truly cemented. About three hundred of us went in their North Bank and basically took it over. Eventually Old Bill tried to pin us in a small pocket to the side of the stand nearest the Underground station. We had Arsenal fans to one side and behind us. This poor attempt at segregation was never going to work, as all our top lads were there, and we attacked the Arsenal, pushing them over to the far side and the back of the stand. Many of them opted out and left for a safer part of the ground or went home. Old Bill were caught in the crossfire and, despite reinforcements, were never able to gain any sort of control, although they did throw a few fans out, both United and Arsenal.

My small group deliberately left five minutes before the end to get back on the tube to Euston Station, where we planned to bushwhack other groups passing through, including any Arsenal on their way home. We got off at Kings Cross, the station before Euston, as we knew there would be fewer police there, and then walked the remaining half mile or so. On the way we came across what we thought was a big group of Arsenal. We piled into them, only to find they were Millwall fans who had been at Fulham and had left the game early to come looking for us. A massive fight broke out, with fists and boots flying everywhere. Police reinforcements quickly arrived and a senior officer pointed me out as a ringleader. Three burly coppers moved towards me, so I legged it down the Euston Road, with them in hot pursuit. I ran straight into some Chelsea, who had returned from an early kick-off game at Derby. One of their lads grabbed me round the waist with one hand and by my hair with the other. This allowed the coppers to nick both me and the Chelsea idiot and cart us off to the local nick, where I was charged with threatening behaviour.

Two weeks later I appeared in court and received a fine. The Chelsea fan was there, sitting outside the courtrooms, and when he saw me he took fright and scuttled off to the toilet. He did not re-appear before I was called into court. There was an amusing ending to that day at Euston. When finally released from custody, I could not for the life of me recall where I had left my car. The day had been one long blur of action and I suppose I was a bit disorientated. With a couple of others, I spent more than an hour trying to find the right NCP car park. The drink didn't help. The *Sun* later carried an article reporting the events of that day and picked up that the Mancs had dubbed us the 'Cockney Reds'. From then on, that was how we were known

As the season wore on United played consistently badly, and defeat after defeat saw us facing relegation. The only good news was that some tough younger lads were joining our firm. One of them was Brian.

BRIAN *On trips with the Cockney Reds I loved what I saw. I learned a lot watching Bob, The Ghost and the others getting up to all sorts at the height of the violent years. I remember one day being at this pub in Whalley Range, Manchester. I was only thirteen so couldn't go in, but I was put to good use. While Bob and others were shouting*

*from outside, goading the opposition fans inside, I was
sent round the back to smash all the windows and distract
those inside. Bob and the others then poured in and it all
kicked off. My reward was probably a glass of lemonade,
a packet of pork scratchings and a pat on the head. It was
my apprenticeship into the big-time violence, and it wasn't
long before I graduated with honours.*

As some left the Cockney Reds for various reasons, more
than double their number joined up. Our ranks came to
include not just Londoners but anyone from the south, especially those who gathered at Euston on Saturday morning.

Most of us were at the dramatic end-of-season derby game at
Old Trafford when Denis Law's back-heel condemned United
to the Second Division. When the Lawman's goal went in, our
whole terrace erupted. A flare was thrown, causing smoke to
drift across the pitch, and a few fans jumped onto the grass.
Word went around about trying to get the game abandoned,
and more fans ran on. The ref stopped play to clear the pitch
and Denis himself went off, looking as if he was about to burst
into tears. Still more fans poured on. I decided to leave via the
Stretford End exit and then re-enter the ground at the main
stand entrance, which enabled me to get onto the pitch near
the Scoreboard End. Despite Sir Matt pleading with us to get
back over the walls, the game had to be abandoned. Half the
crowd seemed to be on the pitch by the time the police formed
a cordon and slowly moved us back. Eventually we left and
took to the streets outside, looking for City fans. Not for the
first time, they crept away, which was probably just as well –
they would not have escaped without a beating.

The game did not restart but the result stood. It was all over
the TV news and a few interesting things emerged. Tommy
Docherty, in an interview, failed to condemn the fans but

did suggest this might be an indication of things to come and might lead to the installation of pitch-side fences, as in Europe and South America. That particular bandwagon would roll on: fences were introduced and failed to stop hooliganism, but were kept until the Hillsborough disaster brought about their eventual removal.

* * *

When that Millwall fan said those words on *Panorama* about looking for a 'piss-up and a punch-up', he inadvertently spoke for many us. Huge numbers of young men were forming violent football mobs. Most were teenagers or, like me, in their early twenties, eager for a fight and to take the other team's 'end'. It was fairly basic stuff: we would fight with fists, or pick up any stones, bricks or bottles to hand, but only a few would ever go tooled-up with weapons. Some older blokes joined us, but most steered clear of serious trouble. Hooliganism became front-page as well as back-page news. Football on the pitch was also becoming more glamorous as coverage of the game increased and families were able to watch the highlights on their new colour TVs, often bought on hire-purchase.

In United's case, the Cockney Reds joined thousands of others to form an unstoppable mass when arriving in the vicinity of an away ground. We would usually all meet up in a convenient place – perhaps a pub or a park – and then strut, army-file, to the ground under police escort, chanting, looking for home fans or to break away from the cordon to chase the opposition. As I have said, often my little firm would break away from the main mob and be more underhand, cunning even, to find aggro. We loved football and always hoped United won the game, but our day was as much about getting boozed up, getting into the away end and dealing with our rivals on the streets before and after. It was what we were all about. It was what we did.

We didn't like being outside the top league, but we were ready for a season no-one would forget.

CHAPTER 5

ON THE RAMPAGE

Stories from the 1974/75 season could fill three books. It was as if war had been declared, and in August 1974 the United army massed to take on the world – or at least the English Second Division. We all wanted immediate promotion but also looked forward to visiting places we had not been before and leaving our mark, as we had done at Halifax and other backwaters previously. At times more than 20,000 of us would descend on a ground that was inadequately designed for such numbers. Inevitably there was mayhem. We did not like the loss of face that being in a lower division entailed, and were determined to show what United were – on and off the pitch. The country had never seen anything like it; no country had.

The first game was away at Leyton Orient, and anticipation was so high that many travelling Reds camped out all night at the ground before the game. I travelled up from Bournemouth, where I was on holiday with my then-girlfriend, dropping her off at home before heading to Euston for the Cockney meet-up. We then moved on in numbers to Orient. Despite an operation overseen by the Met, no plans could cope with the crowd size that day. There was trouble before, during and after the match, mainly between United and Old Bill. I was grabbed during the first half of the game by some coppers as I charged a fence, and they led me away to throw me out of the ground. We had only gone a few yards when a group of my mates attacked them and I escaped.

Joe joined us for the first time that day. I already knew of him through the gang scene around Sutton.

JOE *This was my first real involvement with the Cockney Reds. As Bob says, I was around the local scene and knew him by reputation, although he was part of another gang. We would often mix with them at Tiffany's in Wimbledon. We were a bit younger than Bob's lot but we all decided football was good for trouble and we wanted some. So I shed my feelings for Tottenham, became a Cockney Red, and the Orient game proved to me that this was just what I needed. It was intoxicating.*

Our second fixture was at home to Millwall. Their violent reputation matched our own, and we knew there would be a large welcoming committee at Old Trafford to see what they were made of. For the younger London element, this season was a golden opportunity not just to follow their heroes to away games, where the ranks of United acted as a huge security blanket, but also to Old Trafford, where rival supporters would be fewer and those inclined could cut their teeth on football violence with less chance of coming to grief. The Millwall game was the first Old Trafford outing for a young Mick Groom, now a long-standing Cockney Red from Essex. At school he had been known as 'Coco' because he always acted the clown, and in his early days as a Red he was dubbed 'White Coco' by the Mancs, as there was already a well-known black lad up north known as Coco (and who henceforth became 'Black Coco'). Now Mick is just plain 'Groomy'.

GROOMY *My friend Tony Howes and I decided to hitch-hike to Manchester for the game against Millwall, after we had had an amazing day in East London for United's first game in Division Two at Leyton Orient. We finished school on the Friday, and after going home, having tea and getting changed, we met up and off we went. This was all done without our parents' knowledge, as we were just a couple of fifteen-year-olds and they would have tried to stop us.*

We were soon on our way, with thumbs outstretched, and after a few lifts we found ourselves on the outskirts of Manchester in the early hours of the morning. Not sure of where we were, we caught an orange bus that was travelling into town and ended up in Piccadilly Gardens. After a hot drink in some café, we asked how to get to Old Trafford, and were pointed in the right direction. Eventually we saw the ground in the distance. This seemed to make us forget how tired we were, and we stepped up the pace.

The ground seemed so big compared to the other stadiums we had been to, although admittedly these consisted only of Orient, Spurs and West Ham. We walked round to the Stretford End, two excited but tired little schoolkids. There was hardly anybody about. We decided we needed a bit of kip, and just plonked ourselves against one of the gates and tried to get some shut-eye. Later, the place started to get a bit busy, and we walked round to the small souvenir shop and passed the time away until we joined the queue, along with the other Reds. Then the gates opened, and we were in. We climbed the steps, and we were there, on the famous Stretford End. We went straight behind the goal and stood in front of a barrier, and just looked about, chatting and waiting for the game to start. The noise was fantastic. It felt brilliant to be there, and soon the game had begun.

The match itself is a blur, but I can remember the roar each time we scored, and ducking under the barrier just as it seemed that everyone was going to end up in the front section. It was scary and exciting at the same time. We won 4–0. At the end of the game, Tony decided he didn't want to hitch-hike home, and said he would ring his parents and get them to pick us up. We only lived 220-odd miles away! After making our way back to Manchester Piccadilly, Tony rang his mum, and as they had been having kittens worrying where he was (my parents were the same), his dad agreed to drive up and collect us. When his parents arrived, they gave us a roasting of the first degree, and then some much needed drinks and sandwiches.

I was woken up outside my house to be met by my mum and dad, who just shook their heads, and in I went. Over the next year or so the hitch-hiking continued, but this time our parents knew. I would often turn up at school the morning after travelling up north to a game in a dishevelled state, tired and not averse to dozing off in lessons. I've been following United since then, although nowadays I either drive up, fly if abroad or go on the local supporters' club's coach!

I have been hanging out with Groomy for well over thirty years and he is as committed as anyone to the United cause, travelling all over the world (thirty-nine countries to date) to watch them. He soon got to know us from attending matches, at first by reputation and then later personally.

GROOMY *After the thumbing experience, I used the trains for a while but had no idea who Banana Bob was. At first I was a Stretford Ender, but later I graduated to the Scoreboard Paddock at the other end of the ground, near* *where the away fans are now seated. It was from that point on, and at away games, that I saw Bob, Tooting Steve, Steve M and Griff in action. They were the real hardcases, but we needed them in those violent days. I'm not saying I didn't get caught up in some of it, but generally I didn't want to know about that sort of stuff. However, I won't be the first to say that these four and a few others were needed to help protect us from attacks from other firms, and we did unite behind them. I didn't see Bob as real nasty, with knives or anything, but for a small bloke he didn't half command respect from us and the other clubs' firms. More than once, faces in these firms would think twice when they faced Bob.*

The Millwall game turned out to be a disappointment, as their much-vaunted firm did not show up and the police needed only two coaches to transport their supporters to the ground. Even then, the coaches were stoned and bricked, and were so badly damaged that some of the Millwall asked to miss the game and be put back on a train. We had watched some of this at Piccadilly before making our way to the ground. We got off the bus at White City and were told one Millwall fan was flashing a knife down by the canals. About twenty of us headed there, and when this mug saw us he tried to climb over a wall to get away, but beyond it was only the canal. He was trapped, but Old Bill arrived to steam into us and save him. Two of Millwall's better-known faces did come into the old Scoreboard Paddock. One was attacked, the other slipped away into the crowd. We later heard of a stabbing of a Millwall fan elsewhere, but their main group were escorted out at half-time and we waved them off. Job done, Millwall sent packing.

On August 31 we were off to Taffland and Cardiff City.

Cardiff is a tough port and we expected serious opposition. We were not disappointed. The roar of violence echoed around the streets as skirmishes broke out on every corner before the game. There were some bizarre sights, like the Red in a white boiler suit, bowler hat and Doc Martens boots, like a character from *A Clockwork Orange*, or blood-spattered fans queueing to enter the ground. The large group I was in was attacked by Cardiff as we neared Ninian Park, but being old hands, we kept out of the main action, biding our time, as there were too many police present. Instead we watched as teenagers knocked hell out of each other. There was real hatred from the Welsh fans, with numerous anti-English chants and references to 'Munich'. Some responded with provocative chants of 'Aberfan', a reference to that terrible disaster that was still painfully fresh in the memory.

United had most of the long side opposite the main stand but, as ever, our aim was to get into Cardiff's main terrace, which was behind one goal. Between us was a no-man's land with two separating fences and a line of police up the steep terrace. Insults were chanted both ways and the occasional charge made at each fence, with a few brave or foolhardy souls even climbing to the top before the cops pulled them down. A group of United did manage to get undetected into the Cardiff section, but were soon rumbled and attacked, before being escorted to our section. They were greeted like heroes. Cardiff responded by tossing over some large wooden stakes, one of which downed a United fan, who was treated by his mates. A lump of concrete went back the other way and hurt one of theirs, quite badly it looked. In fact I had never seen so many injured fans strewn across the terraces. The St John Ambulance did their best, but most casualties were carried away by their mates to a kind of makeshift triage area near the turnstiles. Some had to be taken away by ambulance.

I had been with Griff throughout and we could not wait to get out of the ground to get at Cardiff, but at the final whistle we were heavily marshalled by the police, who were desperate to keep us away from the local hooligans behind the goal. Instead of leaving the terrace and being taken by the shortest route, which would have meant meeting Cardiff fans coming out, the main United group was escorted around the far end of the ground and along the other side, which took several minutes. From there we were to be led towards the railway station. Despite the police efforts, however, the Cardiff stood waiting, and threw a few missiles as we left the ground. My group did not at first join the main United escort, and so about thirty of us were able to rush Cardiff at their exit. We did what we could, but when they saw how few of us there were, they turned around to attack, so we had to fall back and join the main body of United. We were still able to pick off some Cardiff trying to target stragglers from our main group. All of this was caught on camera, and photos appeared in the national Sundays the next day.

As we neared the train station in a tight group about a thousand-strong, we saw our chance and surged though the police lines and into the Cardiff. I damaged a few Taffies with some flying punches before we were shepherded onto the station concourse, where there had been fighting even before our arrival. We ended up being forced onto the train for London. The carriages were so packed that some of us got off at Newport, just to seek somewhere safer to stand along the train. The British Transport Police were out in force and tried to stop us getting off, but I broke clear and ran along the platform. I then tried the door of another carriage, but it would not open. The train began to move off with me still clinging to the door. I was grabbed by the coppers and pulled away into the waiting room, where I was cautioned and had my details taken before being put onto the next London train. A couple of weeks later I received a fine through the post.

THE GHOST *This was the day when I met 'Popeye'. We met at Paddington for the 9am train, a top turnout with three hundred-plus making up our firm – United fans drinking Tartan bitter and light ales, all singing. We pulled into Cardiff at noon, at the same time as the Manchester trains arrived, and the noise as we came together with the Mancs was deafening. By then we were about a thousand-strong. We headed to the exits, where Old Bill was trying to control the flood out onto the concourse, and smashed through the police lines. There waiting was this massive firm from Cardiff. It kicked off big-time and we were into it toe-to-toe, with hotdog stands going over and an off licence ransacked. Fair play to Cardiff, they were proper having it.*

We then went under a bridge and in front of us was another firm, who we thought were fellow United fans. As we got nearer to them we saw a big bloke in front of this mob, and a few barmies ran towards him and his mates. As they got closer this geezer, who we nicknamed Popeye because of his massive forearms and tattoos, started ironing out four or five of our barmies. We realised this was a Cardiff firm. We ran to take them on, with bricks and bottles flying between us. We were about ten to fifteen feet away when Cardiff suddenly stopped and start pavement dancing. It lasted a few seconds before a brick flew past me and my mate, Pancho from Stoke. I ducked and it hit a North London Cockney in the canister and put him down. Popeye was now to the right of us, bricks were flying at him, and a couple hit him in the boat-race. He wobbled, about to fall, and United steamed into him.

We were then into the rest of Cardiff as well and they had it away on their toes.

We got to the ground and swarmed over the turnstiles, ending up in a top corner, next to a fence that separated us from the Cardiff terrace. It seemed like every two minutes we were bombarded with bricks. At half-time we went to the toilets and a big roar went up, as it had kicked off again, and Old Bill arrived to sort things out back by the fence. As the second half began, Cardiff started chanting 'Munich', so we attacked the fence, while some United responded with 'Aberfan'. This really upped the ante, and Old Bill got it from both sides. We couldn't get at Cardiff through the fence, however, so many of us left to wait for them outside the ground.

As we came out, their main firm was already waiting at the end of the street. We ran towards each other and the fighting that followed went on for almost ten minutes. We pushed them back and they eventually legged it, perhaps to wait elsewhere. We had taken loads of casualties and huge numbers were nicked as the police eventually gained control in the road, although fighting continued elsewhere. We then hit the train station to make our way home, another end of a day in football.

A special court sat that evening to deal with those nicked, both Cardiff and United, with Popeye apparently one of them. This was something of a watershed moment in policing football violence, as people started getting bird instead of small fines, yet the big clampdown still was some way off. As far as them singing 'Munich' and us 'Aberfan', two wrongs don't make a right, but it was again the start of something that became a norm and continues to this day within the game.

Three weeks later came the return game at Millwall. None of us wanted to miss this, even though, oddly, the fixture was scheduled for a Monday night. If the idea of moving it to a working day was to reduce the number of United fans travelling, then the authorities did not comprehend how many of us lived around the south-east. It may also have been intended to cut down on the drinking hours available, with most being at work in the daytime, but had the unintended consequence of making attendance available to the hardcore hooligans of other London clubs, who would have been watching their own teams on a Saturday. Now they could all rock up.

I caught a train down because my car was out of action and bumped into some mates at New Cross Station. From there we went into the Cold Blow Lane end at The Den. It was a forbidding place, especially as we were not with the rest of the United fans, as we had arrived late and didn't know the ground well. One of our lads, Roy, who came from the Old Kent Road area and looked just like Elvis, even arrived wearing a United T-shirt, something we Cockneys never did. We told him he must be mad and would be a target for all the faces there from different clubs. 'I don't care,' he said. 'Fuck 'em.' Millwall's hardcore were in a side terrace but some were able to climb over a low fence to get to the United section at the other end from us. I later heard the United numbers were swelled by a good number of others, mainly from Chelsea and West Ham. They baited each other throughout, but with a line of Old Bill with dogs between them, no United were going to try their luck, as they were short-handed; the special trains had been stopped en route due to damage done by the Mancs.

I was acutely aware that some Millwall on my section of terrace might know my face, and the evil mood darkened further when Gerry Daly scored a penalty early in the second half for United. By then I had become separated from my mates after going for a slash at half-time and returning to find they had moved. I wasn't bothered, and stayed on until about fifteen minutes from the end, with the score still 1–0 and us never looking like conceding a goal. By then it had dawned on me that Millwall would be looking for United fans the second the game ended, and if recognised I had no back-up. Given that quite a few Millwall lads knew me, I decided for once that it might be a good idea to slip away early.

And so the season went on. At Nottingham Forest we were given the whole Trent End rather than the usual away end, so we were one up on them before we even started, which did not go down well. This was done so that the police could get us out of the ground and off towards the railway station after the game without us coming into contact with the Forest mob. This was common practice at most away grounds but hardly ever worked, as we were always in such large numbers that the police could not cope if we attacked their lines. This day was no different. We broke through the police cordon as we were led out into the streets. Forest fans, smarting from a 1–0 defeat, lined up against us and there was the mother of all fights right outside the main stand. Traffic cones were picked up and thrown and bottles rained in from both sides as ordinary fans scattered in terror. It was all of thirty minutes before the police could form a wedge between the opposing fans and shepherd us towards the bridge over the Trent and away to the station.

Home games were not free from trouble either. Sunderland have always had a big away following and brought thousands into Victoria Station, where we were waiting for them. One unlucky bloke was singled out and took a real hiding. At the ground I entered the paddock beneath the main scoreboard, beside the Sunderland fans behind the goal. A group of us then broke into their section and they had to climb into the seated area above to escape. I saw the bloke we had attacked at Victoria, who had a cut above his eye, bruising to his cheeks and bloodstains all over his bomber jacket. That didn't stop me piling into him and blacking his other eye for good measure. He got away from me and tried to escape onto the pitch, but some young Mancs pushed him to the ground and kicked his legs for good measure. Not his best day out – and his team lost 3–2. With such large crowds it was relatively easy to get away with such antics. There were no stewards then and the coppers just did not have enough bodies to deal with multiple outbreaks of fighting in various parts of the ground.

Sheffield Wednesday away was something else. With Hillsborough being a big ground and not far for the Mancs to travel, it was a chance to take truly huge numbers and gate-crash all areas of the stadium. We were allocated one end but simply took the other, with a large number of the Cockney Reds also getting into their terrace along the side of the pitch. It was the largest takeover of another side's ground I ever saw. The trouble started when we went 3–1 down in the first half. The abandoned game against Man City was still fresh in our minds from the previous season, and the shout went up to invade the pitch and disrupt the game, in hope that the result might be invalidated.

Despite so many United being in the Wednesday end, the police were only patrolling the opposite, away end. Some of our lads climbed over the pitch-side wall and ran towards the United end, calling on those there to join in. In response, mounted police crashed through a gate at the end of the terrace and charged those milling on the pitch in front of the United end. Fans were flattened or kicked by the horses and fell over each other as they tried to escape. It was a wonder no-one was killed or badly hurt. Fans attended to the injured strewn along the pitch and those crushed by the swell on the terrace (shades of what was to unfold years later), with no help from the first-aiders. It looked like the aftermath of a battle, with fans lying everywhere. Eventually strong-arm police tactics restored order and the game resumed, ending in a 4–4 draw.

Cardiff had been more violent, but this game showcased a different facet of our hooliganism. Sheffield was basically invaded and the police caught off-guard by so many United fans getting into the ground without tickets and taking over the terracing on all sides, something not done before by an away crowd at such a big stadium. It also exposed poor police planning and led to public calls for fences to prevent pitch invasions and attempts to stop matches, coming as it did after that City game and a similar occurrence at Newcastle United. Without doubt, most of the clubs in Division Two would be pleased to see the back of us. Fortunately for them we breezed through the season to win the league and were back in the big time.

A number of stalwarts, including Joe, joined us that year. Another was Micky W, from South-east London.

MICKY W *Born in 1962, I started going to United games when I was twelve. This coincided with United's stint in the Second Division and the start of real violent times. Like Bob I was drawn into all this excitement and me and my mates hitchhiked to games that season at places like Millwall and Orient. We were drawn along with the crowd, marching as one to and from the grounds, and it was only a question of time before we got more active. I would travel by train up to Manchester or to away games with about fifteen others, people like Coomber, Didi and some boys from the Peckham area. Occasionally it was on the Cockney Reds' own specials, where it was carnage, but more often than not on a scheduled train and always the* *same one if going to Manchester, leaving at just past 9am and coming back on the 5.30.*

I looked up to Tooting Steve and The Ghost back then, until I noticed Bob later into the Seventies. The strongest group amongst the Cockney Reds in the mid-Seventies was the Finchley firm, who put out about a hundred every week. They were very menacing and always put up a good show. I made great friendships over more than forty years and many of us are still good mates.

Throughout that season every game had its own story, and there were many funny moments – or at least, we found them funny! For some reason my little group always enjoyed a day out in Norwich, mixing with the country bumpkins, or 'carrot-crunchers' as we called them. In January 1975, me, Griff, Tooting Steve and some other lads travelled up there with more than just the football in mind, as we planned to make a day and night out of it. It was the second leg of the League Cup semi-final, after the teams had drawn 2–2 at Old Trafford. We went on to lose 1–0 at Carrow Road but, for once, there was little trouble at the game, with a relatively low turnout of United fans.

Part of our plan was to visit the Scamps nightclub in Norwich after the game. Its sister club in Sutton was one of our favourite haunts, with good punch-ups on a regular basis and where it was easy to pick up girls. Before heading on there, we found a small pub in the city and downed numerous pints. We were in high spirits, despite the defeat, and became rather loud, which upset the pub landlady, a fearsome-looking woman around about five feet tall but with arms like a wrestler and attitude to match. Then some Norwich fans turned up. They quickly realised they outnumbered us two-to-one, and started making threatening noises. Given that Griff was with us, I knew this could turn ugly, as he was not afraid to use his knife, so I looked for a way to get us out of there without losing face. I decided to throw a bottle at a large mirror behind the bar. The landlady ducked to avoid the bottle, which shattered behind her, and in a fury threw down her tea towel, lifted up the bar flap and headed towards me. I flew out of the door, quickly followed by the others, leaving the irate lady shouting abuse at us. In fits of laughter, we headed off down the road.

On entry to Scamps we found some of our football players at the bar and ended up chatting and buying drinks with Lou Macari and Stewart Houston. I had met Houston more than once on the train back to London after games at Old Trafford, as he was still living in the capital when he first transferred to United from Brentford, and occasionally gave him a lift from Euston to Victoria. Meanwhile Griff and Tooting Steve approached Alex Stepney, who came from their old stamping grounds in Mitcham and had played for Tooting & Mitcham United, to talk about old times. However, Stepney blanked them. I thought Griff was going to punch his lights out, and we had to pull him away. To avoid any further nastiness, we said our goodbyes to the players and led Griff towards the exit.

And so that epic season came to an end with promotion, but the violence was to continue as the decade wore on. Indeed things were to become much worse, with the country being riddled with more strikes, rubbish piling up in the streets, the dead not being buried, punk rock providing a raucous voice for the disenchanted and the football terraces reflecting the wider breakdown of society.

CHAPTER 6

IT GETS WORSE

There were times in the Seventies when killing another fan seemed just one step away. We went out with intent to harm the opposition, and when you – and your rivals – have that attitude, anything can happen. In August 1974 an eighteen-year-old from Blackpool was stabbed to death by a Bolton Wanderers fan during a half-time skirmish underneath the Kop end at Bloomfield Road, in what was regarded as the first hooligan-related fatality of the modern era. A number of lads had already started to carry knives or other weapons. There has never, so far as I know, been a shooting at a game in England, but it has happened elsewhere, notably during a clash between Feyenoord and Ajax fans in Holland. Plus foreign police are usually armed and have also been known to fire at fans. I often look back now and realise I came very close to being in very serious trouble, both inside and outside football. When you are young you don't think so much about the potentially terrible consequences.

One of our bloodiest encounters came at the start of the 1975/76 season with a game against Wolverhampton Wanderers at Molineux. Fourteen fans were stabbed that day. I drove up there in my Rover 2000 to meet the lads, and the tone was set when we arrived outside the ground, where we spotted a black guy wearing the gold colours of Wolves. He was also carrying a hand axe, like a sawn-off version of a normal axe, and was swinging it around as he walked along the street. His eyes stared like a demon, as if he was in some sort of trance, and he was shouting abuse at anyone who came near; not that you could get that close, as the axe swung in a such a wide arc. Everyone, including his fellow Wolves fans, kept well away at first, until eventually, no doubt tired from his exertions, he stopped threatening to cut off people's heads and held the axe down by his side. Sensing an opportunity, we grouped together and charged him from behind. He fell forward, stumbling, but managed to keep his balance and turned around, spitting anger at us and raising the weapon above his head. We stood off as if beckoning him forward, although inwardly we hoped he would see sense and leave. The axe looked seriously sharp. He took a step forward, stopped, took in how many there were of us, then turned and ran off down the road. We all sighed with relief.

The atmosphere remained threatening, with Wolves geared up for what they knew would be a big fight. Some United occupied the terracing along the side of the Molineux pitch but most were packed in behind one of the goals. Nevertheless, we scouted the ground to see if we could get into the Wolves end. This was to be Tooting Steve's finest hour. I followed him as our little team led the rush to get into a section of side terrace full of Wolves. The Ghost was with me.

THE GHOST *This Wolves game was when Tooting Steve did his so-called suicide action by diving into their end. He was the top boy that day, make no mistake, leading twenty or so of us into the middle of the ground where the Wolves firm were. He told us that when we got to the top of their terrace, to scream and shout and start punching and kicking. Well, he went off on his own into their lot and the* *crowd split right down the middle like a wave. We followed and got down to the pitch level, only for this black geezer that we had seen earlier in the street to pull out his axe and hit one of us. Fortunately one of our lads, Sammy, came across and proper ironed the geezer out, and we all climbed over onto the pitch. This was before the game had even started. It was mayhem in and out of the ground.*

Worse trouble came after the game, with businesses being attacked and looted and windows smashed up and down the side streets near the ground. Some shops had boarded up their fronts, but we tore the boards down, smashed the glass behind and took anything worth grabbing – we even cleared out the club shop. The area around the ground resembled a war zone. And all this was after we had won with two late goals; God knows what we'd have done if we had lost. The Old Bill summoned horses, dogs and reinforcements to eventually hem us in near the Molineux Hotel. Hundreds were arrested but my little team was able to get away and head back to the car.

It all made the TV news, with a host of confiscated weapons put on display. They included the infamous axe, a meat cleaver, scissors, steel combs, an assortment of knives and even a hairbrush. Sir Matt Busby was interviewed about the behaviour of the fans and said, 'We don't want them, they should be grabbed and thrown in the river.' The *Daily Mirror* started to run a regular league table of hooliganism, which showed United way ahead of anyone else. What sparked so much media fury was the collateral damage to both commercial and residential property, particularly people's homes. We didn't care about any of this, about the cost of any repairs or whether the locals were terrorised. The hooligan ruled, and nothing was standing in his way. As our ranks swelled, many older, more law-abiding fans began to stay away, not wishing to run the gauntlet of constant violence. Young kids would also be kept away by their parents, and you rarely saw a woman at a match. Football violence thrived on this breakdown of tradition and the hooligan was able to take over the popular terrace.

Other factors were fuelling the rise in violence. Drink was a major one, although I was the same with or without it. Some needed it to give them bravado, but a drunk loses his edge and sharpness, so there is a fine line as to its effectiveness when it comes to a fight. Others talked the talk after a few pints but rarely walked the walk; booze made the gobshites sound off even more. It also seemed that the criminal world was taking an interest in football. High-profile villains like the Krays had always been around sports like boxing, snooker and horse-racing, but now they were finding an outlet in football. Even bigger white-collar crooks, like the newspaper magnate Robert Maxwell, were buying clubs. Partly this was ego-driven but there was also money to be made in the game by rich men who took large sums out of clubs but rarely spent much on their grounds or even the players. Some of the supposedly 'top' grounds were in a dilapidated, unsafe state and the fans were treated like cattle. Many of us responded by acting like animals.

My next run-in with the law came in August 1975, as I made my way back to London from a game at Stoke City. There was massive trouble on the train, with few of us having valid tickets. The ticket inspector took exception to being messed about and had the train stopped at Bletchley, in Buckinghamshire. I was pointed out to the police as the ringleader and was carted off, protesting, to the local nick. It wasn't too bad: I was kept in for twenty-four hours and fed three times – each time eggs and chips. The coppers said I was held because they had an outstanding warrant for me on their system and had to check it out. It turned out to be an error and they released me, but I did end up later at Stony Stratford magistrates on some made-up charge for the trouble on the train and copped another fine.

A month later we played against Manchester City, a fixture that was perhaps the worst derby game for violence up to that time. Our leader that day was Geoff Lewis, the short, tough, ginger-haired Manc who had adopted us and had a fearsome reputation. We arrived in Manchester by train in the late morning and headed to the Waldorf Hotel, near Piccadilly Gardens, where we met up with Geoff and a few hundred thugs and started drinking. More and more crowded inside the bar, with other United lads filling pubs all the way out to Maine Road. Geoff called for us to move out at about two o'clock and we formed a large mob as we snaked along Oxford Road towards the ground. As we passed the various pubs along the way, more United streamed out of them or joined us from cars and buses, and by the time we approached Maine Road we were almost a thousand strong.

City's boys didn't come out (they never did) in any numbers because they knew they would get obliterated. However, it still kicked off before the game and there were two near-fatal stabbings. One fan was done in the neck, and if the blade had gone through the carotid artery he would have been dead in a short time; luckily for him it narrowly missed anything serious. It happened on an area of wasteland outside the ground, when United chased off a small group of City. One of them stumbled and was held down by a Red. He recovered and grabbed our lad by the hair, but another Red pulled out his knife and stabbed it into the guy's neck. I arrived on the scene to witness the bizarre sight of some of our blokes trying to wriggle the knife out so they could use it again. Unable to do so, they lost themselves in the crowd as a St John Ambulance man and the police arrived.

The day became famous for one of the best ever ruses to get into a home section. The crowd was 47,000, with City's main faces in the Kippax, us to their left and the police in-between. To the right of the City fans, however, was another group of United, mixed in with them. We knew they were there but City did not. Some of the United jam-packed into our terrace pretended they were being crushed and gasped for breath, so the police let them onto the pitch perimeter to find a less congested place to stand. They promptly ran to the City section, jumped over the wall and steamed in. This was the signal for the Red group who had already infiltrated that area to attack from their side too. Then more simply piled out of our section and flooded into the City mob. The day was a total triumph, and outside the ground afterwards we never saw City at all. That was typical them – they like to go home early for their tea. They might come out occasionally when most of us have gone home, and claim a little 'victory', but that's it.

By the time we played West Ham at the end of October, we were top of the league. The Hammers at Upton Park, deep in the East End, was always a good trip, and this one brought back memories of a previous visit, when we had got off at Plaistow, the stop before Upton Park, to try to surprise their firm. They had heard about it and were waiting, armed, when we arrived. A handful of us got out of the small station but were attacked and at least one was stabbed. Some of the few coppers there were literally shaking with fear at the level of violence. We had to back off into the station, where we picked up handfuls of fruit and veg from a stall in the foyer and hurled them at West Ham. It was little match for their ammonia, bricks and bottles, but we returned fire with what we could and held out for more than five minutes, which believe me is a long time when you are under the cosh. The police would not let us out, and eventually forced us onto the train to go to

Upton Park Station. The 1975 game turned out to be similar in its intensity, and goes down as one of my finest moments.

THE GHOST *This was when we saw Bob at his best, at the front leading the charge. Some West Ham came out of their 'chicken run' terrace and onto the pitch, but these were mainly the innocents trying to avoid getting smashed as United swarmed into that section of the ground. 'United' chants seemed to be coming from all four corners, then fighting broke out behind the goal, where the two sets of main fans were segregated, as many of us were in their part. To be honest we were taking a hammering, outnumbered but fighting hard. We formed into a group and were being pushed back towards the exits, but there was Bob, holding the line, not taking a step back. We all wanted to leave but we stood by him and he spurred us on and saved us.*

I just did what I thought was right. Of course, I was wound up with drink, but this was at a time when I was at my most violent. There was also something about the Hammers that got to me; I had previously had a run-in with some of their top faces (see Chapter 16) and was well-known to their Inter-City Firm. They outnumbered us heavily as they advanced towards us, and some United were edging towards the exit to avoid a real slapping. I did not blame them. Even The Ghost shouted something like, 'Come on, Bob, there'll be another day,' and someone else said, 'Let's wait in the street and catch them when they come out.' Two young lads at my side paused and looked at me, as if for guidance.

That did it. I snarled, 'Let's get at them!' and moved towards the baying West Ham mob. Surprisingly they stopped, as if unsure what to do next. I ran forward with a shout, punched a West Ham lad on the side of the head and booted his shin.

The Ghost suddenly appeared at my side, as he invariably did, and then it was all off. Headbutts, punches, elbows, knees and boots flew everywhere. The raw close-quarter fighting must have continued for almost five minutes before the police drove a wedge between us. We had held our ground, and we proudly gave them a parting chant before being escorted out into the street.

United were still top of the league as late as the end of January, but faltered through February to fall away over the final stretch and finish third, while Liverpool won eight of their last nine games to take the title. Still the Red Army continued to terrorise all and sundry, and towns and cities came to dread the day we played there. Many of the country's more tranquil spots had never seen anything like it. One of these was Norwich, where United rocked up for a midweek game in March 1976. Among those who experienced the Red Army at first hand was Steve Little, who I later got to know and who became the ghostwriter for this book. Steve was shocked by the behaviour he witnessed that day.

STEVE LITTLE *Although I am a Burnley fan, I was born and bred in Essex. I also had many friends who followed Manchester United, and used to join them for visits to grounds like West Ham and Fulham in the Sixties, when there was little trouble. In March 1976 I was living and working in Norwich, and had a small office near the train station, which has the Carrow Road ground just behind. Making late morning business calls on foot, I came across a crowd of fifty United fans swarming out of the station and heading towards the city centre. What astounded me was their ages. This was not school holiday time, but some were only about nine or ten and the oldest of the group looked no more than fifteen. I had worked in London and knew* *the accent well, and these kids were definitely from the capital, or near it. They all wore red and white, some had beer cans and these were either cast into the nearby river or thrown on the pavement when emptied. Shoppers gave them a wide berth. As a twenty-six-year-old bloke I didn't fear them, but others looked scared and the louts preyed on this, abusing passers-by and spitting at or arguing with anyone who showed any sign of disapproval. At one stage the group started kicking a ball around on the four-lane road, bringing all traffic to a halt. Blaring horns were met with V-signs or spittle on windscreens. I later heard that the group pushed an elderly man to the ground when he took issue with them.*

I had to call into the shop of a mortgage broker, the office of a recently retired top referee, Norman Burtenshaw, one of those that no fans seemed to like – he had even been stabbed by a Millwall fan as he left the pitch at The Den some years before. I told Norman what I had seen, and he went off on a rant about United hooligans and what he had witnessed of them whilst a ref. He was clearly also not a great lover of Tommy Docherty. Later I went to the Market Place, where colourful stalls sold their wares, and ran into the same group. They were no less threatening but had been joined by much older youths, probably late teens and early twenties, also what the locals would call 'Cockneys'. There was blatant stealing from the open stalls until the police finally arrived and the United group dispersed. Other groups poured from the station all afternoon to gather in the city pubs and cafés.

Nevertheless I had decided to go to the game. On my way to the ground the United army was now over three hundred strong and marched down towards the ground, mostly in the middle of busy roads, holding up the commuter traffic.

Being in jeans and bomber jacket myself, with longish hair, I latched onto them and they didn't seem to notice. Most had cans of beer, bottles of vodka and other spirits. One youngster was pouring Bacardi into a half-full bottle of Coke so that it looked like he just had a soft drink. Their route happened to pass Burtenshaw's office. His name and face were emblazoned on advertisements in the window. That was enough for the United boys: someone heaved a block of something through the window. Some lads dived in and threw office chairs into the road, amid a great cheer, then scattered paper documents onto the footpath. One kid picked up a long shard of glass and jokingly threatened his mates, before throwing it back into the shop.

I was amazed that no police had bothered to accompany this large group, bearing in mind what had happened earlier in the day. At the ground I could see why, however; the police were there in force to handle all the arriving United fans, corralling them on the station forecourt and into the car park and road nearby to escort them the few hundred yards to the ground. The game passed off without incident on the terraces with United fans escorted out before any from Norwich and shepherded to the station.

The next day I dropped in to see Burtenshaw. He was seething and using industrial language worthy of a red card about the damage and United generally. His mood was not helped when the new window fitters dropped a huge sheet of plate glass into the road while taking it down from the side of their van, and had to order another. This was my first experience of what a scourge on the game hooliganism had become. I later realised that these kids bent on causing trouble were serving their 'apprenticeship', learning from the older ones.

* * *

By the time the long, hot summer of 1976 approached, I was almost at the end of my sentence in Pentonville for the attack on the building site foreman. It meant I missed United reaching the FA Cup final against Southampton. I would have loved to have been at Wembley, and even thought about making a break for it, as there was an outside work party was being sent from the prison to Holloway in North London. If selected for it, I figured I could slip away, gate-crash Wembley and then given myself up afterwards. It would probably add six months to my sentence, but might be worth it for the fun. I'm glad now I didn't bother.

Instead I followed the game on a small transistor radio. What excited me ahead of the game was the prospect of an easy win, after all it was only Second Division Southampton. They were 5-to-1 against to win, unbelievable odds in a two-horse race, such was the money going on United. Assuming United were to win, I could then look forward to a Charity Shield outing in August against the Scousers, as they had won the League. I had a side bet for some tobacco with a face in the nick, but lost when Bobby Stokes, yards offside, scored for a 1–0 Southampton win. I was not a happy bunny and even less so when the Cockney lads told me what they got up to on the day and what I had missed. The Tooting firm, for example, met at Waterloo Station to hunt down arriving Southampton fans they might be able to relieve of tickets.

JOE *We were desperate for tickets, so we hung around, watched them get off the train and followed them out of the station. They went in a pub just around the corner, towards where the London Eye is now. We mixed in with them at the bar, but they didn't know who we were*

– London accents and no colours or scarves. We pretended to be Saints fans and asked if they had tickets. They said they did. We said we didn't believe them, so they showed us. Silly sods, because we then knew where they kept the tickets on their person. We made an excuse to get a few of them outside and, once there, we held them down, beat the crap out of them and nicked the tickets. We didn't take their money or wallets or watches – just the tickets.

We got about half a dozen, but by the time we arrived at Wembley off the tube there were thirty or forty of us who wanted to get in. A few managed to crash through the turnstiles two at a time, after showing just one ticket; the men on the gate weren't going to argue. In those days you could also slip the gateman ten quid and he'd let you in. And any tickets could be thrown back out to be used again.

THE GHOST *We were standing at the stadium end of Wembley Way, milling around and wondering what to do next, as some still didn't have tickets. They were resigned to buying absurdly overpriced tickets from a tout, when Bobby Charlton appeared and asked, 'Any United supporters here?' He had about six tickets in his hand. 'Yes Bob,' we answered in unison, in our London accents. 'No, you're not from Manchester,' he said, and moved on. A proper melt, I thought, and I have never forgiven him.*

JOE *Despite losing, we had a great night and laughed that Bob was stuck in clink and missing it all. We went up West and you'd have thought we'd won the Cup. All evening we fought with Southampton, running up down the streets, attacking them at will and escaping by diving in and out of pubs.*

I was really upset to have missed all this. Prison was chastening, yet only seemed to make me worse. Mum and Dad did visit regularly but my sister, who was married by then, quite rightly chose not to. My parents retired to Seaford, in Sussex, that summer of 1976. I really did appreciate them visiting me and felt guilty that I was letting them down. As soon as I came out of Pentonville, I moved into a flat in Waddon, near Croydon, for six months, then my parents rented me a flat in a house they owned in Sutton that had been divided in two. I was comfortable there and eventually bought it off them about ten years later, after I had met my wife.

As far as the Cockney Reds were concerned, the time in prison raised my status within the group. When I came out I was even more of the dog's bollocks, and I felt good about it. Looking back I could, and should, have done things differently but back then I didn't care. I was dangerous, awful, really terrible. I was so out of control I might easily have killed someone, or been killed myself, if circumstances had been unkind. I still felt I was no leader – I wasn't into ordering people about and all that crap – but my actions probably did make me someone to follow.

I was released from prison into the famous long summer of '76. I made the most of the glorious weather, working outside – some days it was even too hot to work in the afternoons, so we stayed in the pub – and at weekends going down to the coast to Littlehampton to camp out and cool off by jumping from the jetty into the Channel. Even the sea felt warm.

I was quickly back in the swing once the 1976/77 season started. At an August away game at Derby, both home and away fans were housed along one side and it was so easy to go into their part of the stand, so eight to ten of us Cockney Reds did so. As usual we wore no colours and laid into them before the game had begun. In the ensuing chaos my shirt was almost ripped from my back before the police restored some calm. Sporadic fighting continued to break out as other Reds infiltrated the Derby section, and half-time saw a major kick-off. The police waded in again not long after the game had resumed, and I was picked out due to my torn shirt. I gave the Old Bill a right verbal volley while trying to wriggle from their grasp, but was slapped to the ground and led away in cuffs. The game made national headlines, with a number of fans being found guilty of threatening behaviour and getting at least three months.

I was one of them. The evidence provided against me came from a number of coppers and, as at the Old Bailey all those years earlier, was largely fabricated, but the odds were stacked against me, so I pleaded guilty. I was, I admit, wildly out of control that day, so couldn't complain about the result. I spent two weeks in Leicester Prison, which was by far the hardest lock-up I had been in to date: the screws were harsh, the food dreadful, fellow inmates unfriendly and recreational opportunities virtually non-existent. I was pleased to be moved to the more low-key Ranby, not that far away in Nottinghamshire, which was comfortable and more like an open prison. As before, I toed the line, kept out of trouble, read a host of books and was released after six weeks.

Following this hiccup, I was told by Dobbin, who ran the excursions for the London Supporters' Club, that the club had instructed him not to let me have match and travel tickets. I did not much care, as there were plenty of other supporters' groups I could use, but I had now become marked out as a troublemaker and was on some list held by either the club or the police, although I was never sure which (maybe both). I actually took pride in this at the time, but my behaviour would continue to lead me into bad situations. As 1976 drew to a close I was twenty-six years old and had already crammed a lot into my life, much of it unpleasant. I was established as one of the leading lights in the Cockney Reds.

The unfortunate city of Norwich hosted United again in April 1977. I always enjoyed the trips up to what we called 'carrot country', often driving up and staying the night. It had top-notch pubs with decent beer, plus a few nightclubs we could get into after the game. We drove up for this, so missed the trouble on the trains and elsewhere which was filmed for a TV documentary. In fact there seemed to be TV cameras everywhere, but we weren't picked out because we never showed who we supported. We ended up drinking, quietly for us, in a pub beside the river close to the railway station not far from the ground.

All Saturday morning, those Reds not travelling by train arrived in droves and wandered through the city. Old Bill had too much to cope with given the numbers and the usual damage and looting was rife. As far as the game was concerned it was a nightmare losing 2–1 when we had been on a good run of results and we were to fall away for the rest of that season despite going on to win the FA Cup. What happened that afternoon has been recorded for eternity as filmed by the BBC and entered the general folklore of football violence. Young fans streamed down the exit steps behind the stand as the game ended – lads as ever with their flared trousers, mops of hair and scarves tied round necks, wrists and waists or just waving them in the air. The Old Bill formed a line just beyond the steps and were soon subjected to a torrent of bottles, and anything else that was solid. Two blokes took it on themselves to climb up onto the stand and one fell through the roof. I was with the fans trying to break through the corrugated sheeting at the back of the stand to get into the Norwich fans. As pieces of this sheeting broke away some were thrown inaccurately towards the police and ended up hitting all and sundry.

A seventeen-year-old Groomy was one of those filmed by the BBC travelling to the match on the train.

GROOMY *I was asked about tattoos by the TV reporter. I only had one or two then, unlike today, but had spent seventy quid on a United tattoo on my back, which was a lot of money in 1977. On the day after the game, the News of the World published a load of pictures they had got from the BBC and put it all over the front page, with me and my tattoo as a feature. I basked in the glory on the Monday at work and told all my mates to watch the Nationwide programme going out that night. That was my fifteen seconds of fame. There was a downside, as there always is. On the Tuesday, my eighteenth birthday, me and Steve M were up for the game at Everton. Celebrating a win and my coming of age, we were blotto, and were travelling on a bus from the ground towards Lime Street when we were spotted by Old Bill, who recognised me from my moment of fame the previous night. We were hauled off the bus, manhandled into a police car, driven to the station and put on a train.*

There was clearly a media fascination with this strange tribe known as Manchester United fans. When we played Leeds at Elland Road the following season, West Yorkshire Police filmed the whole day from their perspective. You can see the film online on the British Film Institute website; it's not that exciting and is rather long, but it's a fascinating depiction of society in the Seventies. How different everything looks compared to today.

First, the lads featured look like they are attending a Bay City Rollers tribute band audition, with their lank hair, United scarves tied around their wrists, and flared jeans either covering their shoes or, in the latest trend, rolled up at the bottom to a few inches above a shiny pair of Doc Martens boots. Second, they all look about fifteen. The cops are in their traditional garb of the day: no hi-vis tops, body armour or communication devices, probably just a whistle. They all seem to have bushy sideburns and 'taches that make them look like a porn stars – or rejects from The Village People. Some are on horses and many are leading dogs. One particular shot, of coppers waiting on horseback at the top of a hill overlooking the ground, makes them look like Apaches about to attack a wagon train.

According to a sheet of cardboard held for the camera at the end of the film, there were 44,500 in attendance and eighty-one arrests, with four coppers injured. Manchester United won 2–0. There are monotonous pictures of United being led from, and back to, the railway station and their coaches, reminiscent of those black-and-white wartime documentaries showing thousands of prisoners of war snaking their way into captivity. We don't see much trouble but there is good footage of those arrested being searched and relieved of their wallets and keys in some temporary police station in what looks like a church hall. Most of those shown are Leeds fans, although there is a close up of a Manc lad with a badly damaged cheek and eye, something commonplace then.

Wasteland around the ground is strewn with debris where it looks like old housing has been demolished. Fans are marched across it, which seems a little careless with all that rubble waiting to be picked up and thrown. The Cockneys are not shown. We would have kept away from the bulk of our main support, but close enough to pile in if something kicked off. If we saw a copper with a camera, rare as it was then, we would avoid being seen. Most of the Cockneys were older, wiser and, having seen it all already, would have been better organised and aware of what was likely to happen, making sure we weren't compromised. The police were predictable then and easy to outsmart and outthink. This game must have been one of the earliest examples of cameras being trained on football fans, and old-fashioned TV monitors being watched by plod in a control centre at the ground. Years later we were to see similar on programmes about the Hillsborough disaster, but a fat lot of good they did then.

Our clashes with Leeds in that period were as bad as any in the history of British football. There was pure, unadulterated hatred on both sides, and how someone was not killed I will never know. One of the Cockney Reds' finest hours came at such a game, at the end of the 1979–80 season. We had to win at Leeds and hope Liverpool lost to take the league title away from the Scousers. Over 14,000 United were there, a huge number of them without tickets, including me, Griff, Tooting Steve and his brother. Many southern fans had bought their tickets through the club and travelled to Manchester on the Friday to join the Red Army crossing the Pennines the next day. We travelled up by train on the day, making every effort to avoid the main groups; we were more of a commando squad, slipping under the radar and looking for a surprise attack.

As we neared Leeds, some of their fans boarded our train. It kicked off and the fighting was intense even before we arrived in the city. We then had to punch our way out of the train station and all the way down the street, encountering more and more groups of Leeds as we went. They had the numbers but we held our own. We were a group of maybe fifty and there were other groups of United, both Mancs and Cockney Reds, dotted all over. We eventually reached a building site, where we tooled up with wood and bricks before moving on to a pub near the ground for a couple of hours drinking.

When we came out, we bumped into a large group of Leeds. We laid into them so badly, backed by other United fans arriving all the time, that they split up and ran off. Leeds, like most others before and since, were having second thoughts. By 2.30 we were heading towards the turnstiles, clashing again with Leeds along the way. Missiles flew and one Yorkie, a big fat bloke, went down unconscious from a brick to the head thrown by one of his own side. We just stepped around him. Thousands of United were already inside the ground and many more outside. None of my group had tickets, but stubs and even full tickets were being thrown back outside from those inside, many of them shaped into paper planes to make them fly. At one point a set of gates were smashed from the inside and crashed down on a group of police officers, with some being injured and having to be taken away.

We lost 2–0, and with fucking Liverpool winning it was a bad day. But off the pitch there would only be one winner. We were shown out of the ground ahead of the Leeds fans, with Old Bill more interested in cracking our heads than those of their own fans, something we always suffered at Liverpool too. As we left the stadium, we organised ourselves. The police tried to escort the whole United contingent back towards the city centre and the train station, but my group was having none of it. We had pre-arranged to turn right and head off to the United coach park, along with those travelling on the coaches, which were parked conveniently at the top of a hill. We waited for about ten minutes to let our stragglers catch up and for Leeds to be allowed out onto the streets, then headed towards the train station, where we knew the Leeds hooligans would plan to go. We used an unusual route that one of the lads knew. About a thousand of us were able to get behind Leeds near the station and surprise both them and the police by attacking from their rear.

We gave them a hell of a ragging. Running battles kicked off outside and inside the station and on every platform, and spilled onto various trains. Us, Leeds, the police and ordinary passengers were all caught up in a maelstrom of running, fighting, shouts, screams, confusion and terror. Many fans ran onto the tracks, either being chased or doing the chasing. Old Bill seemed at one point ready to give up, but at just that moment reinforcements arrived and started arresting anyone they could grab. It was pot luck as to who they targeted – you could be grabbed if you stood out or were shouting, or weren't quick enough to dive back into the crowd or run faster than they could catch you. We eventually chased Leeds off each platform, with Old Bill always one platform behind. Only once we had cleared our Yorkshire enemies from the station did we board our trains and sit down, ready to leave.

By then I had got to know Joe very well. He had become one of the main faces in the Cockney Reds, a good man to have by your side in a fight. He recalls the first time he and I really teamed up on the terraces, at a match at Chelsea in the late Seventies.

JOE *We all met up in a pub opposite the ground. We were not wearing any colours, and with our London accents could pass for Chelsea fans. About a hundred of us went over and got into the Shed, where we split into small groups and started to mix in. What we didn't know was that another lot of Cockney Reds had got in separately. Someone gave a shout and it went off like you'd never seen. We backed Chelsea right down to the bottom of the Shed, but when they realised there was only just over a hundred of us, their main firm started coming back at us. It was toe-to-toe for about ten minutes, with Bob leading the way. The Mancs in their own section were all cheering and shouting us on.*

When the fighting stopped, the Old Bill walked down the middle of the aisle and said, 'If there are any Manchester United supporters in here, we will give you an escort to the other end to be with your other supporters. Or we'll leave you.' No-one moved, and there were even a few scuffles as an inspector walked down the middle and made another plea. We finally moved out into this gap and were shouted and spat at by Chelsea. The Old Bill then walked us along the side of the pitch, with Bob at the front – it was like a triumphal march as we waved like a conquering army to the United terrace, with Chelsea throwing coins and shouting abuse. We had got in their end and won the day, and from that point on Banana had my respect.

CHAPTER 7

AWAY DAYS

Every team has certain away grounds where they always seem to get trouble. Our trips to Southampton were usually lively, with bad blood between the two sets of supporters dating from our loss to them in the 1976 FA Cup final. In February 1977 we were drawn to play them away in the same tournament. I drove down with Griff, Tooting Steve and a couple of others, and we duly parked up and went to meet some other Cockney Reds who had travelled down in vans. After a few beers and the odd skirmish, we made our way into the ground, choosing to enter one of the side stands rather the designated away end. It was packed – some fans were even clinging to branches of trees outside to get a view – but I managed to locate some other United in amongst the Saints fans. Trouble erupted when United scored, with our fans invading the pitch in celebration. I went on the pitch again with hundreds of others at the final whistle and chased after the Southampton. They legged it and we followed, attacking everyone in our path as we spilled out through the gates and onto the street.

Southampton seemed to have had enough and all ran off. About thirty of us hung around for a while to see if they might return, but when they didn't show, we headed away from the ground, with some police officers walking in front of us. One of our group became detached behind us. We heard a commotion and turned to see that he had been jumped by some of their lads. We ran back to help, with the police now behind us instead of ahead; they had their hands full with another group of United and left us alone. Our mob of thirty chased off the opposition, helped our mate to his feet and headed off towards our vehicles, which were parked in side streets.

We drove off in convoy, only to come across the group we had just been fighting. We knew they were top faces, not young kids, and that they were tooled-up, but then so were most of us. We stopped, our lads jumped out, and I drove around a corner to park the car. It was a residential area with few spaces, so it took me a while to find one, and by the time I returned it was clear many Southampton had been injured. One was slashed so badly on the top of his head that it looked life-threatening. Still their boys were well up for it, and those of us not armed looked for anything we could use, with the fighting as savage as any I had seen. Soon police cars and ambulances whined towards us, and I headed back to the car with my group, while the others piled into their vans.

We set off again but had not got far through the city when I was pulled over at a police roadblock. They were treating this as a major incident, due to the seriousness of the injuries; apparently it looked like the slashed bloke might not make it. I blagged my way past the coppers and was soon out of the city but not before I saw a cut-throat razor, almost certainly the weapon used in the attack, being tossed out of another United car window. We found out a week later that one of those arrested had given the police a number of names, including my nickname, and a copper asked one of the Cockneys who had been nicked, 'What do you know about Banana Bob?' This mate replied, 'Isn't it a type of milkshake?' I can't have been fully on their radar, as there was no comeback on me, but they now had a name. The bloke with the cut head survived.

Major rucks could happen anywhere, often at the most unlikely of games. The Cockney Reds were keen on any trip that might bring a spot of action, even when United were not involved, and London was ideal for making short, impromptu visits to other grounds.

JOE *When Wimbledon were elected from the Southern League into the Football League in 1977, they became eligible to enter the League Cup, and this particular year they had an away game at Gillingham, the first leg of two. Having grown up close to Wimbledon, some of us followed their fortunes and liked the club. They had no hard fans and were a friendly lot, so we decided we would go down to Gillingham with them to see if we could have a good evening out. The Gillingham firm had a bit of a reputation in a lowkey way, so we put a little firm together and headed off on the train. We found other small mobs from Chelsea and Millwall travelling there with the same idea.*

We got chatting and one said, 'Why don't we team up? We could put on a right show.'

I'm up for it,' I said, and those with me agreed. 'But let's not say who we are,' I added. 'The fuckers won't know what hit them.'

Some of the Chelsea lads were hardcore and one, who was already very drunk and shouting the odds, suddenly produced a handgun. He waved it above his head, opened the carriage window and fired out. We were all on the floor by then. Fortunately he walked off down the carriage and we didn't see him again, so God knows where he went. It definitely was going to be one of those nights.

From Gillingham Station we all headed for the Railway

pub, where the heavy drinking started. After a while some scruffy down-and-out approached us and offered to sell a crate of beer and spirits he had nicked from an off licence the night before. We expressed interest, and he led me and a couple of others down an alley beside the pub to show us his stash. We gave him a slap and sent him on his way, taking his booze to refresh us at the game.

About fifty of us eventually congregated in a small side stand. The Gillingham lads could see us but had no idea who the hell we were, as we were separate from the Wimbledon fans, who stood mainly behind one goal in what was a small crowd. Gillingham must have been intrigued, because when the game ended they were waiting for us outside – two or three hundred of them, prepared to take on this unidentified crew. They ran straight at us, but no-one moved – we just stood still like the infantry. Most of us were so pissed we couldn't have moved fast anyway. We went toe-to-toe and had a right punch-up. A lot got nicked and, to be honest, I was relieved when I was arrested, as we were being overrun. Interestingly it was the first time I'd ever seen the police filming a fight.

We were taken to the police cells and all let go at different times of the night. I had to wait until dawn before there was any transport for me, and was none too happy, but one mate, Eric, a great teller of jokes, had the Old Bill in such fits of laughter that they took him out of his cell and summoned everyone in the station to listen to him. A couple of weeks later, we all had to go to Chatham Magistrates on a threatening behaviour charge. We all pleaded guilty, as it would have been too much hassle to contest the charge at Crown Court and we might have ended up with a stiffer sentence, such was the evidence against us, much of it on camera. We were all fined.

Nevertheless, when the second leg was played, we all went down to Wimbledon's Plough Lane to give it to Gillingham big-time. They were in the ground early and took the Wimbledon end, so we had to sort that out first – and we did. A funny thing was, the Gillingham could not work out how Wimbledon had such fucking awful fans, when everyone thought what a nice little club they were. We never let on we were Cockney Reds.

We made a similar trip in 1978, when I gathered together a tasty little firm from Tooting, made up of few Cockney Reds, some Palace and a couple of Chelsea, to visit Millwall's Den for a cup quarter-final. They were playing Ipswich Town, who had a great side then and a good following, more violent than you might imagine for a load of country boys. Once again we joined more lads from other clubs, all there for the same reason. We stood among the Millwall support along the side of the pitch to avoid the packed Cold Blow Lane End. Ipswich were behind the goal at the other end, baiting the home fans. We joined in with Millwall's vocal response. With the game still to start, two Ipswich lads ran onto the pitch and up to halfway, beckoning to the three sides of Millwall. A few Millwall climbed over the perimeter wall and ran towards the centre circle, and realising their plight the two Ipswich legged it back to their end, by which time the coppers had intervened.

Tension simmered throughout the game. Millwall were thrashed 6–1 and as each goal went in the crowd trouble worsened. Bottles, darts, iron bars and concrete slabs rained from the sky into both the Ipswich and Millwall terraces and dozens of innocent people were injured. My firm came to the fore as the game ended, clambering over the wall to join Millwall fans already on the pitch and running towards the Ipswich end. We could see Ipswich backing up the terracing, causing a crush as they tried to pour out of the back of the stand. Some were even trying to remove parts of the back of the stand to get away. What they hadn't factored in was the fifteen-foot drop from there to the road behind, and many were injured as they jumped or fell down. The police did their best but were short-handed, as most of them had already left the ground in preparation for keeping the departing fans separated in the streets and at the nearby station.

With about twenty others, I headed for the same station. We arrived to find a good number of Ipswich already there, pushing to get to the safety of their platform to catch the train to London Bridge. Millwall had chased them down but a strong police line held between the two sets of fans, leaving Ipswich corralled on the concourse and on the platform stairs. We needed the line back towards Croydon, so we used a different entrance and ended up on the opposite platform to Ipswich. They saw us and assumed we were Millwall, prompting a dozen or so to come over the tracks and onto our platform for a row. Every credit to them, but it was a move they regretted as we attacked, causing significant injuries to some of them. We left them in a heap and climbed onto our train. That day doesn't feature in any hooligan books but it deserves to be in any compilation of the worst football incidents, and again showed some eight years after Sutton how we sniffed out violence in and around London, even when United weren't playing.

We made another unusual trip to a backwater of the game in September 1977, when we trooped down to the West Country to see United play the French team St Etienne in the UEFA Cup. The first leg, in Paris, was such a riotous affair that it has been called 'the night soccer hooliganism was introduced to France'. Sadly I was not there to experience it, as I was short of readies at that time, but apparently an hour before kick-off, five hundred United fans gathered behind one of the goals and launched an all-out assault. 'Armed with bottles, sticks and knives they went for the supporters of the French team,' *The Times* later reported. According to the magazine *Goal*, 'Gripped by panic, the home fans sought refuge by climbing the grills surrounding the field, which broke under the sheer weight of bodies against them and led to more supporters piling onto the pitch. It was in the midst of this solid iron twisting and breaking that the majority of the 33 injuries, including five serious, occurred. Local reports at the time indicated that it was fortunate fans were nimble enough to climb the grilles, else there may have been multiple deaths.'

A disgruntled UEFA awarded the tie to the French due to the violence. United were furious, blaming fans who were not part of the official Supporters' Club but had travelled under their own steam. Most of them did not have tickets and so had either gate-crashed the turnstiles, bought from local touts or paid (most unlikely) on the gate. The Sports Minister, Denis Howell, became involved and claimed some of the blame should be directed towards poor policing and segregation by the home club. United appealed the decision and were successful in that the second leg was approved, provided it was held more than two hundred kilometres from Old Trafford. The venue chosen was Plymouth, which was about as remote as possible. I'm sure Plymouth Argyle's owners rubbed their hands at the prospective income, but then they had to contend with more than 25,000 United fans from all over the country waking up their sleepy backwater. There was a full house of over 31,000 and we duly won the match and the tie. No French put in a show, and most of the local yobs hid behind their curtains.

I went down with Griff, Steve W and some others in my Jaguar XJ6. The game itself was fairly uneventful and afterwards we set off home, but quickly had to pull over for a piss. Griff, being Griff, somehow managed to pick an argument with some locals who were 'staring' at him, so we piled into them, leaving several in a heap. We then drove off, only to be pulled over by a police patrol car on the Cullompton bypass. The numpties we had attacked must have phoned them. We were taken to the local nick, where the police ran a CRO check and found yours truly and Griff on their database. The officers had been friendly towards us up to then, but their mood suddenly changed and they slung us in a cell. I was eventually released but Griff was held in custody on remand and then taken to Exeter, where he received a visit from Southampton police for the earlier serious incident in the cup game at The Dell. He was shown photos of the badly injured Saints fan.

'You did that,' a copper said.

'No, I didn't,' Griff replied. 'That's nothing to do with me.'

They asked if he was the same person named as the attacker by witnesses. 'There are a lot of people with my name in this world,' he replied, which did not go down well. Police subsequently raided his home in Mitcham to confirm his address and found an axe, which they deemed was an offensive weapon. They also found some drugs, so he received a six-month suspended sentence. But he was never charged with the Southampton incident, which really pissed off the police.

Another game around this period brought one of our invariably lively excursions to Norwich. Some of the regular Cockney Reds decided to meet up at the house of Steve W, who lived in Gants Hill, Essex, which is just off the A12 on the way towards East Anglia. We went on the Friday so we could have a night out at the Talk of The South club down at Southend. Steve couldn't put us all up so we stayed in a bed-and-breakfast, from where I drove the next day with Steve and

Griff. Passing Ipswich, we saw a couple of tasty-looking birds thumbing for a lift. We picked them up, and it turned out they lived in Norwich. They were chatty and seemed to like us, as they offered us a bed for the night if we got stranded for any reason. That was too good an offer to pass up, so we took their address and phone number.

We spent a few hours drinking at a pub near Norwich Station, a short walk from the ground. The usual hordes of United were there and we met a few other Cockney Reds who had come by train. A few locals got a bit mouthy, but we saw them off and then left for the game. The police presence was enormous, and they obviously hadn't forgotten three years earlier, when they had taken a bashing. The game was followed by a return to the pub, where I became more than just drunk – I was all over the place. However I was still committed to driving us all home, due to the hire car's insurance being in my name. We decided to get some food to 'soak up the booze' and stopped at a burger van, before returning to our car, which was in the open-air part of a car park. I went into the covered part to have a piss against one of the pillars. A copper appeared as I did up my flies. There was a splash up the wall and a pool at my feet.

'Did you do that?' the copper asked, pointing.

Griff, standing nearby, shouted over, 'No, it was done by a dog.' Which as it turned out was not that helpful. The copper grabbed me, I instinctively flung up my arms and by chance knocked off his helmet. I slurred an apology and, fair play to him, he saw the funny side and appeared content to let us go. So we jumped in the car and drove off. We had not gone far when a patrol car pulled us over; the first copper must have radioed his mates. I pulled over to the side of the road, opened the door and tried to leg it, but was so pissed that I stumbled and fell, and two coppers soon had me in hand. I had left the keys in the car and one of my mates had moved into the driver's seat, so I denied that I had been driving, and refused to take a breathalyser test. But the cops had seen me at the wheel, so I was stuffed.

The upshot was that they took me in and I spent the night in the cells. Throughout the night a procession of United fans were brought in, most of them for being drunk and disorderly or for threatening behaviour. Some had apparently unhitched a load of barges on the canal, which had floated off. Griff and the others, without their driver, decided to ring the two girls we had met to find out how to get to where they lived. I was so drunk that I cannot remember clearly what happened, but I assume I was tested at the station the next morning, then released. Later I received a one-year driving ban and a £100 fine, not for drink-driving but for refusing the breathalyser, which was a better option for me to plead guilty to.

Going on these away days sometimes meant not watching United or lying in wait at the other team's end to try to take it over or, if outnumbered, just create a ruck. It was a thrilling experience, but meant that sometimes we risked taking 'friendly fire' from our own side.

THE GHOST *If we went to Arsenal, Chelsea, in fact any of the London grounds, no-one could tell we were United. We would go to games when United weren't playing there, get in the home end, keep quiet for a while and then start a fight, and the Gooners, or whoever, wouldn't know what had hit them. Mostly though, we went to watch United.*

One year we were at the bottom of the North Bank, in amongst the Gooners, waiting for our chance to attack, when United's away contingent came out of their end and across the pitch, right in front of us in the penalty area. Many of us were shit scared, make no mistake, as they wouldn't have known we were United, and with us just a few in number, it seemed we were about to be on the end of an attack by our own. Fortunately they stopped and went back.

Having lost a cup semi-final one year, we played Watford in a third-place play-off at Highbury. A lot of Arsenal were in that day to look after their North Bank. It was kicking off big-time between us, and because the crowd was a bit sparse there was loads of room on this terrace for us to charge each other. They had no idea who we were and seemed to think we were Watford. It was chaos.

Sometimes we were not exactly welcomed by our own supporters.

JOE *The one and only time I went on a coach organised by a supporters' group was from Epsom to some United game. The Reds in Epsom didn't like us lot from over Sutton/ Tooting/Croydon way. I turned up for this trip and got on this almost empty coach and took a seat. A few around me were the anoraks that go on these types of trips, so I wasn't expecting any trouble on the journey. I sat back, closed my eyes and relaxed, only to be disturbed by some geezer hitting my shoulder.*

'Can't sit there,' he said. 'That's my seat.'

'It doesn't look like your seat, 'cos I'm sitting in it, mate,' I replied.

'No, no, no, we've all got our own seat.'

'Well, let me tell you something's fucking changing, because I ain't moving, so you'd better go and find another seat.'

I half stood and put my head against his. He got the message and found another seat. No-one spoke to me on

the rest of that trip and the coach people wouldn't let me
travel again, so that was that.

Most of the non-United games we attended would be in the
London area, when big rivals like Leeds United were down.
They played a few games at Selhurst Park that we turned up
for, memorable days with a few old scores settled.

One away day further afield was when about three hundred
of us went on to the seaside after a derby game against Man
City was called off. We heard the news and all decided to
catch the train on to Blackpool, who happened to be playing
Sunderland. They had a few tidy firms and Blackpool
always offered plenty of other entertainment. We arrived at
Bloomfield Road at half-time and, as usual, no-one knew who
we were. We easily got amongst the Sunderland and had an
almighty ruck.

Another postponement, of a game against Queens Park
Rangers, caused some of us to head off to the Arsenal versus
Newcastle game at Highbury to try to get in amongst the
Geordies. The majority, however, went to watch George Best
at Fulham, as many United fans did that season – showing
how popular he was, even when playing for another team in
Division Two. I can't recall the Cockneys ever causing problems at those Fulham games, perhaps due to the respect we all
had for George.

* * *

Throughout the Seventies I worked on building sites but also
made extra cash by selling items I had either nicked when going
to games or bought for re-sale from mates. Times were good,
and although I was drinking too much and mixing with some
shady types, all seemed well in my life. The country, however,

seemed to be tearing itself apart. Unemployment was rising to the highest levels seen in fifty years and some lads turned to any means necessary to make a few bob.

MICKY W *With society in a state, many of us in the Cockney Reds devised all sorts of ways to make money. My little group made a tasty living out of working slot machines. It involved the use of lawnmower string that you could use to manipulate the credits, allowing you to keep on playing until you had emptied the machine. It helped fund our days out to football and plenty of nights out in the week. Drugs were another thing. Some blokes I knew were supplying gear to well-known sports and TV people. Snooker players seemed to love cocaine. One day I saw two leading players of the day, now dead, sniffing cocaine in a mate's flat; the next day they played before millions watching on TV. A huge amount could be made by dealing or just acting as a go-between.*

Roy Downes and his mate Tony C, who came to games, were professional pickpockets and very good at it. Their trouble was, they would just as likely lift from United fans as anyone else. One day when on a trip back from Bristol there was trouble on the train when the buffet bar was closed, so we Cockneys opened it up and drank or nicked everything there. The train was stopped at Swindon due to this and to fighting on board, and as we disembarked onto the platform, there was Tony dipping someone in the crowd. Later we moved onto a hotel and he was dipping people in there too. Roy did the same during a football trip to Bulgaria but was nicked by the local cops, who subjected him to sleep deprivation and various other deeply unpleasant measures to discourage him from trying it again. It was so bad that it affected Roy mentally for the

*rest of his life. He was rarely seen at United games after
that and was never the same again.*

Roy Downes and Tony C were two of the most prominent
black faces among the Cockney Reds, along with another
big hitter from Wandsworth known as Black Sam. There
was a lot of racial tension at this time. Pro-white groups like
the National Front and the British Movement were gaining
support at a lot of football grounds, while the Afro-Caribbean
community suffered from racism, high unemployment and
feelings of injustice that exploded in riots in Notting Hill
in 1976 – which inspired the Clash song 'White Riot' – and
Brixton in 1981. Manchester United fans generally never
fell for the racist stuff, partly I think because of the club's
longstanding Irish-Catholic connections. In fact some of the
lads became quite prominent in taking on the racists when
a group called Red Action was formed in 1981. Despite the
name it had nothing to do with Manchester United, but was
a group of left-wing activists prepared to take to the streets to
confront far-right boneheads and groups like the NF and the
Britain National Party. Some hard-nosed football hooligans
had joined these groups and we came across extremist right-
wingers at a number of games, notably at Spurs and Millwall.

A Cockney Red called Mick O'Farrell became a leading
light in Red Action and took with him some like-minded
United fans, both Manc and Cockney. This added spice to
the conflicts around football, as we saw when confronting
Spurs in particular. There has always been a strong Irish presence at United, including a good number of Cockneys with
Irish backgrounds like Micky W and Brian. They hooked into
Red Action too, which was pro-Republican as well as anti-
fascist. I was also asked to join but had enough going on at the
football and declined, despite my own Catholic and pro-Irish

background. It was not really for me, although I did witness them in action. I also felt joining them might make me a target for the Law, and was proved right when many of the leading lights of Red Action were arrested.

One thing I can say about the Cockney Reds is that we embraced all creeds and colours, although we still had the odd idiot, like all big groups do.

STATUS QUO TONY *We were on a train coming back from a game and the West Ham players were on it. Clyde Best, West Ham's Bermudan striker of the Sixties and Seventies, came into the buffet bar and we were milling around, quite happy to be rubbing shoulders with a top player. Out of the blue a United twat called Clyde 'a big black cunt'. We were horrified and really berated the fella. To his credit Best just took it and went away with a smile – he had probably become used to it. None of us liked this sort of thing and I've seen less of it with United than anywhere else, but that's not to say it wasn't there.*

Perhaps because we were used to ethnic diversity in London, the Cockneys especially were welcoming to all within our various groups. Not many football firms can say that. I have fond memories of Roy in particular. He was a quiet bloke with an air of mystery about him. Some said he was wealthy, perhaps from the proceeds of crime, but I don't know for sure. He moved in all sorts of circles and knew many United players. He even once sat on the bench with Tommy Docherty at a Wembley final. How that came about I don't know – he was indeed an enigma. I was sad to see him so shattered after that Bulgaria experience. He became hooked on drugs and went into rehabilitation several times. I will always remember the fact that he rarely mixed with our crowd standing on the terraces, preferring the comfort of a seat, but outside the ground he would back you up in any fight.

Euston was the place where we would clash most often with other London firms as they travelled to and from away games. We would look at the fixtures to see who was likely to be there on any particular day and plan ahead. On match days we would fill all the pubs in the vicinity and take over the place. Trouble would break out both in the pubs and on the streets – I've seen pool balls being thrown through windows and at other fans. It was like a warzone at times and the police could rarely cope, although they once corralled us in a back street for two hours to stop trouble before a game at West Ham. It seemed almost every week we clashed with Arsenal, sometimes joined by other club's fans, depending on who was travelling through. Some Cockneys just turned up for a fight with no intention of going to the game.

THE GHOST *There was one time at Euston when loads of United fans going to a Tottenham game were accosted from nowhere by a small firm, all 'sweaty socks' (Jocks), climbing up the steps. They were Hibs fans. Their team had played a friendly at Millwall the night before, with the usual smashing of heads, and they were shouting the odds at how they had seen to Millwall down at The Den, which was most unlikely. We steamed into them and they had it on their toes all the way back to Russell Square.*

JOE *We would pick a fight with anyone, and Euston or Kings Cross/St Pancras were real battlegrounds. I don't know why, but we often seemed to clash with Arsenal. For some reason we also reserved special attention for Aston Villa, with whom we had a memorable stand-off on the way home one Saturday. During a lull in the fighting,*

*one of their number said to me, 'Fuck this for a game of
soldiers, why don't you put up your best bloke and we'll do
the same for a one-to-one to sort it out?' For one moment
I thought I might take up this challenge myself, but as I
looked around I saw other likely lads who might put up a
good show. Then I spotted one, something of a gobshite,
who always talked up how good he was in a fight, although
the rest of us knew better.*

'Right,' I said to him, 'it's you.'

*'But Joe, I need to get off,' he pleaded, looking at his
watch. The other Cockneys watching knew what I was up
to and called for him to man up.*

*'You bastard,' he angrily shouted at me, as we pushed
him forward. All skin and bone, he was up against a man
mountain and duly took a hammering. We were in hysterics
as he eventually stumbled away and headed down the steps
to the nearby tube station. We did see him again, but he no
longer talked up his prowess in a fight.*

Of course, every home game was an away day for the
Cockney Reds. Our usual return train was the 5.30 from
Manchester Piccadilly to London, not necessarily straight
home to our loved ones but perhaps to a pub or club close to
Euston, or, before we had domestic responsibilities, a nightclub somewhere close to home in South London for a late
one. Occasionally the lads would stay up in Manchester for a
drinking session and catch the last train back, which normally
meant a decent snooze in a quiet carriage, recovering from the
exertions of a long day. There was rarely any trouble on these
journeys but one did throw up the famous 'incident of the
missing shoes', when one well-heeled traveller came upon the
Cockney Reds in transit and would never forget the experience. The Ghost was there.

THE GHOST *This is one of those stories that has become the stuff of legend and shows the more humorous side of football travel; not that the victim of this particular little joust found it remotely funny. Not all memorable incidents require the bashing of heads and running battles. Some of our lads were coming back to London on the last train from Manchester on a Saturday evening. They included two of my best mates, their friend Pat and a Scottish pal of his. They had been on the lash all day, seen us beat Leeds 2–0, then continued drinking into the evening at Mother Mac's and Monroe's in Manchester. When they finally stumbled into their train carriage, they found it almost empty and sat down at one end with some cans. Their only company was an elderly couple sat up the other end, with thirty or more empty seats between them and our lads. The trains in those days had windows above the tables which slid open a foot or more. The boys started playing cards.*

A smart-looking bloke gets on wearing a pin-stripe suit, a hat with a pheasant feather in it and a rucksack over his shoulder. Instead of sitting away from our lads, he sits at the table right across the aisle from them, gets out a pack of sandwiches and leaves them on the table. He then takes off his shoes, rather expensive brogues, and puts them on the table too. He ignores our boys and dozes off once the train gets going. Pat's mate gets up, walks off and comes back laughing but says nothing. The other three of them, who are also dozing, stir when they hear his laugh but soon return to the land of nod.

As the train nears Milton Keynes, Pat's mate gets up again, walks the other way along the carriage and comes back laughing once more. The others still doze but the old couple watch his every move up and down the aisle, and give a little wave and a laugh as they take in what he does. He makes one more trip, this time to the toilet, returns and sits down. One of the dozing boys looks up to see breadcrumbs round this lad's mouth but thinks nothing of it and closes his eyes.

By now they're approaching Watford and the bloke in the pin-stripe is still asleep. He wakes up, looks out the window, looks round the carriage and suddenly shouts, 'Who's nicked my sandwiches?'

'Don't know what you're talking about,' Pat's mate says, with the crumbs still around his mouth and the stain of a big blob of salad cream on his jumper.

The bloke then says, 'Where's my bloody shoes? Come on, give me my shoes back.'

'But I can't,' says Pat's mate.

'Why not?' says the bloke.

'Well, one's somewhere near Stoke and the other's at Milton Keynes, coz I threw them out the window before I ate the sandwiches.'

The bloke went mental. 'Do you know how much those shoes cost me?' he shouted.

Pat's mate just shrugged and said, 'No idea.'

The guard arrived as the train neared Watford and hears the bloke's tale of woe. Once the train comes to a stop in the station the guard looks for Pat's mate, but he's moved to another part of the train. Sitting in a more crowded carriage this mate spots some Transport Police looking to board the train, so he dives for the exit and legs it down to the tube before they can get to him.

The police come aboard but find our lads asleep or more likely feigning it. The old couple didn't take much interest, and both sat quietly reading books. The posh bloke was really annoyed and padded up and down the aisle in his multi-coloured socks, muttering and swearing and our lads kept quiet, still pretending to be asleep.

The officers woke the lads to tell them the Met would be waiting for them at Euston. Once the train arrived there, the coppers appeared, and the posh bloke points out one of the Cockneys. Our lads are escorted from the train and the old couple let them pass with a smile. At the door Old Bill grab the lad who's been pointed out as he steps onto the platform and tell him he's under arrest. Another's held and also told he's being arrested.

'But we've not done anything,' one says. 'It was someone else who got off at Watford.'

The posh bloke is fuming and frustrated. Back inside the carriage the old couple are slowly making their way to the door, where they stand to watch the goings on between the Cockneys, the coppers and this bloke in his socks, rucksack over his shoulder, still clearly upset.

One lad offers to explain what might have happened, although he admitted he hadn't seen anything. Even the Old Bill seemed to find it amusing and started laughing. This sets the bloke off once more and the coppers try and calm him.

'Look,' he says, 'ask those people over there. He points at the old couple. 'They probably saw everything.'

The couple hear what's said and walk over.

'Excuse me, officers, can we help?'

'Tell them about this lot and my shoes!' the man shouts.

The old chap ignores him, walks past and says quietly to the officers, 'Are you concerned about this strange man who got on the train at Manchester?'

'Yes,' says the officer. 'Do you know anything about this?'

'I do,' says the old man, 'what I can tell you is that he

didn't have shoes on in the first place.' And with that he walked off.

The Old Bill could hardly contain themselves and said to our lads, 'You'd better be on your way before we do decide to nick you.'

The posh bloke was not happy.

Another funny incident involved Groomy on a day out in 1980:

GROOMY *Despite the odd little problem away from football, I haven't caused much aggro at games, with my only offence being nicked for swearing in a home game against Carlisle in the 1970s. However, I had a run in with a copper outside The Bullseye pub in Basildon in late 1979 which led to a custodial sentence for ABH. Early the following April, I was released from Wormwood Scrubs on a Monday morning, after serving four months, and the very next day was offered a job above the entrance to Goodge Street Station, doing a bit of general renovation work, to start on the Wednesday.*

Lunchtime came on day one of the job, and I thought I would pop along to St Pancras to see the lads on their way to Nottingham Forest. I slipped my club-hammer and bolster into my new donkey jacket pocket and took a leisurely stroll down Tottenham Court Road. A few beers later, I was 'manhandled' onto the train by Gurney and Neil Collins (better known now as 'Captain Vile'), and the jib began.

After escaping the clutches of Mike Dobbin and Graham Castle, who were collecting fares for the official United Travel Club, we arrived at Nottingham Station and strolled out into the street. I hid my tools in the front garden of a rather posh-looking building – I later found out it was the British Transport Police gaff – and we proceeded to find a 'cheap' off licence. Twenty minutes later, three Cockneys with three stolen bottles of Smirnoff Vodka were in the small queue to enter the Sportsman's Bar, which was the Forest Supporters' Club, adjacent to the City Ground. Entry was gained, and we strolled to the bar, where Gurney ordered the round, in a creditable Scottish accent.

Gurney: 'Three lime juices, pal.'

Barman: 'Lime juices?'

Gurney: 'We're driving.'

Barman: 'What, all three of you?'

'Aye,' we all answered.

Finding a table, we proceeded to down vodka and lime until it was time to go to the game, still laughing at the memory of the barman's face. A successful jib by us all, a 2–0 defeat and a free train journey back home, complete with the retrieved club-hammer and bolster. Needless to say, I was unemployed again on the Thursday!

Among a number of things Groomy and I have in common is that we are partial to the odd tattoo. For me it's on the legs and the front and back of the upper body – discreet but all over. Groomy is less covered but, you might say, more adventurous, or perhaps creative, and is known as the most colourful character in the Cockney Reds. It is rumoured (and he has never denied it) that a few years back he had a little message tattooed onto his John Thomas that said it was 'The property of ...' and then his first wife's name. After they split up, and not wanting any future conquests to see the message, he had a red devil imprinted over the top of it. Now that is commitment to the United cause. He also, in a moment of drunken madness, had an eye tattooed onto each cheek of his bum – I'm not sure even he knows why. Anyway, these eyes featured alongside the match report in the *Daily Sport* when we played Barcelona in Rome not long ago. Groomy flashed his bum at the photographers and that was the result.

At games now you will likely see him in some garish outfit (he got married wearing a bright red suit and also wore it to a game in Milan). For a while he used to wear a kilt and at a match in Milan was seen in his infamous mankini – not a pretty sight, even after a good few drinks. These days he is often in a green-and-black hooped top and even at a game at Chelsea in 2017 was standing on a parapet waving and was picked out on a YouTube film wearing this awful garment. But disastrous sartorial choices are not his main claim to fame. Many years ago, he unfurled a banner which read:

UNITED, KIDS, WIFE

Believe it or not, his then wife was there at the time to witness the unveiling. She was not overly amused. In more recent times 'IN THAT ORDER' has been added underneath.

This flag has been a permanent feature at games. Gary Neville has said how he always looked out for it when playing and even contemplated using the phrase for the title of his auto-biography, but valued his marriage too much. He did mention the flag in his memoir, as did former player and manager Wilf McGuinness. If you don't spot the flag look out for Groomy in his top and, by the way, he nearly always has a bright red goatee – as you do. He's a top Cockney Red, not so involved with the more violent stuff over the years but a good ally.

GROOMY *I always see ways I can get my thrills without the buzz of whacking someone or taking on Old Bill. Many a time I've calmed a situation when my mates have been totally legless and gone at Old Bill, have led the boys away and been thanked by the coppers. There are other ways you can get one over them if you wish, and that includes stewards in the ground. We once played Fulham at Craven Cottage, a ground where previously I had done some work and had come across an old black-and-white baseball hat with 'Fulham Catering' printed on it, which I kept. At the subsequent game I had it in my pocket and was also wearing a fluorescent orange bib, similar to those worn by football stewards. We'd had a few beers in Hammersmith and needed a freshener at half-time at the Putney End of Craven Cottage. As I headed to the bar beneath the Cottage with a mate, we found Old Bill had made sure the stewards blocked any United fan from getting there. Some were arguing with the stewards and it looked like it might kick off, so I put on my Fulham Catering hat, held my mate's arm up his back as though I was escorting him out, and the stewards let me through. We had our beer. Later in the game there was a bit of disorder in our crowd and a steward, seeing my orange top, shouted at me to do something. I shouted back, 'Fuck off, I'm watching the match.' The bloke's jaw dropped in shock.*

There have been many characters like Groomy over the years, but they are a dying breed.

CHAPTER 8

ONE CRAZY BASTARD

By 1982 I had a long track record of violence and been involved with a series of major incidents stretching back to the beginning of the Seventies. Add these to my time spent in the nick and my hooligan rap sheet was as bad as any within the Cockney Reds. We were now a well-established firm, respected in Manchester and building a reputation across the country. On a personal level I was still working as a brickie on various sites around the south of England, for an outfit based near Croydon, and lived on my own in the same flat my parents had arranged for me a few years earlier. I was seeing a woman who had three children, but our relationship was on and off and there were other women. I was thirty-two.

The country had fought a real war that springtime, when the Argies were given a seeing-to in the Falkland Islands by our lads. Then came the World Cup in Spain, where another type of army went to set about whoever got in their way. It would later emerge that Margaret Thatcher even wanted to pull England, the Scots and the Northern Irish out of the tournament, concerned that we might come up against Argentina and that English hooligans might disgrace the country. It was only a few weeks before the start of the tournament that our troops landed in the Falklands, and the surrender took place the day after the first match. Thatcher ultimately decided to let our teams go and is as it turned out there was quite a bit of trouble in various towns but nothing as bad as had been feared. England and Argentina were both eliminated without having played each other.

In May 1982, with the season all but over, many of us were at a loose end so went to watch a young United team play at Watford in the second leg of the Youth Cup final. We had a strong team, with future stars like Clayton Blackmore, Norman Whiteside and Mark Hughes, but Watford had some promising youngsters too, and had won 3–2 at Old Trafford in the first leg. We set off for the evening kick-off with a short train ride to the north of London. Not many Watford bothered to turn up and we had the run of the place. We lost on aggregate, but with only a couple of Old Bill there, we were all able to swarm on the pitch and lord it around and mix with the players. We'd been drinking all day and once back on the train we found the buffet shut and the staff in the seats busy counting a mountain of cash from the day's takings, bearing in mind they'd had a busy trip down from Glasgow. The staff were annoyed to see us and ushered us out of their carriage, but one of our mates, from Coventry, slipped behind them, grabbed all the cash and jumped off the train just as it was leaving. We settled down and the staff made a fuss about the money and when we arrived at Euston Old Bill packed the platform and they had us lined up searching all fifty of us but were pissed off when they found nothing. We were let go and our mate had got away with it all and despite the result, it turned out to be a most profitable day for him!

After the Falklands War, someone came up with the idea of a United pre-season friendly in the military town of Aldershot to raise money for the South Atlantic Fund, set up through the national press to provide support to bereaved service families by public donation (over £20 million was eventually raised).

With Aldershot being a short distance across the Surrey border, it seemed an opportunity for a night out in the height of summer with plenty of booze and to mix it with the locals, including squaddies from the town's huge Army barracks, who were always up for a fight. We were sure that once they knew we were in town they would come out – it was second nature to them.

We congregated in tee-shirts and shorts outside a pub on a roundabout close to the football ground, and it was good to see a large turnout of Cockney Reds after the summer break. At this time of my life I was more than binge drinking, and it was only a matter of time before this got the better of me, either by damaging my health or landing me in big trouble with the law. I was out of it well before the game started.

It became clear in the pub that a few lads from other clubs had had the same idea as us. A Gooner came into the bar, and in my drunken state I gave him a volley of abuse and ripped off his Arsenal shirt. This seemed to set things off. Some of the Cockneys nicked all the bottled beer stored in crates in a side passage of the pub and carried their booty over the road and into the ground. It was there that we came upon some Army boys and were soon in amongst them. Various skirmishes kicked off, and we eventually chased them out of the ground just after half-time. One chant was, 'If you want some fun with a tommy gun, join the IRA' – that went down well! What an irony that we were there to provide for families of dead service people and yet spent our time attacking members of the armed forces.

After the game we went back to the pub for a while to await our trains. All of those stolen bottles had by now been drained and many of us were well gone. More trouble broke out in the roads from the pub to the station. The Army had had enough and retreated back to their quarters but small gangs of

Arsenal, Chelsea and others were still up for it. The worst was a gang of local black lads who attacked us near the station. They ultimately came off second best and legged it, but they'd had a real go by then. It was a great warm-up for the season about to start, another one I would never forget.

One thing I had not so far added to my record was a game abroad with United. This was to change when me, Tex, Roy Downes and the Peckham brothers decided we would take our first foreign football trip to watch the second leg of a UEFA tie against Valencia in Spain (the first game was drawn 0–0). These were top lads, especially Roy the pickpocket, an amazing character. In 1982 he looked like Michael Jackson in his Jackson Five days, all afro hair and slight figure. He was pretty furtive and we never knew exactly how far he moved in dodgy circles, but he was certainly seen by many as one of the leading Cockney Reds at this time.

I went to a travel office in Wimbledon Broadway to buy flight tickets, but when we arrived at Gatwick Airport we found the flight had been overbooked and we were bumped onto a later flight to Malaga, some 290 miles from Valencia. The airline told us to get a taxi when we got there, keep the receipt, and they would pay us back later. I had only a small carrier bag with me and was wearing tee-shirt, jeans and trainers; it was September and warm, and we knew it would be even warmer in Spain. We had not booked any hotel rooms: the plan had been to do so when we arrived at Valencia, have some drinks, watch the game, then stay another night before our flight the following morning. We had no tickets for the game, but we knew these could be bought at the ground or from a tout.

Instead we arrived at Malaga Airport, nicely mellow after downing a few at Gatwick and then more on the plane. We had not bothered to change our pounds into pesetas, thinking we could do that once in Spain, but by the time we got there all the exchange shops were shut. We managed to blag a taxi to Valencia, which was quite a feat of negotiation given that the driver faced a 600-mile round trip and we had no local currency. Somehow we also persuaded him to cram four onto the back seat, with me in the front. The driver was a good bloke and took it on trust that we would pay him when we could eventually buy some pesetas. He even treated us to a meal during the eight-hour drive through the wild Spanish countryside, telling us that it was where the spaghetti westerns had been made with Clint Eastwood.

We arrived in Valencia at about seven in the morning, and paid the driver as he had been so good to us we didn't have the heart to mess him about. We had barely slept on the journey and had not eaten much, but after visiting the ground and securing tickets – for the Valencia section – we hit the first open bar we could find. By mid-afternoon I was more pissed than I had ever been, and the others were not much better. Other Mancs were milling around and there were flashpoints all about the city. I would like to remember exactly what I got up to, but I was so out of it I have no idea. I do know I became split up from the others who, I later found out, went into the ground without me. Drunken confusion overtook me in the early part of the evening, with night setting in quickly as it does there, and I somehow decided that I had already been to the match and needed to get to the airport. It just shows how bad I was. I staggered to a taxi and off we went – until I heard the match commentary over his car radio. I asked the driver to take me back to the ground and fortunately we hadn't gone far.

I was surprised to be let in, given the state I was in, and was ushered through to the lower tier of a stand behind one of the goals. The ground was far from full and I could sit where

I liked, so I looked around for Tex, Roy and the others, but couldn't find them. There was segregation in the upper tier of this stand, with the main United group one side and Valencia the other, but as I was below I couldn't properly see what was happening up there. As for the match, I was told we were 1–0 up from a Bryan Robson goal, but it was all a daze.

Then Valencia scored, and suddenly it all kicked off above me. The Spanish fans set about United and the police waded in – but not against the locals, only the visitors. Bottles and parts of seats were thrown, some falling down to where I was. I stood up and might have shouted something – I don't know – and before I knew what was happening, the police were pointing at me and some of them started to climb over the perimeter wall towards me. I was an easy target: pissed, in a tee-shirt, showing tattooed arms with the Manchester United crest on my left forearm. One copper grabbed me from behind and another slapped on some handcuffs. They also hit some Mancs nearby who had done nothing.

Swearing and squirming, I was dragged to the back of the stand to a police control post and beaten about the head. A senior officer came up, shouting in Spanish into my face and I gave as good back. I was still handcuffed and crouching, almost kneeling, on the terracing as he towered above me. He smashed his hand against my head not once but twice, but on the second hit reeled back shouting and hollering – he had broken his own hand. This made him and his colleagues even madder and they seemed to be making out as if it was my fault. I was pulled to my feet, manhandled out to a police wagon, thrown inside with a few Mancs and driven off to the local nick. I seemed to be getting special attention and of course my behaviour towards them was far from friendly.

I was put in a cell with a couple of Mancs, but they were soon released, apparently to be escorted to the airport. One cheeky twat even said, 'Lend us a few pesetas to tide me over.'

'Fuck off,' was my heated response.

I was in such a state that the coppers left me to sleep it off, and I took well over twenty-four hours to sober up. No-one spoke to me and I was left alone for much of the next day, by which time I was starting to worry. We had all heard about foreign jails where they lock you up for years for not doing much. I was told I was being charged with assaulting a police officer, and knew from my Old Bailey case that the outcome could be twice the usual sentence, or worse, if a copper was involved. I was left in the cell that night with a Spanish prisoner who spoke a bit of English, but I felt alone and feared this was not going to turn out to be much fun.

This was a first foray abroad for some other Cockney Reds, as one, another Bob, from Hayes in Middlesex, records:

HAYES BOB *Born in 1960, I started out at United games in the 1974/75 season and by the time 1982 arrived I was a fully-fledged Cockney Red, travelling to most league and cup games. Due to our lack of European qualification, my first chance to travel abroad came in the 1981/82 season. An early round in Poland was a trip too far but Valencia in September 1982 was right up my street. Travel then was cheap because most of us purchased books of Inter-rail tickets, which gave you a kind of block booking for all sorts of travel, including air fares over a certain time period. It should be remembered that the game was only four months after the Falklands War. Feelings in Spain ran high against the Brits and when we arrived in Valencia, via Alicante, Argentinian flags were being waved at us from all quarters and abuse directed at us by all and sundry.*

At the ground, we were shepherded into the upper tier of the stand in one corner by very aggressive police, who also seemed to have taken up the Argie cause. The steep stand had perfunctory plastic seats – not that we sat in them – and the surge when Bryan Robson scored to put us ahead in the tie meant we fell dangerously towards the pitch in celebration. The police saw this as some sort of aggressive act and charged into us with batons flying. Older United fans complained but we youngsters just accepted it all as part and parcel of the football experience. Spanish police on horseback charged us as we made our way to the coach park after the game, and on the coach out of Valencia we were attacked and our windows were smashed by huge chunks of masonry. Many of the older fans wrote subsequently to UEFA to complain but received no reply. You would think this a chastening experience, but it wasn't, and we couldn't wait to get abroad again the next season, after this early exit from the competition. We didn't hear anything of Banana Bob's problems until days later.

I had meanwhile been shifted to a proper prison. They did not seem to bother with formalities like searches, and I still had my camera in my pocket, along with my passport. Like a fool I offered up the camera when I arrived at the prison. It should have kept it: there were pictures of the match-day fighting already on it and I could have taken more in jail, then made a few quid selling them to the tabloids back in England when I got out, or even used them as a bargaining tool in the clink.

What worried me most was the uncertainty. It was not like at home, where you could be up before the magistrate the next morning for threatening behaviour or breach of the peace, cop a fine and be sent on your way. This trumped-up charge of assault made it different. I did get a visit from some chinless bloke from the embassy, but he did not seem too impressed with what our fans had been up to on his patch. He did get word back to my parents, who managed to write, and I found I had made the TV news and the front page of the *Daily Star*, as well as a report in the *Independent* that blamed the police and the Valencia fans for the trouble – which probably didn't help my cause if the Spanish read it. My dad organised a locally-based lawyer who spoke English and he came to see me after nearly two months, by which time it was November. The next time he visited was February.

There were constant comings and goings in and out of the nick. My first regular cellmates were two Spaniards who spoke little English. After a week another Spaniard and a Franco-Spanish guy called Michel replaced them. Michel had good English and we became close mates and looked out for each other. It was nothing like a nick back home. For a start we had an *en suite* toilet – hardly fit for a king but at least a bit private. There were showers in a block on the ground floor. The food wasn't bad, and money could be sent in to buy extras. We could get clothes and drinks but had to do our own washing. All I had was the tee-shirt, jeans, shoes and under-wear I had travelled in, but I was soon able to get some new stuff. There were all sorts of criminals in this nick: murder-ers, gangsters, drug dealers, bank robbers, rapists, along with some just on short-term remand – they were not split between prisons with different security levels, like at home. I must have been on remand, although I was never told.

During my first days inside I was shown local newspapers with reports of the violence at the game – blaming us, of course. Michel translated for me. The papers did admit that Valencia fans stoned United coaches on their way to the airport and said all the windows were smashed except the drivers'. I later learned that David Smith, secretary of the official supporters' club, blamed Spanish militia for most of the trouble, and warned of the danger of United fans being killed at future European games. I settled into the day-to-day routine, making friends despite not speaking any language other than my own. They all had a good smattering of English. Up the corridor from our cell was a French-Algerian burglar and a Belgian bank robber who was a bricklayer like me. I got on well with them both and we used to swap stories, but their criminal lives seemed a world apart from any thuggery around football. The only prisoner we had a problem with was this Kraut who seemed to upset everyone, making threats to all and sundry for no apparent reason. He was tall, muscular and imposing, with this shock of blond, almost white, hair; a typical arrogant German with a nasty streak. He goaded me once, saying that I would still be in the nick the following Christmas. I would normally have cuffed him one for that, but I chose to steer clear of trouble. Thankfully someone else took a knife to him as we queued for dinner one day and he was moved to another wing.

The sun filtered into my third-floor cell for most of the day, keeping it warm and pleasant even when winter set in. Overall it wasn't a bad place, as we were allowed into a yard for long periods to chat and exercise and I even got a tan. Each morning we would enjoy cups of coffee and doughnuts while the unfortunates without money raised cash for their snacks by queuing for us in a mad scrum. There was TV on the ground floor in a communal area and we could watch football and have a few side bets. In fact there was more football on Spanish TV than anything we received at home in those days.

There were many incidents, but one springs to mind. A tower stood above the wired fences and walls flanking the exercise yard, and guards kept an eye on us from behind a mounted machine gun, although this deterrent was never actually trained on us. There might be as many as two hundred men milling around that yard, and one quiet weekend some of them tried to escape. In one corner of the yard, a group found they could use the right-angled junction of the two walls to climb to the top by standing on their mates' backs and grabbing a ledge at the top. Beyond was an open space to an outer wall, and in that space a gang of workmen were putting in some extra security mesh, and had erected scaffolding which almost reached the outer wall. The prisoners scaled the scaffolding and rocked it so that it swayed far enough towards the outer wall for them to jump onto it and have it away. We all cheered like loons as they cleared both walls. Fortunately the guards didn't fire, instead raising the alarm by walkie-talkie. Of three prisoners who went over the wall, one got stuck on some barbed wire and was soon recaptured, while the other two escaped. They were apparently rounded up in the surrounding countryside, but we never saw them again and assumed they had been put into a more secure prison. One of them owed my Belgian mate a fair bit of cash, and he was seriously pissed off that he wouldn't see a peseta of it.

Messages and various items, including drugs, were regularly thrown over the walls into the yard by prisoners' families and friends. On one occasion a fight broke out over one of these items and four blokes started throwing punches and wrestling each other to the ground. The guards let it happen while we stood watching and egging the men on. It was three onto one, so the single bloke pulled out a knife, only for the other three to do the same. A few of us wanted to pile in to even the odds but we held back. Screws back home would have been in there hitting all and sundry, with more punishment to follow in front of the governor, but in Spain it was a case of letting it sort itself out, which it did. The staff did not even bother to take action against any of those involved.

It was a lax, carefree environment where nothing was done today if it could be put off until tomorrow.

Soon after the escape attempt, my French-Algerian mate and the Belgian came to my cell, closing the door behind them. They looked furtive rather than threatening.

'Bob,' the Belgian whispered, 'you must know a few criminals back home. How about putting us in contact? We'll make it worth your while.'

I didn't really want to get involved but, as they were mates, said, 'Look, I would like to help but my line is more football. However, I do know some faces that know some faces, so give me your details and I'll see what I can do when I'm released.' They seemed satisfied – anything for an easy life. I did write a letter to each when home, saying that I couldn't help.

I largely kept out of the arguments and sporadic fights and spent my time playing cards or dominoes for money. There were all sorts of devious dealings, unseen by the screws, who didn't seem interested anyway. One tidy little earner involved beer. A bottle would cost me seventeen pesetas and I could buy three twice a day. I would store these up and sell three for as much as two hundred pesetas to mates desperate to hit the booze in such vast quantities they seemed permanently pissed – it was their way of coping. I could then use that cash to buy other luxuries only a few could afford.

I received regular letters from Mum and Dad and one or two from the woman I was seeing at the time. Not much was heard from the Cockney Reds, but I liked to think they were concerned for me – then again, they might have been having a good laugh at my expense. Each day I hoped to hear something about release, and finally a letter from Dad arrived, saying that the lawyer I had seen was working hard on it. After more than two months it was something positive, but I remained anxious about how long I was going to be kept there. My mood was not helped when Christmas came along a month later and nothing further appeared to have happened. This was when I was at my most depressed, missing those back home, family, mates, football ... women. There were celebrations over Christmas of course: the quality of the food improved for a couple of days and my mood lightened, but I thought of my nice flat in Belmont, my girlfriend and her kids, the Cockney Reds enjoying a good piss-up before a game and then cracking a few heads. I even thought of my Mark 3 Cortina left in the flat's car park – it was a heap of junk really, but I missed roaring around South London in it with a bird in the front seat.

The New Year arrived with a celebration on our wing, but the weather turned cold and it was no longer pleasant being outside in the yard. The shorter daylight hours made the days drag more and by six we were always back in our cells. These were, thankfully, well heated and I liked to settle down in the evenings to read – during my time inside I probably read more books than I have since. Dad sent a few and there were some English ones already in the library. I kept fairly fit, apart from a bout of raging athlete's foot that took ages to clear and was a sodding irritation. Intermittent violence continued throughout the various wings but I kept my nose clean, despite itching (and not just from my feet) to get involved on occasion.

News from home, including some newspaper cuttings, continued to come through. I now had the *Daily Star*'s front page and a picture of me in handcuffs being set upon by the police. I didn't know it then, but this photo was to be my salvation. I also found out that up to thirty Reds had been arrested that same night in Benidorm after fighting in a night club. They were lucky enough to be shipped out of the country almost immediately. It made me feel even worse for having been picked on for something I hadn't done.

At least I enjoyed my birthday in the January, when my mates on our wing made sure I was well and truly pissed. I was on the bog for most of the next day and this French-Spanish bastard kept throwing water over the door and onto my head for a joke. With a thumping headache and stomach out of control I felt so fired up I could have killed him, as my frustrations had built up so much by then. Fortunately for him I daren't get off the bog, and I am sure he knew that.

Then, one day in early February, this brief turned up and said he would not be leaving the nick without me. I couldn't believe it. He had found evidence – the picture from the *Star*, I assumed – to show I could not have struck the copper, as my hands were firmly in cuffs and I was on my knees. They had to let me go. After a few quick goodbyes to my wing mates, the lawyer took me to an airport hotel for an overnight stay, before a flight to Gatwick the next morning. I thought I might be questioned on arrival, as I had been away for months and might have broken rules about time spent abroad, but I sailed through passport control without any problem. I headed back to Sutton by bus, relieved to be home.

Looking back now I should have gone straight to the *Star* and offered them my story, but I didn't and probably missed the chance to make a few quid. Life quickly returned to normal. My old job at the Croydon firm was still there and I linked up again with the woman I had been seeing and her kids. I also met up with the Cockney Reds and we were soon in action on the North Bank at Highbury. Those four and half months in Spain suddenly seemed far away.

There was still one important job left to do from that ill-fated trip. I had kept the receipt for the taxi from Malaga to Valencia and turned up at the travel agent's shop to claim the refund. As a precaution I took a very large mate from the building site for company. Built like a brick shithouse and with a look more menacing than mine, his mere presence ensured no argument and the money was swiftly forthcoming.

My mum, dad and sister were great about it. How they stuck by me I don't know, but they did, and I see now how lucky I was to have them. The British Government were of course anti-football and staunchly anti-hooligan, and although they could have got me out they didn't give a damn. I put it all down to life experience. After all, I had been in jail before and, apart from not knowing my fate for so long, it was strangely a lot of fun.

Someone writing on an internet forum in more recent years called me 'one crazy bastard' and they are probably right. I was soon back into the swing of things, but did I learn my lesson from Valencia? Did I bollocks!

CHAPTER 9

ALL ABROAD

The close season of 1983 left me bored, with no football on TV to speak of. I was still working on the building sites and moving from job to job. I should have set up my own business and now wish I had concentrated more on that than making trouble, but I would go wherever there was work. A little group of us would hear of jobs and do our best to keep together as a team. Most of the work was short-term but sometimes a longer job would come along. When a new Marks and Spencer store went up not far from where I lived, it gave me two years' work. That was a dream of a job, as at the time I had no driving licence after another year's ban, and it was handy to hop on a bus to get to work.

United did have a pre-season warm-up tour to the Netherlands coming up and, although it was not something I would usually go on, I couldn't resist this one, especially as it was in Amsterdam, just a short hop across the North Sea. It was to be a four-team competition, in August, and we were up against Ajax and Feyenoord from Holland and Roma from Italy. It was beyond belief how the organisers could put Holland's two best-supported teams, who absolutely hated each other, up against one another *and* send in United with their thousands of rowdy fans, many looking to make their mark in one of the most laid-back cities in Europe. Roma had a violent reputation too.

We caught the train up to Harwich from Liverpool Street and joined about three hundred United on the ferry to the Hook of Holland. On arrival we bumped into forty Everton fans getting off a train from Amsterdam to catch the ferry home from their own tour. This was not long after one of our lads, Jobe Henry, had been slashed at Old Trafford and needed something like two hundred stitches. We were keen for revenge and rushed at them. Outnumbered, they legged it, to a chorus of jeers. We were pleased to have had this little warm up ahead of the main event.

We had drunk heavily on the ship and continued when we arrived in central Amsterdam. By late morning (all this on the day of a match) I was as pissed as I had been in Valencia. We had found somewhere to stay but had no tickets. The day is once again something of a blur, but I vaguely recall watching some mates play pool for big money, and really pissing them off by picking up the balls off the table and throwing them across the bar, smashing glasses, hitting punters and messing up the game. It was not long before the police arrived, handcuffed me and shipped me off to the nick. They also confiscated a small knife I had bought that morning, and which seemed to convince them I was some sort of crazed killer. Fortunately my mates paid for the damage at the bar and at lunchtime the police let me go. They were probably glad to see the back of me.

I joined hundreds of United in Dam Square, all drinking, singing and ready for trouble. A mob of us eventually marched off down a side street and someone slung something heavy through a jeweller's window. I helped myself to four white gold rings and a gold lighter. We then legged it and caught a tram to the football ground. Some smashed their way in but I remained outside, fighting, although I can't remember much about it. All too predictably, I was arrested again. I was taken to the same police station as earlier, and their equivalent of a desk sergeant greeted me with the words, 'Oh no, not you again.' This time the nick was heaving with United fans and I spotted Roy Downes, but we were kept apart. They told me to empty my pockets, and found the rings and lighter. There was no way I would be getting released this time. I was stuffed.

I was eventually moved to a prison on the edge of the city with four tower blocks: three for men and one for women. There I had a visit from a bloke from the British embassy, who asked about my circumstances at home. I laid it on thick, saying I had a woman and three children dependent on me and a good job which I needed to get back to. He said he would try his best and left. I was moved once more and spent time in another, bigger local prison, and began to fear the worst. I did meet a mate there from Cannock, Harry, who had been arrested at the same time, but most of my other mates had been released or had not been nabbed.

It eventually became clear that the Dutch police wanted rid of me, as it seemed too much bother for them to take me to court. Perhaps the bloke from the embassy pulled a few strings. After six days, I was told I was being sent home. I still had my return ticket to Harwich and was expecting to be taken to the Hook of Holland, but instead the coppers hand-cuffed me, took me to the airport and shoved me on a normal flight. In the holding area at the airport they even offered me my knife back. I threw it into the box for unwanted items before being led to my seat in cuffs. I was then formally released. The other passengers must have thought I was some sort of major criminal and there was plenty of muttering and tutting. At Gatwick I was held for a while for routine questioning and then let go. I did manage to keep this incident away from Mum and Dad, who would not have been impressed so soon after Valencia.

In the following 1983/84 season, we drew Juventus in the Cup Winners' Cup. Turin is a tough city and the Juve fans had a reputation. Before the game they would cruise around on their Lambrettas, pass close by groups of English fans standing in the street or outside bars, slash you with a knife and zoom off. One of our lads, Black Sammy, got stabbed up the arse, which was one of their favourite tricks – it won't kill you, it'll make you bleed a lot and make shitting and sitting painful for a few days after. It was also our own Griff's speciality.

There was a ban on the purchase of tickets for the away game other than through the official supporters' club, but a black market would see many United in amongst the Juve. Elsewhere there were running battles everywhere, with United taking over the centre of Turin in the hours before the game. A number of trams were smashed up. The *carabinieri* were not exactly subtle in how they handled us, yet did little to stop the Juve fans. The fighting became so bad that at one point he British consul showed up to try to calm everything down. He failed, and beat a hasty retreat after being hit on the head by a flying bottle.

Getting home (after a defeat) was equally chaotic, with many Reds swapping flights with each other just to get away earlier. Some even travelled to a different airport to get an earlier flight home. The newspapers and TV had a field day reporting on the English football hooligan disease – the authorities and the Government were being stirred into doing something about it.

Both at home and abroad the Cockney Reds would normally come out on top in any fighting. Our numbers helped, of course, and we had some tidy faces over a long period of time. But there were occasions when we were second best. The odd battle was lost, and one of those occurred ahead of that

Turin trip in 1983, as a fellow Cockney Red, who wishes to remain nameless, relates:

ANON *As Banana has said, it wasn't always United in the ascendancy. In 1983 against Tottenham, I got my nose broken. It was the same night Alex Ferguson's Aberdeen won the Cup Winners' Cup and I wished I had stayed at home to watch that instead. I remember meeting in the bar at Euston with about fifty Cockney Reds. We waited for the train from Manchester to come in, but only Black Coco and a mate got off. They went straight down the Tube and it was obvious we weren't going to have any more back-up. We got off at Seven Sisters and walked to White Hart Lane without too much incident until we got to the Corner Pin pub opposite the ground. A mob of Tottenham came out and steamed into us. We retaliated and they ran off. I then jibbed over the turnstiles into the ground and thought I was having a great night.*

After the game there was a mob of Tottenham waiting outside the Spurs' shop, and I got punched on the nose out of nowhere. Tottenham were suddenly all over us. I stumbled through the crowd, my eyes watering and blood spurting all over me. Somehow I managed to get together with the rest of the Cockney Reds and we started to make our way towards Seven Sisters station, but Tottenham were in front and behind, and we were massively outnumbered. We retreated to Bruce Grove overground station and went up to the platform. I thought that was a great idea – just get away from them. But no, someone decided we were going back down onto Seven Sisters Road, and off we went like lemmings. It was a long walk back to Seven Sisters station and we were attacked all the way. We took a real pasting, which was most unusual. But you can count these low points on the fingers of one hand.

Foreign trips in the days before internet booking, budget airlines and open borders were often a logistical nightmare and fans would go to extraordinary lengths to see their team. Hayes Bob is one of many Cockneys who braved all sorts of obstacles to follow United, and his recollections accurately portray the kinds of experience many of us underwent at one time or another.

HAYES BOB *In October 1983 a group of us had the chance to sample the delights of the Communist Bloc with an away tie, first leg, in the Cup Winners' Cup against a team called Spartak, who played in Varna, on the Black Sea coast of Bulgaria. The nearest airport, at the capital, Sofia, was some fifty miles or more away, and at that time flights were costly, but to show our dedication to the cause – or stupidity – we decided to travel overland and by sea. Four of us were up for the trip: me, Dave Holdstock and John Taylor from the south and Steve from Salford.*

We travelled straight from United's Saturday game to Victoria Station in London to catch the boat train to Dover, only to find the ferry crews had gone on strike. Some enterprising small-boat skipper approached us and offered to take his vessel across to Calais. It could hold just him and the four of us, so you can imagine how small it was, and a rough crossing did not help our stomachs. Four green-faced Reds alighted at Calais port to walk the two miles or so to Calais Station for our pre-booked Paris train. Unfortunately we were now well behind schedule and had missed our service. We also missed the Paris connection to Germany. At the Paris station we were told our only chance to get to Bulgaria on time was to catch the train to Milan, then another via Venice into Slovenia, then Yugoslavia and the capital, Belgrade, then on to Sofia – a trip of twenty-nine hours! We went for it.

Entering Communist countries and passing checkpoints was surprisingly simple on the train, where there was only a cursory passport check. We arrived in Belgrade just after midnight looking to get something to eat but nothing was open. So, we waited for the train to Sofia in what was a shabby city left to go to pot by the communists. Eventually a nearby café opened up and we had some egg dish to fill our empty stomachs. It turned out to be dodgy and we all ended up with dicky tummies. We found a waiting room to catch up on some sleep, but this was difficult as it stank of fish from the adjacent market, which was open for early morning trade.

Our final trip was on a Moscow-bound train via Sofia, where we would need to catch a different train to Varna, itself an hour from the capital. We were told there was little chance of us getting to the game on time, as the railway timetable bore little resemblance to reality. These trains were something else. At various stations all sorts would get on, including men with a few cattle, which they herded on board to mix with us. In Sofia we found the demand for tickets had been so great from other travelling United that only two were left for the train to Varna, so we had to pay £200 for a cab (no one accepted the local currency, the lev; only dollars, francs or pounds). Our driver must have broken all speeding laws as we urged him to go faster. We flew through run-down villages that were little more than shanty towns, to eventually arrive at the ground five minutes before kick-off. We had been travelling from Saturday evening to late Wednesday afternoon, and this with dodgy stomachs.

Our ordeal was not over as we produced our tickets to get into the ground. The armed police, perhaps aware of the British hooligan disease, refused us entry there and insisted we go elsewhere in the ground and at extra cost – it was a scam, but we were too tired to argue and they looked like types you would not pick a fight with. We paid to end the nightmare and, at last, were inside what was an impressive ground with 40,000 fans. We watched as United won, to take a 2–1 lead back to Old Trafford. The United faithful were there in numbers, but with a strong-armed presence and probable travel tiredness, the game passed off without any real trouble.

The return journey through Germany went without a hitch, but I still had to face my boss. I had been refused time off for the trip as others had booked holidays before me, so had phoned in on the Monday before travelling to say I had a tooth abscess. This boss knew I was pulling a fast one and asked that I produce a sort of dentist certificate to prove it, something I had never heard of. I managed to blag my way out of it. I didn't like the job anyway and planned to move on, which I did a few months later. Despite all this hassle, Reds fans both Cockney and Manc would never be put off – it was all an adventure.

The second trip was to watch the game against Videoton in 1985. Being a Cockney Red means many things, but the greatest must include devotion to the cause. And nothing can demand more devotion than a trip to Székesfehérvár. It's in Hungary, and not somewhere you would choose for an early spring break. In 1985 it was still behind the Iron Curtain, nestled south-west of Budapest, the home of Videoton FC. Yet in March, after a 1–0 win at Old Trafford, we sought out our atlases and planned our route: boat to Ostende and train out through Belgium down to the south-east corner of Germany, across Austria and on to Budapest.

It was another long journey. We were on the piss all the way and rocked up at this ground which was little more than non-league standard. The crowd was supposed to be as many as 25,000 but I doubt it was anywhere near that. Reds fans swelled the numbers though, and we took over the place. Their local police had no clue how to cope with an influx of noisy, pissed-up English fans, although the game passed off without too much incident off the pitch – bad enough, the locals might say, but nothing compared with what happened on other trips. Disappointingly we went out on penalties to this tinpot team.

What was interesting about this particular trip was how my travelling group of forty or so, which included my mate Mandy and her friend from the Manchester area, managed to blag its way past ticket inspectors and border officials, using travel permit cards with specific journey usage that we had altered to multiple usage and so cut the group's costs. On our return journey we were worried we might struggle to get past the more stringent examination of these tickets that might occur elsewhere. Austria was lax but as the train approached Rosenheim, in south-east Germany, Mandy and I were increasingly aware that our document looked decidedly dodgy, what with the amateurish changes to it we had made. Worried about being carted off to the local nick, we fled down the train away from the officials and out onto the platform. They sensed what we were doing and made some attempt to follow but we sprinted out of the station and they gave up the chase.

The train's next main stop would be Munich, so we decided to try to hitch a lift there, where we knew our mates would be changing trains and there would be a decent stopover wait. A man driving a two-seater MG stopped and probably having a young woman with me helped attract his attention. Mandy sat in the front seat while I had to curl up in the space behind. He dropped us off on the outskirts of Munich, near a station to catch a local train into the main station. Thankfully, we were re-united with our group and the journey continued without a hitch.

Such was life for the travelling United support through Europe: dodging police batons, flying glass from coach windows, attacks from local fans, blagging past security checks, but most of all the camaraderie of a group whose passion and devotion to United would know no bounds.

I did not make the Videoton away game, but another of our lads who did, Micky W, said the boys had more trouble from the Hungarian equivalent of the KGB than from the local gangs. This was the height of the Cold War era, the Russians had just boycotted the Los Angeles Olympics and there was massive tension between East and West. The Hungarians were almost certainly looking for spies hidden amongst us as much as for football thugs, and the boys were followed wherever they went by menacing-looking men in trilby hats and long macs. To be fair Micky and the others weren't likely to cause too much trouble as the possibility of being sent to some gulag or other was enough to put anyone off.

I know the fans of many clubs have similar tales, but with United the numbers travelling seemed so much larger, and in the successful Ferguson years the opportunity for such travel was only to increase. This exposed us more often to foreign police, armed with tear gas and guns, who could summon water cannons and even fired rubber bullets on one occasion. They would whack you even if you were innocently going about your business, as many of us found to our cost. Football

On my first motorcycle at the age of seventeen. I was in my rocker phase, with quiff hairstyle, and ran with a violent biker gang, before football took over.

An original card for United's London and District supporters' club from 1969. Many took out memberships in the early days for the organised coach and train travel, but gradually more and more fans became 'unofficial'.

With my mates on the way to Wolverhampton Wanderers in 1975, where we came face to face with the 'Mad Axe Man'. From left: Ian, Tooting Steve, me, The Ghost and Dave.

A dismayed Denis Law looks on as police clear the pitch at a game between United and Arsenal in August 1971. It was played at the neutral venue of Anfield due to previous misbehaviour by our fans, so we took the opportunity to storm the Kop end. *PA Images.*

Trouble breaks out on a packed terrace at the old Highbury stadium in November 1975 as we infiltrate among the Arsenal fans. We had many a punch-up with their Gooners firm. *PA Images.*

United fans lined up by the police outside Euston Station after fighting before a London game in 1979. Euston was our regular stamping ground and a place where we often met up, whether playing home or away. *Mirrorpix.*

United's firm, including Mancs and Cockneys, marching down Oxford Road on the way to Maine Road to play Manchester City in the early Eighties. Our derby rivals could never handle us.

Sharing a drink with the legendary Geoff Lewis
in a gathering at Swiss Cottage, North London,
before a game. Standing from left: Tooting Steve,
me, St Albans Steve and Geoff.

The lads always
come out in
force to face
our hated rivals
Liverpool. Top,
walking the
train tracks to
Lime Street
Station before
a game at
Anfield, and
below, heading
to Wembley
to take on the
Scousers. Note
the absence
of any club
colours that
might identify
us as United
fans, even on a
cup final day.

Groomy (left) and Tank, two great characters, at Wembley in 1979. Tank lived in Northampton but was a staunch Cockney Red, while Groomy is one of United's best-known fans and has watched the team in nearly forty countries.

That's me in the bottom corner being coshed by a Spanish cop at Valencia in 1982, my first foreign game. I was held for four months for police assault.

Passengers disembarking the Dutch ferry *Koningin Beatrix* under police escort at Harwich, after it had been forced to turn around due to a violent brawl with West Ham fans in 1986. *PA Images.*

At Barcelona for one of the greatest night's in football history, the Champions League final against Bayern Munich in 1999. What more can I say?

Groomy modelling swimwear in the San Siro stadium, Milan. He now goes for a more conservative look of dyed red hair and goatee. *Empics.*

An innocent United fan is left bloodied after being coshed by riot police at a Champions League game at AS Roma in 2007. Many were injured by the out-of-control carabinieri. *PA Images.*

On the lash in Madrid in 2013 before a game against the 'Galacticos' of Real. From left: Stevie B, Budgie, Roy, Mitch, me, Billy, Fat Jack, Big Si from Manchester, and Joe. These are staunch lads, and all know how to enjoy themselves.

The Cockney Reds out in force for the funeral of one of our pals, Kilburn John, who died suddenly of a heart attack in 2012. More than 300 United lads attended and raised money to help his family.

Enjoying our current pre-match ritual of a quality meal and a bottle or three of fine wine in Manchester before a Champions League tie against Barcelona. It's all a far cry from bunking on trains, nicking butties and swigging from cheap cans.

In Manchester before a game in 2019. Soon to enter my seventh decade following United, I will always be a Cockney Red.

pitches would be surrounded by fencing and sometimes a moat too, so jumping onto the playing area to celebrate a win was often impossible.

I did get on the Old Trafford pitch, however, in March 1984, when we played Barcelona, with Diego Maradona and all. It was the second leg of a European Cup Winners' Cup tie and we had lost the first leg in the Camp Nou 2–0. Bryan Robson has gone on record as saying this was the greatest experience at Old Trafford he has ever witnessed, before or since, and I can't argue with that. Barca's fans probably thought they were through already and didn't bother to turn up so, for once, we could concentrate on the excitement on the pitch. To win 3–0 and go into the semis was monumental. With no fences at that time at Old Trafford, I was out onto the grass cavorting around like a loony, hugging everyone. For once the buzz came from the football as we hoisted Robson and Frank Stapleton, the goalscorers, onto our shoulders and took them down the players' tunnel.

CONSEQUENCES

B y 1984 I was approaching my mid-thirties, established
as a bricklayer and earning very good money, both law-
fully and by working on the side. My love life was more
settled too, as I had met my wife-to-be. She came from Epsom
and knew me from frequenting the same social scene in the
Seventies. She had been married previously and had two young
boys. I took to them and they to me, so perhaps that impressed
her enough to take me on. I am not sure how much she knew
of my past but she maintains that I have a softer side that few
see. I was still heading off to games and went so often that she
thought at first I was a player and not a fan – and certainly not
a hooligan – or at least, that's what she says. Later she was to
literally get a wake-up call when the police raided our home
during a conspiracy witch-hunt. She was not at all impressed
and has been aghast at some of the things I have been involved
in since we got together. Still we have stuck it out now for over
thirty years.

Soccer hooliganism was reaching its peak – and with that
came tragedy. None of us wished to see innocents hurt at a
football match, and we certainly did not want anyone to die,
but there is no denying that crowd disorder brought unintended, harmful consequences for many non-participants.
In 1980 at Middlesbrough, two elderly Boro season-ticket

holders were killed after a game against United. Irene and Norman Roxby were leaving the ground by a corner exit when a brick pillar crumbled, bringing two gates down with it, and they were crushed. Some witnesses blamed it on a group of United supporters, saying they had rushed the gates after the match and caused the collapse. In their defence, the United fans claimed that the rush was sparked by efforts to get away from an over-excited police horse. Subsequent reports said that Middlesbrough's safety certificates for the stadium had not been kept up-to-date, though the club claimed that any violation was merely technical and that all safety requirements were either met or exceeded at the time. Perhaps it was a combination of several unfortunate factors coming together. To this day, however, football message boards criticise us for the tragedy and for later labelling Liverpool fans as 'the Murderers' when we have 'blood on our hands' too.

No fan would want to see innocents dying just because they went to watch their team play. For me, the attraction of football violence was about hand-to-hand fighting between willing rivals: us against them. Among the 'firms' there was a general respect for those fans who were clearly not looking for trouble and were entitled to be left well alone, although I won't pretend some were not caught up in it against their will on occasion. That was part and parcel of going to football in those days. I also believe, however, that holding away fans inside grounds after the final whistle can in itself create animosity and worsen the atmosphere it is intended to improve. At Millwall's New Den I still hear of away fans from big clubs being kept inside the ground for more than half an hour after the game has ended. It only needs a spark, and a gate to be battered down, and we are back to Middlesbrough in 1980.

A similar tragedy, which had ramifications for the Cockney Reds, occurred in November 1982, when an eighteen-year-old

Spurs fan died in a crush at the bottom of a seventy-foot escalator at Seven Sisters tube station after a game against United.
The station had filled up with fans of both clubs and there was
some sort of confrontation, in circumstances which are still
unclear, causing people to overbalance on the escalator and
fall to the bottom in a heap. Scotland Yard first said the accident was caused by a sudden halt of the escalator, which
pitched the fans forward, but later revised this and said it
had been immobile at the time. Little concrete information
came out until later, but I recall the immediate aftermath that
evening. We had been to the game and then moved back to
Euston for a few drinks. We heard a fan had died but no-one
at first knew if he was Spurs or United, and the atmosphere
was subdued. Some claimed that the lad had been stabbed,
others that he had become entangled in the escalator machin-
ery by his hair, but none of them really had a clue.

The day had been one of high drama, culminating in pitched
battles up and down Seven Sisters Road after the game. The
tube station then became a gathering point for both sets of
fans in huge numbers. My little firm within the Cockney Reds
had moved on to the next station, to wait for any train loaded
with Tottenham, before the fatal trouble occurred. Due to
events at Seven Sisters all the trains were then stopped, so we
eventually chose to go back to Euston by bus and taxi. No-one
I knew was on the escalator or near the incident itself, so I
had no idea of what had happened until word began to filter
through on the bush telegraph.

A number of United fans were subsequently arrested and
a Cockney Red, Black Sam, was charged with manslaughter and held in Wandsworth Prison. He was later released,
however, when the circumstances of the death became clearer.
For years afterwards there would be speculation that the death
was United's fault, despite the police clarification. It certainly

highlighted the increasing amount of what might crudely be called 'collateral damage' around soccer hooliganism.

I personally witnessed a number of fights where deaths could easily have occurred. One was the 1983 League Cup final, when we set about Liverpool fans on the way back to Wembley Central Station. It was like a scene from *The Football Factory* film, with bodies everywhere, many covered in blood and some unconscious. I did not hear afterwards that anyone had suffered permanent injury, but that was more by luck than any restraint by those involved. Such was the intensity of the vitriol and antagonism around certain football rivalries by the mid-Eighties.

The 1984/85 season brought a level of hooliganism not seen since the lawless days of the mid-Seventies, while Maggie Thatcher's government duked it out with Arthur Scargill's miners in the background. The police did not cover themselves in glory dealing with the miners, and for months the trouble was front-page news, but by the end of the season football violence came to dominate the headlines once more. On the pitch, Ron Atkinson's team were challenging across all competitions, including the UEFA Cup. This brought some lively away ties across Europe, including an infamous visit to play Dundee United in December 1984.

A lot of Jocks came down to Old Trafford for the first leg but we comfortably saw them off. For the second leg, we all fancied a jolly in Dundee, Scotland's fourth-biggest city. The sister of a mate's partner had a sports bar up there, so that would be our base. We all travelled up on the train but I missed the one I intended to catch, and so lost a chance to meet my hero, Denis Law, who bumped into my mates on the journey. That pissed me off for a start. The sports bar had pool, gaming machines and multi TVs, and we almost drank it dry. Many of the other Cockney Reds and a few Mancs spent the day of the match in the Bee's Knees club in the city, where apparently it was chicken-in-a-basket and beer downstairs and porn videos on the go all day upstairs. Apparently Dundee and Dundee United often teamed up to take on outsiders but, despite a capacity crowd, we encountered few of their lads either in the town or outside the ground. We had given them such a spanking in Manchester that they must have decided not to come out. We had free reign before the game, and during it there was a pitch invasion and scraps with the police. I doubt sleepy Dundee had ever seen such an invasion, and we won the tie with a 3–2 result.

BIG K *I was with a firm of Cockneys looking for some Dundee before the game. We were well up for it, having been drinking non-stop for what seemed like days. With hardly a turnout from Dundee, we took it out on anyone we could find. This programme seller was fair game after he swore at me; I cuffed him and relieved him of the money he had collected, and he ran off with his programmes into the stadium. We then stormed some food vans, throwing food everywhere and nicking their cash. Eventually I was arrested for causing an affray or something like that, and picked up a £750 fine. Down south it would have been £100 max. Another one of our lads ran on the pitch to celebrate when we went 5–4 up on aggregate; he was carted away and later did time for it, being dealt with far more severely than some of those arrested for seriously injuring people in England.*

Many of those arrested were lucky, however, in that they never reached court. The Dundee police rounded up more than a hundred United in some factory outbuilding and took them off in groups to Perth nick. With fifty or so still left, a message came through to the coppers that the nick was full and those remaining should be sent on their way, and no more should be arrested at the ground.

Progress in the FA Cup brought us a sixth-round tie in Manchester that March against West Ham. Their Inter-City Firm had become so notorious that they were being followed around by a TV documentary crew. A couple of years earlier they had done well against our best and held their own, led by faces like Cass Pennant and Bill Gardner, at a game I missed due to my detention in Valencia. This time we were better prepared. We tore into them all day. On the subsequent documentary, *Hooligan*, you can hear some of their main boys desperately exhorting others to stand and fight. It was the same after the game, when we attacked their trains.

In truth this was a warm-up for the games to come against the reviled Scousers. The end of March brought a league game at Anfield at which the Old Bill threw us off the train at Edge Hill, some three miles from the ground, onto buses. It might have seemed a sensible idea, keeping us well away from the city centre, but it did not stop mass violence outside and inside the stadium. Two weeks later we had Liverpool again in the FA Cup semi-final, to be held, of all places, at Goodison Park. This was not the best choice by the FA, given that Everton were in the other semi and their fans would be leaving the city to travel down to Villa Park that same day.

We drove to Manchester to catch an early Saturday service train to Lime Street, Liverpool, guessing that the police would probably stop the separate supporters' special trains short at Edge Hill and make them walk the rest of the way along the roads, without those buses this time. We were about half a mile from Lime Street at a tunnel entrance when the train was stopped. We were later to find out it was held up to avoid us meeting Everton fans setting off to Birmingham, plus the police were trying to clear Liverpool lying in wait for us outside the station. When it looked like the train was not going to restart, we all jumped off onto the 'live' tracks and milled around for a few minutes, before the majority decided to walk on to Lime Street. Old Bill arrived and tried to usher us back to Edge Hill, but they were bombarded with large stones from the trackside and backed off. We went through the tunnels towards the platforms only to be met by more coppers when we emerged. They were now really pissed off, and when we had almost reached the platforms we could see they had been reinforced by their riot squad. We came to a standstill as they lined up in front of us. Beyond the platforms and on the concourse, Everton fans were arriving for later trains and, as chanting started up, we pushed the police line, but it held. They eventually let us out onto the concourse ten at a time, while holding Everton back, but we broke out into the Scousers, with flares being thrown and fighting on all sides. We were able to back Everton off as more of us were let through. Some Everton ran off away from the station and others jumped onto their trains. We had enough numbers to now force our way out of the station and confront a mass of Liverpool fans, who had gathered to await us and had seen off police attempts to remove them.

I pitched into the Liverpool but was immediately arrested and thrown into a police van. I tried to blag my way out, saying I was with my son (I wasn't) and needed to find him, but they were having none of it. I was taken to Liverpool's main nick, charged with threatening behaviour and bailed. I missed the game but caught up with my mates back at the car in Manchester after the game for a subdued journey home. The game was drawn, and the replay was to be held the following Wednesday – at Maine Road. We were ready for the Liverpool response but, on the night, the Scousers made a very poor show: both their team and their fans were well beaten.

Big Ron was to lead us to the FA Cup final in 1985, and a clash against Everton. We had always found the Blue half of Merseyside to be a handful on their own patch, but away from Scouseland they weren't nearly so confident, and in a period when their team enjoyed great success on the pitch, they sometimes over-estimated how well they might fare against us off it. On this day we met at Swiss Cottage, with maybe 1,000 or more spread around several pubs. At about two o'clock in the afternoon we made the trek to Swiss Cottage station to catch the train and were jammed ten deep on the platform. Old Bill had about a dozen officers there and were trying to maintain control, but as more and more United poured towards the platform it all kicked off and the officers were attacked. Some ran off in fright, something I had never seen before, while others took a kicking on the ground. At that moment, a train pulled in full of Everton fans. The doors did not open so some United tried to force them, but were unsuccessful and the train left, greatly to the relief of the scared looking Evertonians on board.

We decided to leave that station and walk, hundreds-strong, to the next one, Finchley Road. By the time our train arrived there, there must have been 1,000 or more pushing to get on. Again some Everton were already on board but the train was not as full as the previous one. We forced our way on and attacked them, causing one to pull the communication cord. Some got off and one or two even tried to escape along the track. Old Bill arrived and waded into both United and Everton. Up in Liverpool the Scouse Old Bill tend to protect the locals at the visitors' expense, but here the police were neutral and would take prisoners from both sides. We eventually headed out of Wembley Park station and someone spotted a minibus full of Everton stuck in traffic. Some of us started to rock it and had almost tipped it over when the traffic moved on and it got away.

I had to travel up to Liverpool for my first court hearing by overnight coach, as even the earliest trains would not have got me there in time. The case was adjourned whilst they waited for reports about me, and I was bailed again. I was summoned to appear again on May 28. A local solicitor approached me beforehand and offered to present a mitigating defence for twenty quid if I pleaded guilty, which I did. He claimed there were mitigating circumstances because Liverpool hooligans had been waiting for us and inappropriate police action had made the situation worse. I got away with a £100 fine, so clearly they didn't take much notice of my past record! I could not have been luckier with the timing, because the very next day saw the Heysel tragedy, and the court's attitude and judgement might well have been very different after that.

The deaths of thirty-nine people at Heysel Stadium in Belgium, at a European Cup final between Liverpool and Juventus, were a disaster waiting to happen. A charge by Liverpool fans through what was supposed to be a segregation fence caused a stampede and fatal crush against a perimeter wall, abetted by poor policing and a stadium totally unsuited to stage a major football match. Six hundred fans were injured. Those killed or badly hurt did not appear to be looking for trouble, as the Juve hard core was actually located at the other end of the ground, and Liverpool fans would later be labelled 'the Murderers' by many United fans, partly as a response to the years of 'Munich' taunts we'd had to endure from them.

Heysel came just eighteen days after the equally horrific Bradford fire, when fifty-six football fans died after a discarded fag set alight rubbish under a wooden stand in Bradford City's old Valley Parade ground and high winds fanned the flames. It was a terrible time for football. With the miners by then battered and beaten, Margaret Thatcher turned he attentions towards removing the stain of football hooliganism for good, laying the ground for an undercover police operation called 'Own Goal'. The authorities had become fed up with magistrates slapping the wrists of the hooligans and sending them on their way with just a warning and a paltry fine. If it could be proven that certain high-profile hooligans were conspiring to cause the trouble, then the courts could apply a much more serious charge of 'conspiracy' which could carry a longer sentence. What we didn't know in the close season of 1985 was just how advanced the Old Bill were with this. Chelsea, West Ham and Millwall were firmly in their sights, and over the next eighteen months or so a large number of high-profile hooligans, such as Steve 'Hicky' Hickmott of Chelsea, were arrested. Some were jailed for up to ten years, although Hicky's conviction was overturned and he received a large payout in compensation.

Why United were omitted from this first batch of targets I don't know, as our reputation was as bad as any. Perhaps it was because we were split into so many groups around the country, with the Cockney Reds themselves being such a diverse collection, that it made us difficult to focus on or pin down. However, our turn would come.

CHAPTER 11

THE BLOODIEST BATTLES

I n March 1985 Millwall's various firms, often referred to generally as the Bushwhackers, had a night in Luton at a FA Cup replay that has gone down in hooligan folklore as one of the worst ever for football violence. Yet of thirty-one people arrested and charged in court the next day, many admitted not being Millwall fans at all, but instead came from a variety of other clubs in the vicinity, attracted by the prospect of a mass riot. I never heard of any Cockney Reds owning up to being part of this, but did hear some were from Luton's arch local rivals, Watford.

The club and police should have been prepared. Luton was a hotbed of racial tensions, with many Pakistanis, Indians and Bangladeshis having moved into the area, and the authorities should have been aware that Millwall, with its renowned hooligan gangs, many of them National Front supporters and racists, would take the chance to make a show. With no proper ticketing control, inadequate fencing and an evening kick-off with many there fuelled by booze, the violence was as bad as could be: a pre-match pitch invasion was followed by a full-scale riot. The resulting national outcry strengthened the Government's determination to clamp down on the thugs and to pursue the conspiracy charges against selected groups of hooligans. Prime Minister Thatcher later confirmed in her memoirs that she effectively set up a 'War Cabinet', so serious did the Government consider the problem had become.

United played at Luton Town the following October. We had by then won all our opening league games of the new season and seemed to be walking the First Division. I was up at a mate's house in St Albans on the Friday before the game and we went on the piss all night. The two violent Peckham brothers were with me and we ended up in the centre of St Albans for a curry washed down with plenty of lager. The next morning, we met the Cockney Reds, Mancs and others, encompassing all of our worst lunatics, in various pubs in St Albans city centre, before travelling the twelve miles to Luton in the early afternoon. Old Bill tried to escort us to the ground, but we broke through their lines while being taken along a walkway outside the station that also led into the shopping centre. We caused havoc among the Saturday lunchtime shoppers – black or white, young or old, football fan or not – and then terrorised the occupants of the terraced houses we passed on the way to the ground, with many a face appearing at a window to see the rumpus, only to cower back in fright when subjected to a barrage of abuse and threats.

The game itself passed off without much trouble, although our win record came to an end with a 1–1 draw. More trouble flared after the game when Old Bill tried to usher us away from the ground towards the station; we again broke away and were able to get into the High Street to confront a big mob of Luton fans, who had been reinforced by disgruntled locals seeking revenge for what had happened earlier in the day. About three hundred of us faced them. Shoppers were caught up in the fighting and kids were being dragged off by their parents to safer areas. A few police were caught in the middle and had no chance. The Luton threw so many missiles that numerous bystanders were hit and injured and someone shouted, 'This is just like Agincourt!' But when we got up close the Luton backed off, not wanting to engage. Griff was hit by someone in a United shirt, who had not realised who he was, which fired him up even more, and we ran Luton ragged. Griff led the way, while keeping half an eye out for his United attacker. Elsewhere hundreds of other United were looting shops and laying waste.

After ten minutes our rampage petered out with the arrival of police reinforcements, so we headed back to the station and onto the train to St Albans. There we were joined by more Reds, and ended up in a pub called the Fleur de Lys in the historic city centre. It all kicked off again there in a row over the disappearance of the pub's charity boxes, and a Cockney chinned a black bloke who gave us some verbals. The injured party left but a near-riot then took off for about ten minutes, before Old Bill turned up. We set about them too. Some of our lads made a beeline for the parked police cars:

BIG K *Together with about half a dozen others, I started rocking these cars. Old Bill were too involved with the fighting further along the road to notice and it didn't take much to tip them over. One car was on its side and the other finally toppled onto its roof, to an almighty cheer. We were spotted by the Old Bill and sped off down the street, and it was then I realised my jumper, with lurid stripes, rather stood out, so I took it off and dropped it in a rubbish bin. The last thing you would want on a night like this was to get nicked. We later joined in with fighting elsewhere. When it began to quieten down we tried to blag our way into a club, but this bouncer was having none of it. So when we turned to leave, I went back towards him and laid him out. What a night, although I have this lasting memory of Steve M being annoyed because all this was happening on his manor!*

All through the city centre the windows of cafés, wine bars and pubs were being smashed and there was by now a full-scale riot. When the police started making arrests, I ran off down some side streets with one of the Peckham brothers and a lad known as Paki Steve, having become separated from the main group. We stopped to catch our breath in a narrow road with cars parked nose-to-tail along its full length. The houses were smart without being too showy, each with bay-fronted windows behind a couple of yards of front garden. The street was lit by lamps and the glow of house lights behind drawn curtains, but we stood in the shadows by a front gate. Suddenly the black bloke from earlier in the pub, no doubt looking for the fella who had hit him, appeared from around the corner, joined by some tooled-up mates. We looked at each other and I said, 'Let's get the fuck out of here.' We legged it as fast as we could and me and the Peckham brother hid in a front garden full of thick bushes, but Paki Steve chose to hide behind some parked cars. Our pursuers must have seen him, and he was cornered. He saw only one way out: he burst from his hiding place, sprinted across the road, hurdled a garden fence and dived head-first through a bay window, showering glass everywhere. Screams followed from inside the house as he landed on a living room carpet at the feet of a family watching *The Generation Game*.

The black guy's gang were dumbfounded. They went over to the house and peered through the window, to see an Asian family in a state of shock. I am sure I heard them apologising; it was bizarre. His gang then moved off down this alley towards us and passed our hiding place, with me curled up into a ball in the shadows under a garden bush. With bigger numbers we could have put up a fight but the last thing I needed was another arrest. The police, who had been chasing the black guy, now arrived at the house where Steve was recovering. Some of them stayed there while the rest followed this gang, but we kept hidden until everyone had left. We then made our way from the garden and found we were opposite the curry house I had been in the previous night. I still had the problem of finding my way back to the car to set off home, but had no idea where it was in relation to where I was now. We went into the curry house, ordered a taxi and had a drink while we waited. I was able to vaguely describe where I had left the car, and the cab driver recognised where it was. We then had to drive round to find the other Peckham brother.

All hell was let loose in St Albans that night and we were pleased to get out unscathed. We heard Griff and Big K had been arrested and taken away to the local nick, and many other arrests followed. The Ghost had a lucky escape.

THE GHOST *We returned to St Albans after the match because our mate Deckchair lives there – so-called because he is tall, tends to wear striped shirts, and looks like a deckchair with legs when he walks. We're all in this pub called the Fleur and trouble started when some charity boxes were taken. This upset the locals, and fighting spilled out into the street. We eventually moved onto another pub, where the fighting continued. So much damage was done that it made the News of the World the next day. I had gone back to the Fleur to find Griff, who had been attacked by this black geezer. When I got there Griff was on the floor, handcuffed by the police. I did not want to get involved but this copper came over to me, pointed at the red stains on my smart yellow top (smart because I was supposed to be going on to a wedding reception later) and, guessing I was involved, threatened to nick me if I didn't 'fuck off'. In* *many ways we outdid Millwall's effort earlier in the year. Also I did get to the wedding reception and received plenty of comments about the top!*

At the heart of the St Albans riot was a solid little firm within the Cockney Reds: the Peckham brothers, Steve M and Griff, Big K, The Ghost, Micky W and another lad called Johnny W. Big K, a child of the Sixties from Peckham way, towered over everyone and had a moody presence. He was particularly aggressive on trains, for some reason, mouthing off about anything and not always endearing himself even to our own. He fell out with nearly everyone at times, but he was another who would stand at your side and never let you down in a fight. On one occasion some dickhead was giving me grief over something and K just chinned him. Fallings out within the Cockneys were not unusual, as you find with all close-knit groups or families, but it normally did not take long to smooth things over, usually with a few drinks. Johnny W was another who could handle himself. At about the same time as the St Albans incident he hit a bloke on a station platform after a game and it was so serious it was deemed worthy of coverage on *Crimewatch*. His mug was even shown on telly from the CCTV, along with three men with him, but they were never caught.

There were all sorts of characters in the Cockney Reds. Some came and went, some have died, but most of us soldier on. One who arrived later and had his fifteen minutes (or seconds) of fame was Robert the Scaffolder. He ran onto the pitch at the end of a game against Wimbledon and kicked Vinnie Jones up the arse, before being taken away by the police. To his credit Jones did not wish to press charges.

Griff, it has to be said, was worse than anyone, as Joe can confirm.

JOE *I met Griff when he was inside for his three-and-a-half stretch for a stabbing, and he was a menace. He was always in trouble with the screws and regularly up before the Governor, often for attacking other prisoners. He was dangerous to be with when we went to matches. He would carve anyone, including me or any other Cockney Red, without a second thought. But this lunatic added to the Cockney Reds' reputation because everyone was shit-scared of us, and much of it had to do with him. He went beyond that line. He would be at the front and do two or three before the whole thing got going. We couldn't control him and I'm not sure he was the full shilling. He was later banged up for one of the worst crimes imaginable, and we disowned him.*

Those battles in Luton and St Albans brought out the elite of the Cockney Reds. They also generated another wave of horror stories in the media, and made the Government even more hell-bent on sorting out the problem. Yet it was not long before an event came along to surpass them for bloody carnage. In August 1986 the Cockneys and a handful of Mancs took a trip that would pass into hooligan history. The destination was a pre-season game against Ajax in the Netherlands, although that was not where the fighting occurred. I missed the whole thing, and am still gutted, although it may well have saved me from a nicking or serious injury.

The ban on British clubs from European competition did not, at that time at least, extend to friendly matches. Pre-season tours in those days were commonly taken to continental Europe, whereas nowadays money dictates that it is usually Asia or the USA. Today's trips are also centrally organised and controlled, whereas in 1986 there were several supporters' groups arranging the travel and match tickets.

Dobbin was our main London Supporters' Club organiser but there were others, such as the London United Club, handled by Teresa, who was very good at what she did. She sorted out the train travel from Liverpool Street in London to the Essex coast at Harwich to catch the ferry *Koningin Beatrix*, which would cross the North Sea to the Hook of Holland, and four or five hundred United nearly filled the whole train.

West Ham were also playing in the Netherlands, but their fans were mostly expected to travel the day before ours, so no-one foresaw a problem. When the Cockney Reds, the Barmies and the Mancs piled onto the train, however, they found forty or fifty West Ham in the front carriage, having done their best to barricade themselves in. The Hammers were outnumbered ten to one but managed to keep our mob at bay, even though at each stop every effort was made to break into their carriage. In response they shouted and gestured through the windows. Our boys decided they would await their chance at Harwich. Cockney Red Big K was there:

BIG K *As soon as we arrived at Harwich, shortly before midnight, West Ham were off like a shot onto the Beatrix. I leapt off the train and chased after them with a group of hardcore United, mainly Cockney Reds. We were delayed getting through the ticket check and this allowed West Ham to run up to the upper deck's small bar, at the top of a narrow staircase. I later heard they had guessed there would be trouble, as they were booked onto a 'United boat' and had upgraded to what passed as first class, where they mixed with the more well-heeled passengers. God knows what they were to make of what they were to witness.*

We massed in the main bar and carried on drinking, as we had on the train journey, and it was becoming more than lively when the boat set sail at about half past midnight.

I was more interested in getting at West Ham and, with some mates, sized up the chances of an attack up the flight of stairs that led to them. It was steep and only about five feet wide. We sent out a scout and he returned to say West Ham were massed at the top of the stairs.

Just at that moment 'I'm Forever Blowing Bubbles' rang out, followed by chanting and then abuse aimed at us, mainly about Munich. That was it, enough time had been wasted. I gathered three dozen at the foot of the stairs. One lad with me shouted, 'Remember our bloke stabbed at West Ham last season, come on!' This was met with a roar from the others.

At first the crew and staff tried to form a wedge between us and West Ham at the top of these stairs, but they were soon frightened off. Behind us in the bar were the rest of the Reds, mixing with a large group of Hells Angels on their way to some gathering in Holland that weekend. West Ham United FC, we later learnt, had warned the ferry company of possible trouble between the two sets of fans but it seemed no precautions were taken, apart from the crew asking these Hells Angels to help keep the peace. They refused. The crew returned to try again to break it up but gave up for the second time, despite calling on some brawny lorry drivers standing in a sizeable group to one side of us to help; they backed off as the violence was about to kick off big-time. I wanted to go to the back of the boat and try a different route upstairs that West Ham would not have had covered, but my mates would not have any of it until sometime later, by which time it had been sealed off by chained folding gates.

Back at the stairwell, about a dozen West Ham were throwing anything they could lay their hands on to stop us getting up the steps. One of us picked up a huge pot, ran up the stairs and hurled it at those at the top, which scattered them for a moment, but they then unhitched the fire hoses and managed to set off the jets in our direction, with the force of the water knocking us all back down the stairs. We clambered back up but, although we were three times their number or more, they were able to hold the high ground above us. Water began to fill the floor of the bar. We stood toe-to-toe as chairs and bottles, pint mugs, sheets of glass and other debris were hurled between us; one Red plucked a fire extinguisher from the wall and threw it at them.

As the fighting got serious, some West Ham pulled out knives and struck out through the banisters. Two Cockney Reds were stabbed and fell backwards. This further inflamed matters and some of our lads flashed knives too. I was knocked over by a mate with a slash across his face and we tumbled to the foot of the stairs, splashing into the now ankle-deep water. Above me a West Ham fan was swinging a rope with a padded end wrapped with metal, or maybe it was a cut-off piece of hose. Whether from this or from the thrown glass, my mate John Paine, a schoolteacher, reeled backwards with his head split open. Blood was spurting everywhere. I stayed with him, placing my hand over the wound, but the blood seeped through my fingers. Someone provided a cloth that I held firmly against the gaping wound but his blood and that of others now flowed down the stairwell and onto the bar floor, mixing with the hose water.

More United from the bar area now became involved and it was at this point I looked for the other way of getting upstairs, but it was too late, so I returned to John to help with his wound and to get him into the bar. Black Terry, along with a few others, had broken into the duty-free to grab bottles, stools and anything they could use as a weapon and we later found out Terry helped himself to some jewellery whilst there too. I saw the captain and some senior crew arrive behind us, but they said and did nothing despite seeing John and others badly injured. There was a sudden lull in the fighting, followed by a tannoy announcement not many of us could hear. The fighting had lasted about twenty minutes before we realised that to get at the West Ham would be too costly in terms of injury, and the whole thing calmed down.

I looked around to take stock. It was carnage. Debris was lying at the foot of the stairwell in pools of bloodied water. John was out of it, but someone had found a first aid cupboard and we wound yards of bandages round his head, from which blood still oozed alarmingly. Someone shouted that the boat had turned around, and soon after the captain confirmed this with another announcement. Our efforts had been in vain, and West Ham gloated from above us about how they had held us back. We had been out of Harwich for a couple of hours, and it would take the same to get back, but there was no further trouble.

When we docked, some hundred Old Bill, many in riot gear, were lined up along the quayside with their cars parked nearby, headlights beaming out to sea. It was a weird sight. Several injured were helped off the boat but only John appeared to be serious and he was taken off to the nearest first aid post and later to hospital in Colchester. I decided to lie low, mixing with a large group of gypsies on the boat and hiding the fact I was covered in John's blood, but the captain picked me out as one of the ringleaders and I was grabbed by a copper, who commented on my bloody clothes.

Along with about forty others, both West Ham and Man United, I was questioned. I explained I had just been looking after John, hence the blood, and they seemed to accept this. I was told I was being kept 'on record' for being involved but without any charges being made. Unsure of exactly what that meant, I trod a little more carefully in the years afterwards. But I was dropped in it when Black Terry told the police that I had witnessed what he and a lad called Burnsy did or didn't do. This was later to lead to a court appearance as a witness after I was subpoenaed to attend.

I was released later that night and caught a morning train back to Liverpool Street, along with some Reds who had hung around. Those not nicked had been put on an earlier train. By the time I arrived in London, most of the BBC and ITV cameras and reporters had gone but earlier in the day it had apparently been quite a scene, with both West Ham and United shown getting off the train with bloodstained clothing, many with patched-up injuries, and some gave interviews. The papers were full of it the next day. The Government condemned the hooligans again and as a result the English clubs got another year added to their existing European ban following Heysel.

Still determined to get to the United game in Holland, I forked out another £80 to get a flight. Still, it was all worth it. That boat incident was an unforgettable experience.

I was hugely disappointed to have missed this. Poor old John did recover from that horrendous injury but was left with an ugly scar. He was to die a few years later, far too young.

The subsequent court case for both sets of fans was delayed until November 1987, largely because the trouble had occurred in international waters and much clarification was needed to sort out the legal complexities. Big K's subpoena took him to court in Chelmsford, where he played dumb, saying he was only involved with helping poor old John and did not see much else. Black Terry and Burnsy both got eight years for affray, assault and criminal damage, with Terry also being done for the jewellery. In all, twelve men from both clubs were convicted and sentenced to a total of fifty-one years. The European ban was also extended to friendlies as a result.

The ferry row was one of the major hooligan events of a decade that seemed to produce more than any other. And the decade was to end with what turned out to be a watershed moment for football, not just in respect of violence. It was to affect the way supporters were protected, stewarded and policed, and would result in much-improved crowd management and eventually all-seater stadiums at the top level. It came on 15 April 1989 at Hillsborough, Sheffield.

* * *

Despite the immense police and media attention after Luton, the Bradford fire and Heysel, and the death of a young fan at a game between Birmingham City and Leeds United, we remained committed to football violence. Some might ask how we could carry on after all this tragedy, especially as we were getting older. In some ways we did rein back, or at least some of the hardcore Cockney Reds and Mancs did, but it had little effect on me. In fact in many ways, I wish I had done even more. I know what we did was wrong, but we did not care what others thought then nor do so now. That streak has never left me.

Our bitterest 'enemy', as ever, was on Merseyside. We had absolutely no time for those we dubbed 'Mickeys' or 'Mickey Mousers'. Many United supporters hate Scousers with a passion and there has never been a game between the two sides without some sort of trouble. As an opener for the season after the Heysel disaster, we played Everton in the Charity

Shield. A few old scores were settled on and off the pitch. One Everton bloke was slashed with a knife and needed multiple stitches and there were numerous arrests for public order offences, theft and even possession of drugs, something new that was creeping onto the terraces.

I don't know exactly when the Manchester–Liverpool rivalry started, but mass violence at a game at Anfield in 1971, in which Liverpool were not even playing, shows how deep it was even then. United had been temporarily banned from playing at home due to a knife being thrown at the Newcastle United goalkeeper and so had to play some games at neutral grounds. One of these was against Arsenal, freshly-crowned winners of the Double, and the venue selected was Anfield, not the wisest choice by the Football Association. Anyone with a clue would have known that the Scousers would not want to give up their Kop to the Red Army, even for a game they were not involved in.

About a thousand hardcore Liverpool nutters, backed by a smattering of Everton, duly took up position to defend their Kop, having put their club under pressure to sell them tickets for the game. They massed at the bottom of that huge end, immediately behind the goal. The few Arsenal that turned up, in a total crowd of 27,000, were given what is now the away section, while we took over the rest of the Anfield Road End. However my firm of a dozen Cockney Reds were intent on 'taking' the famous Kop, and managed to get on there before kick-off. With Griff at our head, we steamed into the Scousers, who quickly realised who we were and swarmed around us. We fought furiously but were vastly outnumbered and had to pull Griff out of the melee to save him from a severe beating. We then climbed onto the pitch and headed to the United section. Our players were out warming up and we had to swerve through them, pursued by a large number of Scousers.

As we dived into the United end, our own support began to climb onto the pitch to take on the Scousers, who smartly turned and ran back to the Kop. The *Guardian* reported that about a hundred fans were ejected from the ground the windows of houses in Anfield were smashed and '600 skin-heads' had to kept in check by police after throwing bricks at the United supporters as they were frogmarched back to Lime Street Station and on to trains back to Manchester.

In my early days following United, Liverpool under Bill Shankly were the coming team. They enjoyed some success in the Sixties, but it was in the Seventies and Eighties, under a succession of in-house managerial appointments, that their star rose, as ours waned. The rivalry became more intense, more personal, and nasty. Their fans would chant that infamous song about the Busby Babes and the Munich air disaster that began with the words:

Who's that lying on the runway?
Who's that dying in the snow?

It was a deliberately provocative reference to the Munich air crash that wiped out half of that iconic young team, and was enough to incite any fan. We often had to listen to the same song from Manchester City, Leeds, and certain other supporters.

If I can identify one thing that marked how great is the hostility between us, it was the sight of golf balls with five-inch nails driven through being thrown at us, along with darts, at many a game. I can still see the image of one Cockney Red running off with a dart stuck in his head. Of course, we threw everything back in retaliation. Our clashes with Liverpool in the late Seventies and early Eighties were as bad as it has ever been at football in the UK; perhaps only the never-ending

Celtic–Rangers feud matched it. There were terrible incidents at every game, many involving weapons such as darts and carpet knives. Trips to their place were always highly dangerous but we felt we had the upper hand when we met on neutral ground.

THE GHOST *It was the 1983 Milk Cup final at Wembley. We always met up at Swiss Cottage before any Wembley final and there were hundreds of us milling around the various pubs. Some in the firm had done some jewellers' shops during the morning and looted a few other shops for essentials like beer and food, before we headed off to the ground. Some of us made the Liverpool end and missed most of the game as we fought toe-to-toe with the Mickeys. We legged it before the end of extra-time and waited for Liverpool in one of the nearby car parks. Most of United had left the stadium and surrounds as Liverpool waited to watch their team be presented with the cup. When they came out they were surprised to find us waiting and were caught off guard. We chased them all the way down to Wembley Central and gave them a right pasting. Upset by this, the Scousers were ready for us when we went to Liverpool the next season and we had to do a lot of ducking and diving to survive: the most interesting point being that Liverpool filth seemed to side with the locals, unlike what happens in Manchester, London or elsewhere. Over the years it's always been the same, with them seeing nothing being done wrong by their own fans – another reason we hate the Scousers so much.*

Then in 1985 came the thirty-nine deaths and six hundred injuries at Heysel. Fourteen Liverpool fans were later found guilty of involuntary manslaughter and each sentenced to a term of three years' imprisonment. One fan was later acquitted on appeal but eleven others had their sentences extended. The head of the Belgian FA was also given a six-month suspended sentence for allowing tickets in Liverpool zones to be sold to Juventus supporters, and one of the officers in charge of security at the ground was later convicted of criminal negligence. The tragedy was described as 'the darkest hour in the history of the UEFA competitions' and resulted in all English clubs being placed under an indefinite ban from all European competitions – the ban was lifted in 1990 – with Liverpool being excluded for an additional three years, later reduced to one.

Liverpool, then still the best team in England, were hit as hard by this ban as anyone; United only missed out on a couple of UEFA Cup campaigns. Of course, the huge ramifications of Heysel and the damage to the nation's image made Thatcher's Government even more determined to stamp out hooliganism in football. Immediately after Heysel we felt some Scouse hardcore seemed to revel in their notoriety, strutting their stuff as much as they had ever done. Four years later, all of that changed.

The Hillsborough disaster, in which ninety-six people died and more than seven hundred were injured at the FA Cup semi-final between Liverpool and Nottingham Forest, was to transform the face of policing, hooliganism and crowd control at football matches. What happened was truly horrific and the families have the greatest possible sympathy I can offer, with so many innocent, law-abiding and loyal fans, who just went to watch a football match, having the life crushed out of their bodies. Those who died were not thugs, they were the innocents, but there is little doubt that the fear of hooliganism was a factor in the immediate police response, which was to prevent fans spilling onto the pitch from the packed terrace, with fatal consequences.

Many fans of other clubs felt it could have been them. I had my own haunting memory of Hillsborough when we played

Leeds there in 1977 in the FA Cup semi-final, and were given that notorious Leppings Lane End. My little firm arrived at the ground without tickets after a boozy train journey and a long drinking session in Sheffield city centre. Other Reds forced their way into the Leppings Lane End without paying; so vast were our numbers the turnstile operators and police had no chance. Many of our fans later told of a horrible crush all along that terrace, and how it was a miracle no-one was killed. I managed to miss it, as me and Tooting Steve snatched tickets off some Leeds fans standing in a queue at the away end and managed to get into a different section with them, even though the tickets had been torn in half when we grabbed them. But I heard the horror stories afterwards.

Inevitably given the abuse directed at us for years, some United fans used Hillsborough and Heysel to take a verbal pop at their Scouse rivals, blaming them in part for what had happened. This became very vitriolic, with mocking names like 'the Murderers' and 'the Victims' being bandied about. Some of the chants from United are just as bad, if not worse, than theirs about Munich. The thing is, it might have been United at that end of the ground on that day and me who arrived late. To be fair, in the years since Hillsborough the Scousers cut back on their Munich chants, but it can all still get out of hand on social media, fan forums and so on. Before the Europa League game in 2016 at Old Trafford, the Scousers were faced with banners all the way along the M62 draped from bridges reminding them of Hillsborough or Heysel. It's not nice, nor mindful of the families who lost loved ones, but I know some United fans cannot ignore the memory of previous insults. And so the rivalry continues. A trip to Anfield is not for the faint-hearted, even today. Some of the Cockneys do link up with a few old-school Liverpool both home and away, but not me.

CHAPTER 12

AWAY FROM THE TERRACES

What is life like for a football hooligan away from his match-day stamping grounds? We were a mixed bunch, mainly working-class lads: builders, factory workers and white-van men, but some were company executives, bankers, businessmen, even members of Her Majesty's constabulary – I was once joined by an off-duty copper at a Tottenham game and we were both taken in for questioning after some trouble in the streets. As a bricklayer I earned good money and my little work gang would often move together to different jobs, passing word around between us of what was on offer. At the time we could pick and choose the jobs offering more long-term employment and so earn a regular, tidy income. Building sites were also not without their scams and we took full advantage, along with many others – the bosses included. Most of the lads in the trade were into football and we would have kickabouts at break times on-site, drink together after work and often meet up on weekday evenings, then go off and support our different teams on a Saturday. There was huge rivalry amongst us and it was not unknown to come up against a work colleague at a game, then be all matey back at work on the Monday.

We rarely stayed in during the week but would invariably go out for a drink, chase women and end up in a fight. Typical of our behaviour was an incident on a Friday in August 1982, a month before my extended jaunt to Valencia. To wind down after a long week, my workmates and I joined a few others, including Cockney Reds, at the Castle pub in Surbiton. I knew the landlord, Barry, and his wife, Linda. They had been awarded Pub of the Year in 1981, served up good beers and plenty of atmosphere, and the place was always packed. Barry made sure he had some attractive women behind his bar, a foolproof way to attract the young male punters. This particular evening, however, the male bar manager became a bit heavy-handed after an argument over a drink order. He subsequently refused to serve one of my mates and it became something of a stand-off, but for once we let it drop and went into the pub garden. A bunch at a nearby table then got busy with us over this argument with the manager, probably because they were regulars. From out of nowhere, one of them hit my mate with a hammer and knocked him to the ground. We hoisted him to his feet and piled into them. This seemed to set everyone off, whether involved from the start or not. Glasses were thrown, tables overturned and innocents stumbled past us to get away.

Anything we could lay our hands on was used as a weapon. I suddenly remembered I had a cut-down machete in the car, which I sometimes used at work, and went to fetch it. My car was some way from the pub, and by the time I got back the fighting had almost come to an end and we could hear wailing sirens not far away. One bloke I knew came up to me and started mouthing off about the damage done to him and his mates. I told him, 'Serves you right as you shouldn't have got involved.' He threatened me and I gripped the machete tight and thought about whacking him with it, but he already had blood pouring from his nose, a cut above his eye which was rapidly closing, and bruising to his face, and given that I knew him, I felt a tinge of sympathy and let it go – which was just as well, as at that moment the police pulled up.

We scattered. Realising I had this dangerous weapon, a fact that would not go down well with the coppers, I slung it in a thick privet hedge surrounding this nearby churchyard and hid whilst things calmed down. After about twenty minutes, with the police gone, we all came out of our hiding places and I jumped into my convertible and drove home. The next day I was working in Croydon but drove over to Surbiton to pick up the machete. I was told Old Bill had come back the previous night after the pub had closed and searched for weapons, but clearly they didn't find mine.

This was not the end of this story. On the Sunday after, I went drinking with a different group, more yuppie-like, to a pub called the Plough at Worcester Park. I knew that some of those we had been fighting regularly drank there, including the one who had fronted me, so I went ready for trouble and was not prepared to let the matter drop. I even put on my work boots to give this bloke a good kicking. As soon as we arrived outside the pub, I went over to an open window, spotted him and shouted, 'You know what happened to you was nothing to do with me, but if you want to make something of it then come outside.' He looked worried but said nothing. I would have gone into the pub and grabbed him as I was so wound up – which was nothing unusual in those days – but my yuppie mates didn't fancy giving me support, so I let it ride, having made my point.

That was me back then, never letting things drop and always wanting the last word. It was typical of my life and it was not just me, because other Cockneys were at it 24/7. Soon after this incident I was off to Valencia and did not return for several months, but by the Easter of 1983 I was regularly going to Barry's pub in Surbiton, often with a mate, Colin, who had his own security business. Colin's firm looked after the snooker star Jimmy White, who lived nearby, and also did the door at Tiffany's. We were in the pub on Easter Sunday and well tanked up after a good session when we saw some faces from that Friday night incident eight months earlier. Another mate, Big Bernie, recognised the one I'd had the set-to with and asked me about doing something, but I said, 'No, not worth bothering about.' Something stirred in me at closing time, however, as I recalled the abuse I had received all that time ago, and my temper got the better of me. So I clobbered this bloke as he passed me at the bar, knocking him to the floor. I then stood over him but his girlfriend, who I knew from way back, pleaded with me to move away and tugged at my arm. I said, 'Well, he shouldn't have got involved back then and needed to be taught a lesson.' I decided to leave it there, even after the bloke rose to his feet and shouted that we should finish this off down the nearby park. I just gave him the finger. He could wait until another day, as our paths were certain to cross again. They did, but not until twenty years later. I was at a wedding when I saw this bloke *and* the same girl, now his wife. To show that times and people change, we shook hands.

* * *

I still had the flat near Sutton and went back to my old job, working alongside Big Steve on a site near the Thames. It was bloody cold after Spain. One day I was in Sutton and I met this bloke, Charlie Capone, who ran a newspaper stall outside the station. He told me a pub over the road was being refurbished, with a restaurant upstairs and bars below, and was looking for some security staff. I was interested and went along to meet the manager, who had been there before it had closed and knew me from old. He also knew that, although not the tallest or biggest,

I could handle almost anything. It could only help that I would also know a lot of the punters, and vice versa. I was hired.

The money was decent and arrived on time, which was rare in the security game – you usually had to fight for your pay. Plus I could drink and eat there for nothing. I knew of some dubious goings-on that I would have to ignore, as is the norm in such places, but nothing much passed me by. Interestingly the bar manager was married to the daughter of a proper villain, a Canadian who had grassed up the Kray twins. This Canadian had previously set up a company and with the Krays' backing, ordered thousands of pounds' worth of goods, sold them on at half price without paying for them, then wound up the company so the original supplier never got his money, a scam known as long-firm fraud.

I needed some back-up to work there and sought the help of my mate Colin, who ran security and was into a lot of dodgy dealings. He was short, bald and round and looked so much like the actor Bob Hoskins that we often called him that. Looks could be deceptive. I saw him upset someone one night and this lad jumped on his back, thinking Colin was nothing; the lad swiftly wound up on the deck on the wrong end of a good kicking. Colin could never make out why I ran around at football when I could have made all the money I needed by doing what he did. I knew I could rely on him to deliver the right person to help me and it turned out to be Andy the Greek, a man mountain of about twenty-two stone but a nice lad. He didn't need to do anything if it kicked off, he was intimidating enough as he was. Through him I met Colin Pates, the Chelsea captain, who lived nearby, and Jimmy White used to come in the bar too. When not working and to get away from where we were known, me and Colin used to go to this bar near Hampton Court owned by a wrestler off the telly. All sorts of villains hung out there. My mate Colin 'looked after' Joey

Pyle, a well-known London gangster and friend of the Krays, and brought with him his cousin, who was a nightmare for causing trouble. So I was mixing with criminals in a murky world, but Valencia had shown me prison was no fun and I did my best to avoid many of the things I saw or heard about.

Despite this being a seven-day-a-week job, I could still get to football and be back between eight and nine on a Saturday evening to work the late shift, when trouble was most likely. The punters knew me too well to take me on, so I had no real problems, although it was clear drugs were being done in the bogs. There is not much you can do about that unless it's really obvious. As time went on Colin Pates and I started visiting the Sussex pub over in Norbury, where he had a mate. He would call me on my day off and insist I join him and we became such good friends that I went to his wedding, after a stag do in a poxy pub called the Burn Bullock in Mitcham. His reception was in a community centre in Pollard's Hill, a bloody rough place. Through him I was to meet several other Chelsea players.

There were many incidents of fighting away from the football, especially with my mates from the council estates near the St Helier Arms, who were always up for a row. We supported many different teams but hung out together, as friendship and loyalty came before football. One night in 1979 we went up the West End to meet United fans coming down for a night out ahead of the 1979 FA Cup final – a tradition then and now. After drinking and fighting with thugs from other London clubs who we knew would be there, we decided to head to the Tiffany's nightclub on our way home, as Security Colin was running the door. Griff recognised some Chelsea face in there and was keen to have a row but I was not that interested until this bloke became mouthy, so I hit him. It all kicked off and Griff knocked out another Chelsea fan, but the bouncers quickly separated us. The dozen or so Chelsea left with their girls, while we finished our drinks. We then went outside via another door and met a group of friends, including Michael B from Sutton, himself a Chelsea man. We looked round for the Chelsea group but were told they had been escorted out of the back exit by security so as not to disturb other punters and to ensure there would be no afters.

In his book *Hoolifan*, Martin King, a Chelsea hardcase, comments on that night. He saw it somewhat differently, although what he says does show how things were in the football fan fraternity away from the game. He says of me that 'he was fast establishing himself as the main man among the United following in London' and he goes on to talk about why some Chelsea held back both that night and on other occasions, as we sometimes did. 'There were unwritten rules, and, in those days, you didn't carry over football rivalries into everyday life,' he writes. 'You had to live and work with people all over London, whoever they were. If people had carried over their terrace wars to the building site, for example, London would never had been fully rebuilt after the war. Starting rows over football in clubs on your own doorstep was asking for trouble. Get into all that and you end up with people turning up at your house and the like.' I agree, and it was especially true with Chelsea, but there were odd nutters like Griff who ignored the rules and were always causing trouble.

As the Eighties wore on we became aware of football conspiracy trials involving several hooligan mobs around the country, and guessed that United would be singled out at some point. I didn't realise it at the time but there were clues that we were already under surveillance. One came when the Cockney Reds had been drinking before a Tottenham game a couple of miles from White Hart Lane, and decided to walk the rest of the way to the ground. After tramping for a mile we were on Seven Sisters Road, about five or six hundred of us. I wasn't causing any trouble but just happened to be leading the group, by accident rather than by choice. There was a bit of a commotion and our group split to either side of the busy road. I became isolated and was immediately set on by the police, for no reason. I did wonder if they were clocking me as part of a deliberate surveillance operation but dismissed it.

For doing sod-all, I was arrested, together with another Red who turned out to be an off-duty copper from Sheffield. I thought I would stick with my new-found mate because I figured the police would be reluctant to proceed against one of their own. What I did not know at the time was they also did not want this to put at risk any long-term case they were making for possible conspiracy charges. However, although the copper was indeed sent on his way, I was charged with threatening behaviour. Before my court appearance I met a Red from Coventry who had been arrested at Tottenham at the same time. As I was pleading not guilty I gave him the details of my solicitor and we appeared together. The charges were thrown out as the police evidence was seen as total rubbish.

I continued to rub up against the police. For a mid-week game at Queens Park Rangers, we finished work on site early, it being winter, and made our way to Shepherd's Bush for the usual pre-match drinking session. The game passed off with some crowd trouble but nothing out of the ordinary. We were making our way back to Shepherd's Bush tube when we were threatened from behind by some QPR, who had waited down one of the many side streets for us to pass. They really should have known better, as we attacked them without hesitation. This led to me being pulled over and arrested. I had some cannabis in my pocket, which I hid in my sock. At first the cops only did a routine frisk and made me empty my pockets, until one, who had been watching with his arms folded, came over and made a more thorough search. When I removed my socks, the little lump of cannabis was there for all to see.

I was charged with threatening behaviour and possession of drugs. This was going to mean two court appearances. I turned up at West London Magistrates along with some of the other Cockney Reds for the violence part, but Old Bill didn't show, so the case was dismissed. A year or so later we realised that they might not have wished to jeopardise the conspiracy case they were building. I was later back in court for the possession charge, but as the cannabis was a fairly small amount, I got off with a fine.

Football formed only part of my life. There were plenty of other ways of getting away from the drudgery of the building sites to enjoy booze and birds, spiced up by never being far away from a fight, a bit of thieving and using my wits to make a few quid on the side. Truth was, however, that I needed to settle down, and it suddenly happened: I found someone I really liked. We hit it off, and married in 1986. Of course, a number of Cockneys came to the evening celebration after our main wedding reception. The blushing bride was not too keen on this, especially with the number of lunatics present. There was some drunkenness and a few arguments, but by and large it went off all right. The Peckham brothers turned up for a time and later used it as an alibi when questioned by the police about a fatal stabbing somewhere else. These two were die-hard Cockneys, serious thugs who were mixed up in all sorts of mischief, but they came from a good home and had been to top schools. Like me, they had a solid family background yet chose the path of football violence and, in their case, things beyond the law outside the game.

For my part, life was settled, with a daughter soon coming along to complete our family, joining my wife's two boys from her first marriage. Things were good – but not for long.

CHAPTER 13

CONSPIRACY

After the Heysel tragedy and the ban on English teams playing in Europe, a hard anti-hooligan line was adopted by the British authorities, and the police were put on our case. Special units were set up to work undercover and infiltrate a number of the more active gangs and to use other intelligence-gathering methods, such as arresting some in the hope they would grass up their mates, filming and photographing us, and setting up CCTV and hidden video cameras.

The 1989/90 season was to bring this to a head for many of our main faces. We reckon the police started intense monitoring of United in 1988 and the urgency was heightened after Hillsborough in April 1989. Chelsea's Headhunters and West Ham's ICF had already felt the heat of the Metropolitan Police wading in and taking some of their top boys into custody, and we knew that our turn would come. Being a much larger and more diverse group than the others, however, with firms all over the country, we also knew it would be more difficult for the police to keep tabs on us and to gain the evidence they needed.

I should have realised something was going on when I was pulled over at Gatwick Airport on the way to Italy for a holiday with my wife, young daughter and stepsons. The security staff wanted to know why I was going there and specifically if it was football related, although there were no games on. Clearly they had checked me out, and with my extensive criminal record, including my incarceration in Valencia, they were suspicious. They still let me catch the flight but this should have set alarm bells ringing that I was a target.

We first noticed how the cops had changed tactics early in the 1989/90 season, when we went to Maine Road. It was the first derby game for some time, as City had spent a couple of seasons in the Second Division. All the boys met at the Grey Parrot, a dump of a pub among the bleak surroundings of Hulme, which was deliberately chosen for being out of the way. Hundreds of us then marched through back streets on a two-mile journey to the ground. It was plain to see we were being extensively filmed by police officers, although we thought little of it.

The game had been made all-ticket in an attempt to prevent trouble but many hooligans had obtained seats through various sources, and the touts did a good trade. We were able to secure tickets for the North Stand. Soon after the game started, fighting broke out in the City end, with some fans even climbing the tall fencing topped with barbed wire to escape. Such was the panic that the referee took the players off for about ten minutes as United fans were escorted out of the City end to their own terrace. On the pitch we played like a load of tossers and lost 5–1; by the time Mark Hughes scored our only goal most of us had left the ground. We waited outside for City and then again in the city centre, and trouble continued right into the late evening. Again, we were constantly being filmed.

In the third round of the FA Cup that season, Mark Robins scored the goal that beat Nottingham Forest and saved Alex Ferguson's job, or so folklore has it. In the next round, at the end of January, we were drawn away at Hereford United, with the game to be televised live on a Sunday. I organised a coach along with Micky W to take us there on the Saturday. This was no ordinary charabanc: it was from the Londoners Coach Company and was the dog's bollocks. About forty of us met and boarded at Euston, from where we were driven out west, having decided to head to Worcester for a pre-game overnight stay, although we had not booked any rooms; it seems an odd route but there must have been some reason for it. Many other Cockneys went via Bristol by train, car or coach, with a stop-over there for a night out in a bigger city.

I have to say that those on my coach journey were the biggest load of lunatics I have ever seen on a trip, before or since. There were some dangerous blokes there, make no mistake. Our mate Prince Charlie was on that trip and as usual had no money, despite being aged in his late thirties. Because all the boys loved him, they chipped in to pay for his coach fare, which he pocketed gratefully. The coach stopped at a service station for us to have a leak and Charlie came back with a black sack. Micky W then collected the money for the coach, only for Charlie to say, 'I ain't got any.'

'But what about the whip we did?'

'I spent it.'

'What on?'

'On these.'

Charlie proceeded to fish chocolate bars of all types from his sack and hand them around. Micky just shook his head and moved on.

It took forever to get to Worcester and we then had to find a place to stay. A sleepy little B&B agreed to take us in but could accommodate only about fifteen of us, so the rest sneaked in and slept wherever they could, some in chairs or on the floor – so forty or more shared the cost of fifteen. It was late when we arrived but some still some went out on the town, clambering through a window so as not to alert the landlady to our true numbers.

MICK W *We shared a few rooms and spread ourselves around, with some sleeping on the floor of the hallways and corridors. In the rooms there were maybe six or seven, but even that is far short of our record, which stands at twenty-two in one room in a B&B in Great Yarmouth when we were up there for a game at Norwich. Those that did book in gave names like 'G. Best', 'D. Law' and 'N. Stiles' to the unsuspecting landlady, and I think the only two that paid were Bob and Griff, because they wanted a cooked breakfast. The rest of us used the windows and emergency exits to creep away. We tried to book the coach we had for the Hereford game for another trip as it was so luxurious but the coach firm told us to piss off.*

That wasn't the only problem we gave various coach firms over the years. Johnny Wynn and Steve M organised some great days out and I helped, along with Bob. It's not surprising we were a problem when you have in your little group people like the Peckham brothers, who, for no apparent reason, slashed a number of seats when we went to a Monday night game in 1993 at Old Trafford, where Blackburn Rovers were presented with the League trophy. It was a surprise any coach firm wanted our business, but for us the trips were great fun. We wouldn't allow anyone onto the coach, which more often than not left from Euston, unless they had a crate of beer and some spirits. We could have gone on the official Supporters' Club trips, which were less expensive but, as years went on, they were strictly controlled and no booze was allowed, so there was no point.

We were picked up on the Sunday morning in Worcester to complete our journey. The police had asked for all fan coaches to register with them so that they could be escorted, but with our trip being unofficial, we didn't bother. We were dropped off in Hereford early without a police presence and moved in force from pub to pub, being joined all the time by more United. Quite a few of the pubs suffered damage. We then heard that the game might be off, as the rain had pissed down for several days and their pitch was worse than usual. The police tried to contain us in certain areas, but we kept breaking out. At one point they kettled us in this town square, so we quietened down as if waiting for an escort to the ground. But as soon as some of the coppers left to go elsewhere, we took our chances – someone shouted, 'Now boys!' – and charged the police line. They split apart and we stampeded through, before dispersing into small groups throughout the nearby pubs.

The game went ahead but the quality was awful and we scraped through 1–0 thanks to a late winner from Blackmore. The passengers on our coach had all been told not to be too late getting back, and when we left town we counted nearly sixty travellers – about twenty more than the outward journey. Some wanted to stop and pick up some booze, so we asked the driver to pull over outside a small, open-all-hours shop. No money changed hands: like locusts we stripped the place bare, taking everything from drink to sweets to birthday cards. When we arrived back at Euston to be dropped off, we didn't need a whip-round for the driver, we just gave him our unwanted items taken from the shop. We later found out that we had been monitored at Hereford, with the police trying to build intelligence and a case against all of us, not just the best-known faces. It was also later to become obvious that some of those nicked at these games, or for incidents away from football, were snitching on others in return for lighter fines or sentences.

We played Man City at Old Trafford in early February, and after the game we again mobbed up at the Grey Parrot pub. It still had not dawned on us how closely we were being watched, but there were once again cops filming, with newly installed traffic cameras also picking us out as we walked from the pub into town, looking for City's firm. At one point during our march, two undercover police officers were spotted in amongst our mob and were quickly engulfed in a blizzard of punches and kicks: when they finally limped away, one of them needed three stitches in a split lip. Another group of fifty or sixty United were plotted up at a bar called Wetherbys, in Port Street, when a lad came in and announced, 'I think there's a mob of City coming down the street.' The next thing the windows were smashed and bricks and bottles rained in on them. They turned over some tables and used them as shields, before throwing pint pots and bottles at City through the shattered windows before surging out and chasing them down the road to another pub, the Crown and Kettle. One United fan had a piece of wood sticking out of his head, but when told he should get urgent medical help shouted, 'Fuck off!' Some City fans got battered quite badly, while a United fan was caught outside the doors of the pub, took a bad kicking and had to be carted off in an ambulance. It was later said to have been the worst violence after a derby match for twenty-five years.

This United lad taken to hospital suffered a fractured skull, according to the *Manchester Evening News*, which also said £30,000 of damage was caused at the Crown and Kettle and a further £20,000 at Wetherbys. Two hundred City fans were said to have 'bombed' the latter with missiles and the licensee told the paper, 'They battered the injured lad outside and he was taken to hospital with glass in his head from a bottle ... in five minutes the place was wrecked. I have never seen anything as terrifying. It seemed to be organised.' A police spokesman called it 'an appalling example of the worst side of football'.

City fans put up a better show that day than they ever had before and were clearly organised. This no doubt reinforced the police view that certain ringleaders were conspiring to set up these flare-ups, as opposed to the random clashes of the past. City have rarely repeated that day, having too few faces to cause us long-term problems; we just overwhelm them. Sure, they might come out at eight o'clock at night when most of us have gone home, and pick a fight with some small groups, but they are no match for us. Nothing changes there.

It was interesting that in that World Cup summer of Italia '90 a load of United, mainly from Tony O'Neill's firm, were stopped as soon as they landed in Italy and put on the next plane home. It shows the intelligence gained against us was proving useful and being passed around Europe. It was not often that United fans travelled in numbers to England games, but a summer trip to Italy had proven too enticing to miss. It was at about this time we found out that our main faces had all been given identifying codenames by the police: O'Neill, for example, was Target Kilo. I never found out what my name was, but I was definitely on the list.

As fate would have it, our next game was at one of the most notorious grounds in the country: the Den, home of Millwall FC, who had been promoted the previous year. We rarely played them, so this was a day out in South-east London to relish. Old Bill, now with their specialised groups, would be on maximum alert, with all leave cancelled, dogs readied, and some coppers buried undercover amongst us. They were much smarter than when we had last visited the Den, in 1974, and we knew the area around the ground would be like a fortress, but we also knew the police could not cover everywhere.

We gathered at the Elephant and Castle, then broke away from the police there by ducking down alleys and back streets. I arrived back in the Old Kent Road at the Canterbury Arms pub, where some Millwall were drinking inside. They decided to clear off and we took the pub over. We left at half past two, clashed briefly again with the police, then headed under a railway bridge, where there was another Millwall pub, the Carlton Tavern. After further skirmishes with both Millwall and the cops, the latter took us further down Old Kent Road to our end of the ground. They were in no mood to take prisoners, preferring to hit out with batons and shields to keep us in line.

We joined the others at the Aldington Road end, behind which our coaches and minibuses were parked up. After the usual ninety-minute interlude while we watched some men kick a ball around a pitch, we were keen to get back out onto the streets for the real action, but were kept in to allow Millwall to disperse. When the cops finally opened the gates, they tried to escort the visiting fans to their coaches or, like me, to New Cross Station. We broke away, and eventually about 1,000 off us arrived back near that Millwall pub under the railway line. The police managed to corral us there, with great difficulty, and forced us to the station. We were put onto a train, but hundreds simply got off at the next stop, Surrey Quays, and began walking.

The streets were filled with hooligans and there was much back-and-forth between rival groups, with the British Transport Police deploying dogs to keep the factions apart. Eventually scores of police were summoned by walkie-talkie, and after repeated clashes they managed to escort us back to Surrey Quays Station. This time officers joined us onboard the train and made sure we did not get off early, as they were aware that West Ham had also been at home that day and that we might head there. More Transport Police awaited us at Euston. I was singled out, taken to a van and accused of leading a mob of fans out of Surrey Quays, where missiles were thrown at the police. Of course, I denied this, saying I had simply got off the train and followed the other supporters, as I didn't know the area. They talked amongst themselves and decided to let me go. In hindsight, I might well have been on their radar and been singled out deliberately. The Ghost was also picked up by Old Bill.

THE GHOST *I got there early, having been up to Euston by 9am so I could meet Tony O'Neill and his firm, who were out in force. Huge numbers had come down the previous night and kipped out in the West End, having run riot there all night. There was no Filth at Euston, and when we formed up we looked a right firm, with so many faces out, ready for a day that Millwall would not forget. We crammed onto the Northern Line and then the Bakerloo, the trains completely taken over by United. There was singing and shouting and some snapped off the hanging handles in the carriage to wrap round their knuckles to carry more power in a punch. The few other passengers looked like they had never known such fear and many left the train as soon as they could.*

At Elephant and Castle tube station we poured out onto the street, like ants coming out of their nest hole. But the Filth were there by now and must have got intelligence that we were arriving early. Out on the Old Kent Road we headed to the Charlie Chaplin pub, but there were no Millwall there. The coppers couldn't cope because, as we later found out, there were problems all over the Elephant

191

and Castle area and they were stretched. We had Micky C with us and this was his manor, so he knew all the side streets, the alleys and the shortcuts, and off we went.

Down one side street all the windows seemed to open as we walked, and we were getting verbals from many of the locals. We gave as good back. We went from the Barnaby pub to the Canterbury Arms and then onto the Tropics, where I met up with Bob and his firm. At each pub we picked up any locals, Millwall or not, and threw them out into the street. One by one Old Bill closed the bars and then turned up with their horses and dogs but there were so many United that had every copper in London been there, they would still have had trouble containing us.

By now it was about a quarter past two and there was a rumour that Millwall had retreated to the Carlton Tavern, near the ground. We were there in no time and this was it – all the Millwall faces were present, everyone we knew, like Bobby Woolford, their main man, and the whole of the Bushwhackers. We steamed in. Bottles were thrown. A fence outside was ripped apart and the wooden slats used as coshes. Old Bill steamed into us – not Millwall, just us. The chant went up, 'Where the fuck were you in Seventy-four?' Some of our faces were nicked and eventually we were forced towards the ground. I remember, too, Bob having a stand-off with Woolford, neither of them backing down – just growling.

After the win we went back to New Cross and I met up with Bob again. We got off at the next stop, Surrey Quays, because some prick pulled the communication cord, but this fucked up the coppers as they weren't expecting it. We left and went into the Warrior pub, threw out any locals and took over. Old Bill eventually showed up mob-handed with dogs, so we piled out into the street and attacked them. I confronted an officer with his dog and he claimed I was United and causing trouble. I said I wasn't and was on my way to visit my brother in Hoxton, East London. He didn't know whether to set his dog on me or laugh. We ran on towards the Tropics, a mainly Millwall pub, where we had agreed to meet up with some mates. The riot police had it ringed and we were ushered through a tunnel under a rail line. The Filth by now were in such a state they would have killed someone given half a chance.

Later, at Euston, I was eventually nicked by another copper and his dog and taken away to the local nick. I was held, kicking my heels for well over an hour, before they let me go without charge.

Back in the FA Cup we drew Newcastle United away. Not surprisingly, the Londoners Coach Company no longer wanted our custom, so my much-anticipated trip, with a potential stop-over in Whitley Bay, never happened. It was probably just as well, as to travel that far with the people we now had in our group would have been a nightmare. We won the tie and our next game was away at Sheffield United, again on a Sunday.

I decided to run a coach from Epsom, near my home. It picked me up and we drove to Euston to collect our normal group, most of whom had been at Hereford – all lunatics looking for a fight. We had loads of drink on board and enjoyed a jolly time on our way up the M1 to Chesterfield, just south of Sheffield, where we were staying over the Saturday night. Once again we had nowhere booked, but the coach driver, who was staying overnight with a mate in Mansfield, dropped us off in the middle of Chesterfield and we found a B&B. Me, Griff and a few others moved from pub to pub, while the rest of the lads from the coach went off somewhere else. We drank with some locals who supported United and had a few Chesterfield FC fans with them.

At some stage during the night, one of our lads came in and said there was trouble at a club door between the bouncers and some off our coach. We followed him back to help out, and mixed it with these doormen. They were strong boys, and after some pushing and shoving and a few haymakers, we decided to move on, having at least made a statement. Things started to deteriorate from there, and we became involved in a few skirmishes with locals in the street and with other doormen when they denied us access.

Soon it was kicking off everywhere. The Chesterfield Reds with us tried to persuade my little firm not to join in, as they obviously knew many of their fellow locals, but we felt we had to support our mates, whether Cockneys or Mancs. It seemed at one stage like we were fighting the whole town, and things became so bad during the night that the Chesterfield Reds even teamed up with their local mates to 'protect' their town, an unforgivable sin. Eventually Old Bill started arresting everyone they could grab and I decided to lead us back to the B&B to avoid a night in the cells. Thirty-seven United were arrested and the local nick was apparently overcrowded. The police even ringed our B&B once we were inside it. Mindful that they had cameras, we stayed in the bar while they remained outside, no doubt pleased to have us trapped all in one place. One renowned Cockney Red was among those arrested:

I had travelled up with Brian and Tommy. We arrived at our B&B at about 5 pm the day before the game. Our landlord warned us not to go to the Spires club in the town, where there was bound to be trouble. We were drinking heavily but were not recognised as football fans at first, as we were there so early. Later we were all blind drunk, Tommy took on a couple of bouncers at Spires and it all kicked off. He was hit by these two manning the doors and Prince Charlie, who had joined us off the coach, waded in. Old Bill arrived. The police treated me fairly but took me in, and at the police station there were Chesterfield Mancs and locals also brought in. Charlie was there too, going berserk, and he had to be restrained by some big coppers and ushered into a cell. He was shouting all sorts and not making any sense. As I was being escorted to my cell, I looked through a glass partition and saw the names of those already put in a cell shown on a board on the wall. This had Charlie's full African name and underneath was written 'mentally unstable'. Believe me, they weren't wrong.

Next day in court, Charlie was going off on one in front of the magistrates, which didn't help his cause. I was out of court by 10.30, having pleaded guilty and been bound over to keep the peace. Charlie received a twelve-month conditional discharge and an article in The Sun had the headline, 'It's Prince Charles in punch up!' It went on to explain that this was Prince Olunoyo-Akinola, an African tribal chief and not the heir to the British throne.

After that season we lost contact with Charlie – perhaps he returned to his tribe. God knows what they would have made of him. He was a character. On other trips he would get up on the table in the bars and sing, 'I am the music man, what can I play ...' and continue with all the instrument sounds. Then he would go around the bar with a pint mug to collect some cash for his efforts.

The next day we were picked up by our coach and headed out of town towards Sheffield. As we did, a car containing the Chesterfield Reds who had turned against us the night before pulled up behind. Some of our lads opened the coach's emergency door to attack them but luckily for those inside the car it was able to drive off. We have never seen them at games since, so they must have been well and truly scared off.

We arrived in Sheffield at about ten o'clock for the afternoon kick-off. Again our clandestine organisation meant the police were not expecting us, but they spotted the coach and sent motorcycle outriders to escort us to the club coach park. Then officers came onto the coach. One of them simply said, 'Have a good day out, and beat these wankers!' Turned out he was a Sheffield Wednesday fan. We were allowed to leave to go for a drink, while the driver parked up and cleared the coach of any incriminating cans and bottles. Nevertheless more police turned up and quizzed him, asking, 'Were you in Chesterfield last night with these people?' Having stayed elsewhere he did not need to lie, and they appeared to accept his answer. He became a bit of a hero for not dropping us in it – although he obviously had his own reasons too – and we made sure he was generously looked after when it came to a tip.

From the coach park we went into the centre of Sheffield. The police were everywhere, but this did not stop huge groups of United clashing with locals around the pubs. If we had not previously been sure before that the police were monitoring us closely, we knew for definite now, as they blatantly filmed almost into our faces. I was even picked out inside the ground by their new CCTV cameras and asked to follow this copper out of the ground and into one of their control vehicles. In the old days I would have objected, but now older and wiser I decided to play ball.

'What's your full name and address?' this officer asked.

I would once have done a moody and given a false name and address, but I had been in trouble so often that I knew they would eventually identify me anyway, and I didn't want to miss the game and not get home, so I gave the correct answer.

He went on, 'Now I want you to look at this list of names and tell me if you know any of these men.'

I scanned down the names, mine included, and recognised them all: top Mancs, Yorkshire Reds, Birmingham Reds and more.

'Sorry, officer, I have heard these names before but don't know any of these people personally or have ever met them.'

'Really?' he said, not convinced. He then went outside. I heard him talking on his two-way but couldn't pick out what he was saying. When he returned, he simply said, 'Clear off and stay out of trouble.'

I later heard that a large number of Reds were pulled in before, during and after the game for probably the same reason. Most were main faces, many of them on that list. So, the police clearly had an agenda and were tracking us, and, as it was to later prove, building some sort of case against us.

* * *

The surveillance continued as we made our way to play Oldham in the FA Cup semi-final at Maine Road in early April. We again met up at the Grey Parrot, this time having gone up to Manchester by train – a coach had become too much hassle to organise. Our shadows in the police still monitored us but seemed to stand off more than usual. I now know they were hoping we would commit more serious offences and were also looking for leaders like me who might be inciting others, enabling them to charge us with conspiracy. I am annoyed now that I sussed this rather late, given what had happened with the Chelsea faces and others. We watched the Liverpool–Crystal Palace semi-final on TV in the pub and were delighted when the Scousers got beat after extra-time. So, in a good mood, we moved on, and managed to avoid committing any incriminating acts, which no doubt further frustrated Inspector Plod and his crack team of detectives.

Prince Charlie was there again, acting up like he did, but that was to be the last I ever saw of him.

MICKY W *Prince Charlie has probably gone mad and is in some institution by now. After the Chesterfield incident, I regularly had phone calls from him that were weird, to say the least. He would call at all times of the day and night, saying things like, 'They're after me – I'm being followed.' He was becoming paranoid about everything. Then, suddenly, he just disappeared. Very odd.*

He was from Hackney in East London and came along with his mate Ernie, a complete pisshead. They were a dangerous pair and far beyond the rest of us in their level of violence. In Bournemouth one year, when staying over to head off to Portsmouth the next day, someone hit Charlie over the head with a baseball bat. It just bounced off as if nothing had happened. All Charlie said was, 'Oops.' I also recall one coach trip on the M1 going north, when the video was showing a hardcore porn film that no-one was watching apart from Prince Charlie. The rest of us were either asleep or drinking and playing cards. As we sped along the motorway, our driver saw a police car pull alongside, as if to look at the TV screen, so he leant forward and switched it off. Charlie jumped up, saying, 'What the fuck are you doing, I was watching that.' We all collapsed in hysterics when we saw the size of his hard-on sticking out through his trousers.

Neil Fredrik Jensen, an outsider who travelled up from London for the Oldham game, later wrote a vivid account of that day for his Game of the People website. I am grateful to Neil for permission to reproduce his account:

On April 8, 1990, I travelled up to Manchester with a car full of United veterans, fans who remembered Best, Law, Charlton, Buchan, Holton, Morgan, Stepney, McIlroy and Pearson. The talk was of games past, of punch-ups, 'running' at Tottenham and hatred of Chelsea and Liverpool. I didn't like to tell them I was a Chelsea fan and that I had always been more City than United – thanks to Colin Bell and Frannie Lee.

It also reminded me of when United were ever in London on a Saturday match day and the 'edge' that seemed to exist at mainline train stations and pubs around grounds. If United were at West Ham, you could bet your bottom dollar that if Chelsea were also at home, there would be some stray Blues fans who would make sure they were near United's journey back to Euston. United had a dire reputation in the 1970s and they really were the forerunners of hooligan troupes. Thankfully, we generally live in gentler times when it comes to safety at football matches.

We arrived in Manchester and headed for the Piccadilly Hotel, which was heaving with United fans, most of whom had southern accents. Everyone seemed to be on nodding terms, the odd handshake indicating old comradeships from the trenches. A short, stocky individual, known as 'Pubby' was walking among his people, handing out tickets, negotiating, grabbing fistfuls of notes. He was chief ticket provider ...

Our contingent was heading for the Grey Parrot in Hulme, an ugly estate pub in an area characterised by burned-out cars, similarly desolate telephone boxes and boarded-up windows. It felt a little uneasy and looked like the type of area that would make a decent 'World in Action' documentary. The pub completed the tableaux – barbed wire on the roof, behind which an over-enthusiastic *and hungry-looking Rottweiler barked at the gathering United fans.*

Pretty soon, the lager-swilling spilled out of the pub and the fans, who had taken up every available vantage, were pressing against the windows. All eyes were on the Liverpool–Palace game, which by now had gone to extra-time. Then mayhem – Alan Pardew headed Palace's fourth goal to win the game 4–3. The United fans went berserk, forcing the large front window of the pub to bow with the pressure. It looked like a nasty accident could happen at any moment.

The Grey Parrot emptied, sending the United hordes to Maine Road. When we reached the environs of the ground, its white plastic roof could be easily picked out among the red-brick 'Coronation Street' houses. Maine Road was certainly no Old Trafford and I was surprised how ramshackle it appeared (to be fair to City, many grounds in the late 1980s and early 1990s looked shabby). United's fans were in good voice – 'Que Sera Sera' and all that – convinced that now Liverpool were out of the way, they could easily win the FA Cup. After all, Oldham were a Second Division team.

But Oldham had other ideas, taking the lead in the fifth minute and eventually drawing 3–3 after extra-time. It had been a cracking tie, but a replay was needed to separate the sides. The two semi-finals had given football a day to remember.

And so, the journey home. This time, we had a new passenger, a 'Cockney Red' with a taste for pushing boundaries. He explained that in the close season, he had travelled to Liverpool, equipped with United scarf, and sat in a pub frequented by Liverpool fans, 'to see how long I would last'. He called it his own 'market research'. A bizarre character who ended the trip smoking a joint – in the car.

It was a day like I had never experienced before, or since. While my curiosity never got the better of me to ask if my fellow passengers were football hooligans, they clearly had campaign medals of their own. It wasn't quite 'Football Factory', but you could tip your hat in that direction. Those that are still around remain United fans, but many of them, exiled by rising prices and rheumatic limbs, are no longer on the front line. When they do watch a game, you won't see any of them taking photos with their smartphones when United earn a penalty...if United is a religion, they are strictly Old Testament.

Fast forward to September 1990. I had enjoyed a summer with the family and the exciting ride our national team gave us at the World Cup in Italy. Then came that fateful knock on our front door at six in the morning. My wife went downstairs to answer it, to be greeted by a bevy of uniformed coppers. Her immediate thought was that something had happened to her son, who had already gone out to do his paper round. One copper asked if I was in and waved a warrant for my arrest. He then brushed past her, followed by about six mates: some local police in uniform and others, from Manchester as it turned out, in plain clothes. My wife told them I was in the bedroom and some of them came in and told me I was under arrest and to get dressed. I asked what it was for and they told me violent disorder, conspiracy and some other stuff. They handcuffed me, took me outside and threw me into a police van, cautioning me in the process, but I wasn't listening. Then they ransacked the house, turning out all the drawers, seemingly looking for knives, drugs and even guns. They also went through our household papers, bills and other mail, and asked my wife what videos we had, saying they were looking for any violent ones and any books on hooliganism.

It turns out these dawn raids were taking place all over the country at the same time. Old Bill's covert operation of more than a year, Operation Mars, was being brought to a head. Top blokes from all our different United firms were hauled in, including Tony O'Neill. I was almost immediately driven up to Manchester to be held in the cells whilst the charges against us were sorted out. It took us hours to get there due to an accident on the M6 and it was hot and unpleasant in the back of the car. The police confirmed we were being done for 'conspiracy' to commit violent crime, or something like that. This was serious. I was held in a cell, interrogated and specifically asked about certain faces: Harry Hamilton for one. All I admitted was that after more than twenty years following United, I 'knew a whole load of people'. I made a short statement saying that I only went to football as an innocent fan, and did not answer any leading questions about other people, places or incidents. Amusingly, when I was taken from the interrogation room and along the corridor back to my cell, Harry, of all people, was being escorted the opposite way.

'Hello, Bob!' he said.

'Hi,' I replied.

The copper looked at me askance. 'Hang on,' he said, 'you just told me you didn't know this Harry fella.'

'I know his face but don't know his name,' I lied.

I was granted bail and was let out with some other Cockneys to make the long journey home. We blagged a free trip on the train by giving a sob story about our plight to the ticket inspector, saying we had no money. I still had the wife to face at home, with her mixed emotions of being bloody furious with me at my arrest, what caused it and what the coppers did to the house, against the fact I was home safe.

Me and Dobbo, one of the other Cockneys charged, decided to use the same brief, which was a mistake because it then implied a possible 'guilt by association', especially if Dobbo decided to plead guilty at some point. Fortunately, he didn't. During our bail period, we had to travel to Manchester to see the lawyer on a couple of occasions. In the meantime, all those arrested and charged were put under curfew and other bail conditions. I had to be indoors from 7pm to 7am – there was no tag, but no doubt the cops were keeping an eye on me. On the day of a United game, I had to report to my local police station at the time of kick-off, meaning I was effectively banned from attending games, nor could I have any contact with the other defendants. This was to continue right through to September 1991. All this added even more stress for the missus, who became obsessed with me being in by 7pm. She would be beside herself when I often rolled in at 6.59, or close to. It was a bugger really, as United got through to and won the European Cup Winners' Cup final against Barcelona in Rotterdam. Now that would have been a great trip, and most of my mates went, but those of us on bail were stuffed.

It soon became clear that all this had been building up with all the filming from as far back as the City game the previous September, and perhaps even earlier than that. It came to light that thirty-four had been arrested in total. Two pleaded guilty almost immediately to a conspiracy charge, added to which was violent disorder, causing an affray and so on. It made for a difficult year, and I was unemployed for some of it. The wife was still not happy with me, not least because my dramatic arrest had been witnessed by neighbours and reported in some of the newspapers. She also had to explain it all to our friends and family. It certainly did not help my cause when a book came out that year identifying me as one of the 'leaders' of United's mob. *Among The Thugs* was written by an American journalist, Bill Buford, who had started going to United matches to research English football violence. He referred specifically to the Cockney Reds and to 'Banana Bob', Roy Downes and Black Sam. Although he did not use my surname, the police would have known exactly who I was.

Being well past the 'young tearaway' stage, with a wife and family, I viewed the case hanging over me much more seriously than I had done, say, in 1970 with the Old Bailey trial, when it all seemed like a joke. I had not yet been informed of the entirety of the police case against me, but was at least fairly confident I could not be singled out from any filming for what I was being charged with. All thirty-two of us were hauled up to Manchester Crown Court in September 1991 for the trial. We were told there would be no jury sworn it until the judge had considered, in camera, the police request to give evidence from behind screens. I packed my bags and drove up with Dobbo to stay with my mate, Doris, in north Manchester. The judge was not impressed by the police argument that their anonymity should be protected so as not to compromise any ongoing undercover surveillance work. My brief had also discovered the coppers had been on some expensive jolly to Italia '90 whilst building up the case, and this fact didn't impress the old judge either when it came out.

My brief had told me that one of our remaining thirty-two was thinking of pleading guilty. This was a serious matter because if he did, it would mean the trial could start despite the legal arguments of our barristers, who were trying to get the case kicked out. Some of the defendants, including me, were approached by their lawyers to explain the seriousness if this fella did this, and were asked if we had any influence over him. It was left for someone to 'have a word' and in the end he saw the light and stayed with the rest of us. The Old Bill heard of this, interpreted it as 'coercion' and threatened to revoke our bail, but could not prove anything, so had to let it pass in the end.

The judge continued to refuse to let officers hide behind screens. He also dismissed some of the conspiracy charges, saying the police had taken too long to bring the case to court, refusing to buy their argument that the delay was due to other work they had been doing which they did not wish to compromise. The prosecution contested his decision all the way to the Appeal Court, but lost there too. The whole business must have cost the country millions: for a start, there were more than eighteen different and costly lawyers representing the thirty-two of us.

I felt under considerable stress while all this was going on. The process was long drawn-out, as these things are. Worst of all, being deemed a major face among the Cockney contingent meant that I faced a potentially longer sentence than many of the others, if the previous hooligan trials were any indication. Yet I knew Old Bill could not have that much on me from recent times. In fact they never divulged what evidence they had against me; they certainly found nothing incriminating at my home. My main fear was if someone was grassing us up. If so they would have to testify from behind a screen at the very least, as their life would not be worth living if we learned their identity. Still, we thought it was unlikely that we had been infiltrated, as we had a great record of spotting any coppers or snitches. And any filming, which if it existed would only have been from the previous year or two, was unlikely to show me as any sort of leader – had it been done in the late Seventies or early Eighties, that would have been a different matter.

The one charge we all feared being convicted of was conspiracy, and I remained on edge until, in May 1993, the Law Lords backed the judge's decisions, and the case against us collapsed. We were free. It was a massive humiliation for

Greater Manchester Police. I fancied suing for wrongful arrest but was advised that my past record would count against me, so I let it go. Old Bill were none too pleased with the outcome and continued to target the Mancs, as Tony O'Neill explains in the second of his two books, *The Men In Black*. And all the groups remained paranoid about being joined by blokes they didn't know, some of whom were seen off, guilty or not, on the suspicion that they might be coppers. I also continued to be a marked man for some time. I thought twice about getting involved in trouble. Most of all, I did not wish to inflict more stress onto my wife, who was still upset by what had happened.

CHAPTER 14

THINGS CHANGE, BUT NOT MUCH

Many people say that the post-Hillsborough period saw a sharp decline in football violence, but there was still plenty of incident. What did change was the handling of football crowds and the security organisation and control in and around stadiums. Perhaps the hooligans mellowed too: most of us felt better off financially, with society as a whole enjoying more affluence than in the somewhat desperate Seventies. Lifestyles and leisure activities changed, and I could see within the Cockney Reds there were fewer teenagers coming off the housing estates and forming little gangs, as we had done. It was mainly the older heads who carried on the fight. Yet police intelligence gathering and the resulting conspiracy trials, jail time and banning orders, combined with the effect of all-seater grounds, where immersing yourself in a huge crowd became more difficult and everyone was filmed, meant that even the most active amongst us felt restricted. Some of the lunatics drifted away, bored and disillusioned and looking for their fix elsewhere.

Not me, though. Even as the decade wore on, our little firm kept some of the old diehards together. It's true that others who came to join us were not looking for a fight every time they went to a game, but even they would stand on when they had to, as one of the lads who linked up with us explains:

> *I'm essentially a pacifist but if someone attacks you, be they opposition fans or police, you'll stand your ground, at least to start with. It was during these times with United at away games that we youngsters looked up to people like Bob and The Ghost, because when caught up in something not of our choosing they were there to protect us, and we appreciated that. We knew who these guys were – we saw them at most games and held them in quite high regard, although never wishing to be involved in the hooliganism we witnessed. It was an odd feeling, as we partly saw them as sort of criminal, yet felt they were looking out for us.*

Despite Alex Ferguson being firmly in control of the club by 1992, we were still underperforming on the pitch. One place where we never seemed to get a result was Nottingham Forest's City Ground. We still went there in our thousands, and there was usually trouble with their so-called Forest Executive Crew. For one mid-week game in March 1992, I bunked off work early and saw the expected dust-up before the game. Their firm then tried attacking us outside the ground after the game, but we chased them off and headed for a pub in town for a drink.

On the way we passed another pub full of Forest, and to their credit they poured out when they heard us in the street. Our fifty Cockneys were outnumbered at least two to one and were forced to back off, eventually heading back towards the train station trailed by both their mob and by the police, many of them with dogs. It was cold and pouring with rain, I was wearing just jeans and a distinctive check shirt, and I got soaked. I was also marked out by the police, having been at the forefront of the trouble, but did not realise that a copper and his dog were on my tail until a Cockney mate shouted, 'Look out, Bob, Old Bill's up your arse!'

I turned to see them about ten yards away. Fortunately for me the dog was distracted by something and jerked the copper away, giving me a split second to run. But the rain had made the ground slippery and I went down in a heap, badly twisting my ankle. I managed to hobble off and hid in a shop doorway, hoping the dog had lost my scent. My train was shortly due to leave, however, and I was forced to come out of my hiding place after a short while, only to see the same copper and dog looking out for me at the station entrance. He must have guessed I would turn up.

As luck would have it, the same mate who had warned me came towards me.

'Wotcha, Bob. You look bloody freezing.'

'I am. Could you lend me your coat? I've been spotted by Old Bill and I need to get past that one over there without him recognising me.' I pointed towards the station entrance.

'Yeah, sure, here take it,' he said. 'Let me have it back at Old Trafford next Saturday.'

He handed over his coat and jogged off. I pulled the collar up so my cheeks were almost covered, parted my soaked hair in the middle to alter my barnet, then advanced for the station, trying my best not to limp. It was not enough; the copper came towards me. Painfully I turned and limped off down the road and managed to get away again, helped by my mate and some others surrounding the copper and his angry dog.

I decided against the train and instead paid £5 for a taxi out to the M1 motorway, where I intended to thumb a lift back to London, as I had parked my car near King's Cross. I went onto a slip road, only to find a couple of blokes already there, standing beside a broken-down car. They said they were trying to get to the nearest service station to organise some assistance. We all started to thumb for a lift, not realising it was illegal on a motorway. A police patrol car soon pulled up. They took pity on us, drove us to the nearest services, gave us a warning and then left. I found a lorry in the car park going to Brighton and the driver kindly agreed to drop me off at King's Cross. It took some time, but the journey turned out to be a bloody sight quicker than my mates managed on the train – they were held up for ages south of Nottingham because the Cockneys had found some tools and commenced to systematically take apart the inside of the train, including unscrewing and lifting up the floor!

We had another big run-in with Forest ahead of the League Cup final the following month. From the time we had twice played Crystal Palace at Wembley in 1990, we had taken to using Kilburn as our staging post before any game at the national stadium. Thousands of United would meet at the numerous top-notch Irish pubs in Kilburn High Road. Although I was trying to keep a low profile after my recent arrest and conspiracy charge, plus my family responsibilities, I was inevitably drawn into some of the battles with Forest fans that day. We absolutely smashed them. Being out of the way in Kilburn also meant the Old Bill overlooked us to some extent, and anyway the support for United was so large that we had other groups dotted all over North London, and the police couldn't be everywhere. We dominated the Forest lads so completely on the streets that I'm not sure they have ever recovered. Even inside the ground many United were in the Forest end, and there was a certain amount of controversy afterwards when it was alleged that their manager, Brian Clough, had sold on some tickets which ended up in the hands of United fans, although it was never proven.

Not long after this, I spent a period in Germany for some well-paid bricklaying work, and so I was away from the football scene and any trouble. There were also times when I would do a few 'jobs' away from the building trade to help out mates. This was cash-in-hand work when I was in the UK, and came about because I was seen as someone who could handle himself.

One little operation was for a mate who ran a business supplying cars to small rental firms. Given the kind of people who get involved in the motor trade, he had a large list of debtors. Most of them were in the south of England but the biggest debt, for £70,000, was owed by a bloke living near Stoke-on-Trent. My mate gave me a Lancia to drive up there and call on him, plus a wage and an offer of ten per cent of any money I recovered, so it would a nice earner if successful. My mate said that as I was often up in Manchester anyway, a detour to Stoke would not be a problem. Nothing too heavy was expected, it was more a case of turning up and suggesting to this bloke that it might be in his best interests to pay. However I took a mate, Ian, with me to act as a 'witness'. Ian happens to be about six foot five and built to match.

We arrived at this bloke's garage and politely explained why we were there.

'This has nothing to do with me,' he said. 'And I'm friends with the Chief Constable. He'll be hearing about you and your threats.'

'I haven't threatened you,' I said. 'I've just given you the message from the bloke you owe money to and suggest you pay up.'

'I don't owe anything and I'm not saying any more without my own witness,' he said, taking a few steps back into his office and towards the phone.

'Well', I said, 'be it on your own head.'

With that, we left and headed to Manchester for the game. I duly reported back to my mate. What we should have done was then pull in some Manchester lads to follow it up for us a day or two later. Instead I agreed to pursue the matter, but it was another two weeks before I could get back up to Stoke. By then we had found out his home address and I tracked him to this place in the middle of nowhere, down an unmade road. He was beside himself when we turned up, and broke away from his gardening to go off on one. He seemed most annoyed that his old lady was in the house and might find out about his problem. He went on again about the Chief Constable, a Masonic friend, and how we were wrong in pestering him at home and even threatening him. It wasn't like that – I was only letting him know that my mate was taking this seriously (and hinting at what might happen if he didn't pay). I said what I had to say, but just before I left added, 'A fire engine might find it difficult to get up this track, you know.' This freaked him out, and we left having done what was asked. I'm not sure my mate ever got much of the payment he was owed; I didn't get my ten per cent, that's for sure.

It wasn't that I had to use my fists or anything, but that I could do 'menace' bloody well. Another time when my so-called muscle was hired to put the frighteners on came when I was due to travel to Blackburn, and was asked to 'drop in' on someone in Greater Manchester. I had some mates who were the real deal when it came to the underworld and who mixed with well-known organised criminals involved in drugs, illegal betting, fraud, indeed anything that made them money. They were also into boxing, snooker, darts and occasionally foot-ball, and many provided protection for sports stars outside of competition. One of their clients was a colourful, now dead, snooker player who was owed money by some fella. There might have been more to it than that, but anyway I was asked by a friend of this star to 'pay a visit' to the debtor. All they wanted me to do was to ask him his name, say I had been sent by this snooker player and to add, 'I was just checking you live here.' I made no threats, but the fella realised he would be in serious shit if he didn't play ball. There was no follow-up required from me, so he must have coughed up.

Despite my fighting at football and occasional forays into 'strong-arm' work, I was something of a changed man by the mid-Nineties. Much of this had to do with the conspiracy arrest and charge that had hung over me and meant I had to try to avoid trouble. I had also been married for nearly ten years by 1995, and had responsibilities to my stepsons and to my own daughter, who was born in 1987. I still had this destructive streak, but I had to deal with things differently.

That's not to say trouble didn't cross my path. One day I took my eight-year-old daughter on the train for a day out to see a game at home against Coventry City. We still have a photo of that day, with me and my daughter outside the stand with Old Trafford emblazoned across its top: she in her winter coat and patterned gloves, linked together with elastic passing up one arm and down the other inside her coat, and me with a lot more hair! I was so proud she was mine. After the game we caught a train home, which was jam-packed with both football fans and ordinary travellers. I sat in an aisle seat and she was next to the window. In the packed aisles I saw a tall, black bloke I knew, a United fan in his thirties who I knew was regularly into marijuana and booze, getting aggressive towards a couple of my mates. He was using foul language and generally upsetting other passengers. These mates and the bloke started pushing and shoving each other, until the bloke pulled out a knife, saying something like, 'Come on then, I'll send you home in a coffin.' My two mates scuttled off down the carriage, some women screamed and a number of frightened passengers in the aisle seats squashed onto the laps of those by the windows – although my daughter didn't seem too worried.

The red mist descended, and I leapt up to try to wrest the blade away, even as I remembered stories that he was known to put poison on the end of his knives. As I moved towards him, he was accosted by another of our lads, called Wayne. He thrust his knife forward and stabbed Wayne in the leg, causing him to yelp in pain. I grabbed the bloke's wrist and, with help, managed to take away the knife and throw it out of a window. After a further brief struggle, he eventually calmed down. The train guard had been called and must have radioed ahead because at the next station the police came on board, took some details and led this bloke away. We later heard that he had been charged but never learned the outcome, although we did not see him for more than a year. We then bumped into him at an FA Cup game at Reading, so he may have served some time inside. A few Cockney lads took him to one side, stood him up against a wall and told him in no uncertain terms to make himself scarce. We have not seen him at a game since.

As for Wayne, there was no poison on the knife tip and he recovered. I later told him he should have gone for compensation, but his girlfriend was well-off so perhaps he decided he didn't need the money or the hassle. As for my daughter, she didn't seem fazed by any of it. Just to be on the safe side, I told her not to say anything to her mum. So what was the first thing she did when we got home? Told her everything, and I got the blame.

This wasn't the only occasion I took my daughter or my two stepsons to a match and this helped keep me out of trouble – most of the time. I did think of taking them to our last game of the season in 1995 but decided against it, as it was likely to be far too lively: we needed a win at West Ham to take the Premiership title. It was likely to be a day of high drama, and like the old days we gathered in numbers at Euston, ready to move on to the East End. The Metropolitan Police, however, had learned a thing or two about match-day organisation and shepherded us off the tube at Stratford and into a large park, where they confined us until about an hour before kick-off. They then escorted us all the way to the ground, and away from it once the game had ended. It was a well planned and executed operation by them, conducted in a firm but non-confrontational manner. And perhaps our enthusiasm for trouble was diminishing with the onset of middle age. To compound the disappointment, Blackburn Rovers won the league when we could only draw.

* * *

Most of the time my particular small group of Cockney Reds now shared cars for our travels around the country. This was not always more reliable than trains. One day we set off to Leeds – me, Big K, Micky W, Steve C and Ads – in a clapped-out, rusting Ford Granada with a dodgy engine. We managed to get it up over 70mph on the M1 near Luton when the steering wheel started to vibrate, a little at first, then more and more, until the whole car was shaking. Suddenly the steering went completely, the car slewed sideways and we hit the central barrier in the middle of a wide grass divide between the two carriageways. We were half on the grass and half in the outside lane with a now defunct engine. Various passing cars swerved to avoid us and hooted their horns as we dashed across the road to the hard shoulder between the fast-moving traffic like scared rabbits. Our driver then realised his mate's work tools were in the boot, so we then had to go back to the car, through the traffic again – more chaos. Some kind bloke pulled up beside us once we had got the toolbox back to the hard shoulder and took us up to the next service station, where we phoned my mate Steve, who had not yet left St Albans. He came to get us and we abandoned the Granada and decided not to sort out a recovery vehicle. We did eventually get to Leeds, one game we did not want to miss, but had to leave straight afterwards as Steve had to get back, so we missed out on the usual post-match ruck in the streets around the ground.

When we passed the spot on the M1 where our car had been abandoned, it was no longer there, presumably having been moved by the police. As none of us was the registered owner (our mate had probably nicked it and swapped the plates anyway), we couldn't be traced and we never followed it up. St Albans Steve dropped us at Watford Station and we hailed a cab to Euston where my car was parked, while Steve C and Ads were going by underground back to East London. We had intended running off at Euston without paying the taxi driver, but the two lads decided to persuade the cabbie to take them all the way home. He smelt a rat and drove to the nearest police station, where they were ticked off but not charged, and where they begrudgingly paid the cab fare.

We were the bane of taxi drivers' lives, rarely paying when we were in a group – we would just leg it when we got close to our destination. Even when the driver radioed up his mates to chase us, we were never caught. One time in Kilburn after a cup final, we had this cabbie who chatted, in a northern accent, about the football. One of us asked, 'What happens if you get knocked for the fare by someone?'

'In Leeds, where I come from, we get on the radio and call up some help,' he said.

That was the wrong thing to say: no way would we pay a Leeds bloke. When we arrived outside a pub in Euston full of United fans, we got out and casually told him to fuck off.

One time when I worked next to a car-hire firm, I rented one of their minibuses to drive us up to a game at Leeds. The

Ghost was one of those with me and complained that my driving at 90 mph in fog was a bit extreme, even for me, and speculated that I had been on the wacky-baccy. They were all seriously getting in my ear and really pissing me off, so I slowed to below thirty and pretended to be drowsy and almost asleep. That quietened them down. I was laughing to myself all the way and later when they found out the truth once we arrived in Leeds, I had to take another lot of abuse. It was all good fun, as most of these trips were, great days out for maintaining friendships that last to this day.

The Ghost has kept his uncompromising reputation right through from the Sixties, even frightening fellow Reds at times. Middle-age took away none of his aggression. In 1993 we played Aston Villa at Old Trafford and pipped them to the title. On the way home the Cockneys stopped off with some Mancs at the Britannia Hotel in Didsbury, south Manchester, to celebrate. The Argentinian Under-23 rugby team happened to be in the bar and, with the drinks flowing, things were looking lively. One of these burly Argies made an inappropriate remark to a girl, and an argument followed, with The Ghost threatening to punch the Argie's lights out. The Old Bill must have been patrolling nearby and received a call, as they soon rushed in. One copper got hold of The Ghost, only to receive an impressive headbutt for his trouble. The Ghost was marched away into custody, looking back with what can only be described as a triumphant smile. He received no favours in the court.

Old Bill had by the mid-Nineties become a lot smarter, often filming us on the streets, in bars and at grounds. They also used undercover cops, mainly young officers in casual clobber who tried to mix in with us, although these were usually spotted and wheeled out. The clubs began to use CCTV too, inside and outside the ground. Most grounds

became all-seated after the Taylor Report, making it difficult to hide among the herd in the aftermath of trouble or to
slip away from arrest. Segregation and ticket control became
stricter, although we all knew blokes who could get briefs for
any game – at a price. The most prolific of them we called
'grafters'. They often hid behind respectable businesses but
had contacts even inside the FA, UEFA and FIFA. Many ordinary blokes had similar contacts and we never went short of
tickets for United games in Europe.

As we passed into our forties, like old boxers we could not
only handle ourselves but were clever with it, knowing the
ropes, how far to go in a fight and not get caught out. Hence
travelling by car, which was more comfortable and flexible
and helped us to avoid the usual police interest. Every so often,
however, we would mob together on a coach. One such occasion was a trip to Everton, with all the main thugs travelling
on a coach from Euston organised by Maverick the Greek. We
had a puncture on the M6, however, and arrived at Goodison
Park after the game had started. Our coach pulled up amid
the terraced houses behind the Gwladys Street End and we
were moved towards the turnstiles. The noise from our group
of less than fifty seemed to echo off the tightly-packed houses,
causing neighbours to emerge from their doors to see what
was going on – then duck back inside when they saw it was
us. Some Everton fans came around the corner and looked
shocked to see us. We laid into them and it took the police
some time to gain control. With the faces we had out that day
there was only ever going to be one outcome.

We had no tickets but gate-crashed the nearest turnstile
before the attendant there knew what was happening. There
were no stewards or police on hand to stop us, and we dived
into the crowd to avoid any surveillance from the police booth
in a corner of the ground. We found ourselves in among the

hardcore Everton, in an area beside the away fans. They were a pretty lairy bunch and we were hugely outnumbered, so for once sense prevailed and a copper guarding a gate in the fencing was persuaded to let us through. We were recognised by our fellow United fans and they cheered us like returning heroes, although we knew we had sort of bottled it – although honestly we'd have been smashed had it gone off. But, you see, wiser with age. At half-time we heard tales of what we had missed in the streets before the game. Apparently it had been mayhem, with much fighting with Old Bill as our lads moved from pub to pub.

Maverick the Greek was a real character in the Cockneys, a well-known tout, with offices in both North London and the West End. He was also a good mate and I often went over to his house in Hampton, Middlesex. He knew Steve Bruce well, and on occasion could get me into the executive area at Old Trafford. He took me for a meal there once and then onto the players' lounge, where Bruce bought us a drink and I stayed on my best behaviour. Maverick told me not to pester the players, but I got Mark Hughes' autograph for my stepson (for me, really!) and met Bryan Robson too. Unfortunately Maverick got into hot water with some serious criminals, to whom he owed money. He was in fear of his life, and sometime after that coach trip to Everton he disappeared, and is believed to have gone to Northern Cyprus.

Not everyone went to every game, but you could always guarantee cup finals would bring out the best in us, on and off the field. In 1994 we played old rivals Aston Villa in the League Cup final at Wembley. As usual we met up at Kilburn and filled the pubs in the High Road. At around two o'clock we set off for Kilburn tube station. A train carrying mainly Villa fans pulled in just as hundreds of us were walking up the stairs to the platform, but most of them did not see us, as we poured on further down the train from them. On the journey we heard Villa setting about some United in their carriage, so when we stopped further up the line at Dollis Hill, we poured off to take them on. They took a total hammering. One Villa bloke had his ear ripped off, and others made off along the tracks to get away.

JOE *I was at that game but took my lad Billy, having got tickets from Wimbledon FC. My seats were not with United fans and I kept well away from my normal mob of Cockney Reds, because I guessed there would be trouble. As I came into Wembley, I got to the bit where we were below the stand in the Villa end. Billy was wearing his United shirt. One Villa fan came over and spat a great big 'greeny' onto Billy's back. I couldn't have that, so I handed Billy over to a copper, ran into the bar on the concourse and smashed this geezer. Then all his mates waded in. I was giving as good as I got but was outnumbered. In the end, the police pulled me out and I took Billy to our seats.*

In April 1995 we played Crystal Palace at Villa Park in an FA Cup semi-final. It was a day of high drama. That January, Eric Cantona had been sent off at Selhurst Park and on his way from the pitch had jumped into the stand to drop-kick and punch a Palace fan called Matthew Simmons, who had run down eleven rows to verbally abuse him. Eric subsequently admitted assault and had to serve 120 hours' community service, and was banned from playing for eight months. A lot of United fans were bitter about this, as they felt the Palace lad was out of order and deserved what he got, and a sense of niggle developed between the two sets of supporters. We already nursed our own grievance against them from a few years before, when a Palace fan had used CS gas against us.

220

For this semi-final scores of coaches, some official, some not, travelled up to Birmingham. My little group had hired a minibus. We had heard there was to be a stop-off point for Palace fans near Walsall, at a pub called the New Fulbrook, and knew that some United would be going to have it out with them. We made a beeline for the place, but arrived to a cacophony of sirens and the sight of ambulances and police cars parked outside, with a lot of lairy United and Palace fans hanging around. We drove on to avoid attention, as it was obvious that we had arrived too late and missed the action, and our vehicle carried a few well-known faces that the coppers would have been only too pleased to detain. We later found out that a Palace fan named Paul Nixon had been in a group attacked by United and has been hit with a brick and then stabbed. As he tried to escape, he fell under the wheels of a coach and was crushed to death. It was a horrible incident, and tensions between the two clubs have remained high ever since.

The next time we went by car to Selhurst Park – this time against Wimbledon, who were then ground-sharing there – we heard that a United fanzine had published a story about Simmons and how his house in Thornton Heath had had to be alarmed, with a link to the local nick. This was because of threats against him from United fans. The fanzine also helpfully printed a map showing where he lived and some pubs he frequented. Me, Griff and a couple of others took a small detour to his house, between central Croydon and the Mayday Hospital. We pulled up outside and sat there, hoping he would come out. We even thought of knocking on his door to give him a fright before he hit his panic button, but in the end decided that the risk of getting nicked outweighed any result. In any case, the place looked unoccupied.

CHAPTER 15

TRAVELLERS' TALES

U nited's success took off in the Nineties and, with the readmission of English clubs to European competitions in 1990, suddenly we had trips abroad every season. We found the police and fans were often hostile, having swallowed everything they had seen or read in the intervening years about the 'English disease'. This was brought home early on during a trip that became one of the most talked and written about ever, to Turkey's biggest club, Galatasary, at their home in Istanbul. The tone was set when arriving United fans were met at the airport with banners declaring, 'RIP Manchester' and, famously (and misspelt), 'Wellcome to the Hell'. Among the visitors was a contingent of Cockney Reds, including Hayes Bob.

HAYES BOB *No-one in Europe seems to like us. My worst experiences for bad treatment by local police, although I have never been a real troublemaker, were in Spain and Belgium, with both United and England. However, the most aggressive fans abroad, together with their police, were the Turks. In October 1993, St Albans Steve organised the Cockney Reds' trip to Galatasaray for the second leg, after we had drawn 3–3 at Old Trafford in the Champions League. We knew we were in trouble with the away goals* *situation but expected even more trouble from the Turks, and proved to be correct.*

Steve had fixed up a three-night hotel stay. The night before the game, thousands of Reds were out on the streets, in the bars and clubs. I was feeling groggy and returned to the hotel mid-evening and went straight off to sleep. Turning on the TV next morning for BBC News 24, it was full of mass arrests of United overnight, with all and sundry coming on to denounce the United fans. We had expected nothing less, as word had come through of provocation from the Turks, with the police simply standing back and doing nothing, as if enjoying watching our fans being smashed up – then only United fans were arrested.

That evening, coaches arrived to take us to the ground ahead of the game. The Turks were out in force along the route and so bad were their attacks that the windows were damaged and progress was slow. Our driver eventually had enough and a mile and a half from the ground got off and walked away. This time the army tried to restore order, but they still would not take on their own people. The coach did eventually move on. The game took place in an atmosphere so dramatic it sent shivers down your spine. I was just glad to get away unscathed and not to have been nicked liked the hundreds of United from the night before. We went out with a scoreless draw and in later years the same referee was banned for life after allegations of match-fixing. We were not surprised, as he had disallowed a late goal that should have stood and would have put us through. Eric Cantona was sent off too and there was trouble in the players' tunnel.

It was the most intimidating place I had ever been to watch football. Their fans had been in the ground for more than two hours before kick-off, being allowed to carry

huge banners including that 'Welcome to Hell' one onto
the terraces and lighting countless flares. When we arrived,
a deafening and threatening roar went up. Yes, we had a
reputation, but the way we were treated was a disgrace.

Gary Pallister, our centre-back, admitted he had 'never experienced anything like it in my life' and Alex Ferguson later called it the most intimidating atmosphere he had ever endured. It also showed the English fans were not always the perpetrators of disorder and could be victims too. 'It was not just the police truncheon aimed against the back of Eric Cantona's head or the riot shield that gashed Bryan Robson's hand,' the *Independent* later reported. 'It was the fact that 164 Manchester United supporters were arrested and flung into a variety of Turkish cells. Many were detained on the flimsiest of pretexts, some were beaten, some had their possessions stolen. Very few actually saw the game.'

Other trips would follow a similar pattern. In September 1996 we were due to play Juventus in Turin in the group stage of the Champions League. I had not yet booked for the trip when I responded to an ad in the London *Evening Standard* offering a flight plus match ticket, although it was not through an official United source. It was handy for me as the flight was from Gatwick, only for it to be changed at the last minute to the less convenient Stansted. The travel firm offered a refund but I managed to team up with some Brighton lads and we jumped on one of those buses that take you from Gatwick, via Heathrow, to Stansted, a bloody long trip in traffic on the M25.

At Turin airport the *carabinieri* were out in numbers and would not allow us out of the terminal without an escort to coaches for the stadium. Our fans were corralled into containment areas controlled by riot police, a hard-looking bunch of bastards, then escorted to the ground well ahead of the game.

The Juve fans, in contrast, were allowed to hang around and seemingly do whatever they liked. This was par for the course in Italy, as we were to find in Milan and Rome. We all know the control certain Italian ultra groups exercise over their clubs and the media and it seemed this extended to the Law as well.

The game resulted in a 1–0 defeat, after which our contingent of over 3,000 was kept in the ground. When finally released we were confronted by lines of police with rifles: three hundred or more of them, and behind them a mass of Juve fans, taunting us. We stormed the police line to get at Juve, and soon police riot helmets and shields were strewn across the stadium concourse. They eventually managed to bring some order and herded us onto coaches to the airport, but it needed some gunshots to bring this about. Many of us had by then acquired bloodied heads, cuts to hands and legs, and torn and stained clothing. Welcome to Italy.

We eventually qualified from the group stage and marched through to the Champions League quarter-final against Porto, against whom we won the first leg 4–0 at Old Trafford in March 1997. Many then signed up for what promised to be a celebratory trip to Portugal's second city for the return leg, looking forward to a bit of sea, sun and a good time.

On arriving in Porto, I found my mates had booked into the Sheraton and the city, which is beautiful, was teeming with United. We all met up in the Ribeira area down near the sea, where numerous bars and clubs are situated. United took over the area. As we drank in the warm sunshine in the afternoon before the game, a huge cheer went up at the sight of Norman Whiteside – who had put on a few pounds – walking through the throng. He acknowledged us and stayed for a few beers.

I was with Griff and the Peckham boys as we headed off to the stadium in the early evening, all pretty pissed from drinking all day. My ticket was in the United terrace, but the organisation at the ground was chaotic. Thousands of United turned up late, as we did, and we missed the first fifteen minutes of the game while the police gave us a hard time, largely due to the vast number of forged tickets. Mine fortunately wasn't one of them. It was the same old story as at many foreign grounds, where getting in can take forever, particularly if there is a spot of trouble or a ticket problem.

The game was drawn and we were through to the semis, but there was trouble as we started to leave. I'd had enough grief from the police in previous months and still remembered Valencia in 1982, so I kept a low profile and stayed under the stands whilst the lunatics above let rip against the riot squad, who had viciously attacked them with batons with little justification. The ordinary, uniformed police were fine, we had no problem with them, but their tooled-up paramilitary-style colleagues were a different matter. Urinals were smashed up to be thrown at them and flares were set off, and the riot squad lashed out every which way in return. At one stage some United tried to turn towards a few Porto fans who had stayed behind. The Porto left in a hurry but the police were having none of it. They opened fire with rubber bullets, and I saw some of our lads running away with wounds in their bums and arms, probably caused by grapeshot as if from a shotgun. I kept clear, but took it all in.

MICKY W *They definitely used rubber bullets as I saw them on the ground. We did manage to do a few coppers in retaliation. The biggest fright for us was when we had been shovelled by the cops into a small area up against the gates, those that are usually open at the end of games to let the fans get away quickly. Such was the crush that we felt the life being squeezed out of us and we then felt how those poor sods at Hillsborough must have suffered. On* *this occasion, we managed to turn on the police and fight our way out, but it was a terrifying experience.*

More than thirty United fans were hospitalised, one with a rubber bullet lodged in his head. It did all settle down eventually and I left with some mates. Confused by drink, we got lost in the city but finally found the others back at the Ribeira, where we drank well into the night without further incident. We had three days there in all before returning home and I have to say that, up to that time it ranked as my best ever trip. Drunk for those three days, on cheap beer, laughs, a bit of a set-to, an aggregate win and into the Euro semis – it hadn't ever been much better than this.

What a time we had that 1996/97 season, with Steve M organising the Cockneys' trips around Europe bringing together hordes across the south-east from St Albans to Croydon to Brighton and beyond. It all came to a bitter end when we lost in the semi-final to Borussia Dortmund, both games 1–0 defeats. For the second leg in Dortmund, our group took the plunge and stayed in the city's finest hotel; me, Steve M, Paki Steve, Griff and a few others. Now, Dortmund's problem as a city is that it is twinned with Leeds, so more reason to make our presence felt.

I was pissed part of the time and, while I am certainly no racist, I have a problem with Turks; I don't know why, I just do. Anyway, I clashed with this Turkish bloke for some reason in a bar, and you know when something is about to kick off and then suddenly you end up in fits of laughter? Well, I went to smash my almost empty Stein glass against the bar to put it to this wanker's neck but the glass would not break. The harder I hit it, the less success I had, until everyone fell about laughing. In the end I gave up and saw the funny side myself. The Turk just looked bemused.

The next day we came across some Germans who claimed to support United and were keen to organise a fight between us and a Dortmund firm. We were suspicious they might be undercover cops, so we pulled up their shirts to see if they were miked up, which they weren't. We still decided not to take up their suggestion and stayed drinking all afternoon instead, before heading off to the ground. There was huge United support, this being the semi, and the Cockneys alone were over two hundred strong as, all pissed, we gathered outside the ground. We surged towards a large group of Dortmund who looked up for a fight but the police were there in sufficient numbers to separate and corral the rival groups of fans. Nevertheless the tension continued to increase, and the police suddenly decided to act. They brought in a fleet of huge buses and, using threats and the odd baton thwack, forced us onto them. Once fully loaded, they were driven off, we assumed towards the local nick. About half an hour before the start of the game, the buses stopped in a huge garage area behind the police station. I managed to restrain myself, but a few blew up at the cops and were taken off elsewhere. I had at least learnt from fifteen years before that being detained for any length of time in a foreign country is not a whole heap of fun.

Fair play to the cops, they supplied us with soft drinks and put up some TVs so we could watch the game, but they didn't let us out. Once the match had finished, they released us in dribs and drabs, and my mates and I returned to the hotel to carry on drinking. I was just pleased I wasn't one of those arrested and detained.

* * *

The following season we were again in Europe, and a trip to Rotterdam on 5 November 1997 to play Feyenoord looked particularly tasty. I took up an offer from some Manchester mates who were travelling by minibus and they picked me up in Kent to drive down to Dover for the ferry. Rotterdam may be the biggest port in Europe but is largely a dump and most of those travelling opted to stay in Amsterdam, where there is plenty to grab your attention. We had a good night out in the city, with no confrontations, and slept overnight in the minibus, which was reasonably comfortable. I wasn't sure whether a criminal case was still open against me for nicking that jewellery all those years back, so I was on my best behaviour.

The next day I drank from lunchtime onwards in a bar with a mixture of Cockneys and Mancs, and managed to get a ticket from a mate who decided to stay in Amsterdam and not bother with the game. Word was out to meet at about 3pm at the main train station to head off to Rotterdam early so we could avoid the police, who in the past had fenced off parts of the station and sent any without match tickets to be held in some army barracks out of town. I still felt this early arrival might draw the attention of the police, and in view of my previous I decided to stay drinking with a small group until much nearer kick-off. Annoyingly we later learnt that more than four hundred took the early train and were able to exit without being detected. Those who had been to Rotterdam before went with some Dutch friends to the area where Feyenoord's firm drank, and fighting broke out before kick-off.

I arrived later with my small group and had a drink in Rotterdam centre before heading to the ground. We had to walk almost the whole way around the stadium to find our entrance and were then delayed getting in due to fighting inside, meaning I missed the first ten minutes of a 3–1 win. At the end we were kept in for a while, then marched over a bridge to a station close to the ground and herded onto a train out of town. I headed back to the bars in Amsterdam with Griff and Young Mark. I decided not to spend another night in the minibus, a bad decision as it turned out because I bunked into someone's room and spent an uncomfortable night trying to sleep on the floor and could barely walk in the morning when my joints seized up. Many of the lads were out late sampling the ladies of the night and a drug or two, washed down with litres of strong lager.

Tired, hungover but pleased with the result on and off the field I headed back to the minibus at the pre-arranged time to meet up with my travelling mates for the trip back home. Looking back, it was becoming more the norm that these foreign trips offered more action than was available at home. That's not to say the Nineties were that quiet in the UK, but things had definitely changed.

As the Champions League campaign went on we were drawn against AS Monaco – a nice little trip but likely to be expensive, given that the French Riviera is not noted for its bargain prices. In the event it was not too bad, and we pitched up in Nice for a right good jolly, spending time visiting Cannes and Antibes as well as sampling the delights of Nice itself. On the day of the game we even took a train trip to Monte Carlo. Glenn Hoddle was staying in the same hotel as my mates in Monaco and must have got a shock when he received his bill on checking out, as the Peckham brothers had put all their drinks on his room tab – the fact that he's teetotal probably added to his misery. Our hotel in Nice was pretty plush and had a swimming pool on its roof. Although it was early March we enjoyed warm weather, sampled the local beers and, for once, steered clear of trouble. We all thought it was pretty warm, so when we arrived at the ground I was amazed to see the locals in overcoats and gloves, while we wore tee-shirts and shorts.

STATUS QUO TONY *Not for the first time I had been mistaken for Rick Parfitt. I should have made a few quid out of being his body double over the years. So there I am on the beach in Monte Carlo with about a hundred of the lads having an informal party. Suddenly a lady comes over, clearly believing me to be Rick, and leads me away to meet her friends. I enjoyed the limelight and they were completely taken in. On the way back, feeling hungry, we stopped off and bought chicken and chips, took it back to the hotel and ate it around the pool. We couldn't be bothered to clear up the bits of carcass when we went inside, but on leaving the bar on the ground floor later, heard this awful din and saw seagulls and various local birds swooping onto the roof to feed off the scraps we'd left. The hotel staff were going mad, shouting and waving their arms. It was like that Hitchcock film.*

Griff and I had a row on the train back from Monte Carlo which carried on once back in Nice. Feelings boiled over until we then became involved in an argument with someone else to ease the tension. All this came to end when for some reason we picked up a motor scooter parked next to the kerb and hurled it along the road. Things never remained quiet for long when we were around.

Unfortunately the return game at Old Trafford was drawn 1–1 and AS Monaco went through on away goals. But the following season was one no Red Devil will ever forget.

* * *

The 1998/99 campaign started on a slow burn, and little did we know what lay in store. After getting through qualification against Lodz, we went into a group that included Bayern

Munich, and at the end of September we were off to Germany. This began my journey through that never-to-be-forgotten treble season. I only decided to go to Munich the day before, so had little chance of a cheap flight ticket to come back within a reasonable time. A weekly return was the best I could get, and I had no match ticket. Since the conspiracy case I was also conscious that, as a recognised face, some jobsworth might stop me travelling, bearing in mind that back in 1994 I had been detained in Gothenburg for over an hour on arrival, due to being a known hooligan.

I flew from Gatwick to Munich without problems and caught a train to the city centre, where I soon heard singing from a bunch of United fans from Brighton. I joined them and ended up following them out of the main station to the Boxer Bar, where we were soon more than a hundred strong, with many Cockney Red mates arriving. We also had our first clash with the police, although it was relatively low key. I met Young Mark, who had booked into a hotel, so I had somewhere to stay for free, though I would be sharing a bed in a room with six or seven others on the floor and one in the bath.

The following day, ahead of the game, we started on the strong beer, and with little food to soak it up, were quickly pissed. There was a heavy police presence, mainly keeping an eye on us, and we recognised some spotters among them. I located some of the lads from South London, and bought a ticket from a mate. To escape the police attention, about forty of us then moved out in small numbers from this packed pub to a bar further down the road. Some of the undercover officers followed us and clearly knew who we were. We spent a couple of hours drinking, then caught a train out to the ground, but got off at the stop before to avoid any police reception. These undercovers followed us, keeping an eye on what we were doing. In the event, Bayern hardly made a show and the whole event passed off with little trouble. European police forces, I felt, were finally learning how to deal with massive numbers of fans from visiting clubs with huge support.

We stumbled through to the quarter-final stage, and St Albans Steve organised our trip to Milan to play Internazionale in March 1999. He was conscious that if any of his 'clients' got nicked it might get him in trouble and, as he was trying to be legit, was worried some of the lunatics in our group would let him down. All the lunatics were indeed there but for once the Italian coppers didn't wade in unprovoked. We were well tanked up but on our best behaviour, perhaps due to Steve's warnings. I had even bought a ticket in advance. Our fans took most of the first half to all get into the ground and as we were already 2–0 up from the first leg, we felt comfortable until Inter got one back. It was on edge until Scholes scored right near the end and we were through. Everyone left the ground in a good mood and, with the Milanese scurrying off with their tails between their legs, thousands of us milled around outside the San Siro to celebrate, before setting off towards the city centre, with Steve pleading with us to keep out of trouble.

After drinking a few bars dry, we headed back to our hotel, where the lounge was packed with United. By then it was past midnight and I was well gone. Alan Parry, the Sky TV commentator, and his sidekick Andy Gray were in there. Gray kept to himself but Parry, who makes no secret of his allegiance to the Scousers, was spouting off to a large group about Liverpool. Someone called me over to tell me what Parry had said during some banter, along the lines of, 'Come back when you've won eighteen league titles like we have.' I couldn't let this pass, so went up and let him know what I thought of Scousers. Parry was taken aback and didn't know what to say. Even the crowd around me went quiet, until some United chipped in with shouts of support. Parry clearly realised he had said the wrong thing. The atmosphere became threatening and I looked at Andy Gray, who was nervously sipping his beer and wishing he was somewhere else and that Parry had kept his mouth shut. A couple of lads pulled me away and some part-time United fan came over, a friend of a friend, to give me some 'advice'. He was himself advised to move away before I gave him a slap. I doubt I would have actually hit Parry, but it was close. He and Gray slunk away, only for former Liverpool player Mark Lawrenson to then be spotted walking across the hotel foyer towards the reception. He was met by a volley of abuse and swiftly scurried off to the lifts to take him to his room. All three kept out of our way the next morning.

Beating Juventus in the semis took us through to the final, where we faced Bayern Munich once more, the game to be played in neutral Barcelona. What a trip that offered, and we weren't to be disappointed. Not only was it probably the greatest game for United in living memory, the whole experience that night was truly awesome. Pity the poor United fools who looked for a quick exit and left when it was 1–0 to Bayern with only stoppage time left as the fourth official stuck up his board saying three extra minutes just as we had a corner!

For a trip to play against the old enemy on foreign soil, albeit in 'neutral' Spain, it was quiet off the pitch. Still, all who went have a story of some kind, whether veteran thug, the good guys or the one-off. The stories of the Cockney Reds getting there, the pre-match build up, the game, afterwards and the journey home are plenty. One lifelong Red, Dave, from the South East, even had a brush with death in his attempt to get to the final. He and some fellow City-types managed to blag seats on a small private plane owned by a mate. After a re-fuelling stop in France they took off again, only for Dave to see fuel spewing out of a storage tank on the wing. Mayday! An emergency landing and repair followed, and they were told that a spark would have blown them to kingdom come. They survived and arrived just as the game kicked off.

Fat Jack was another with a tale to tell:

FAT JACK *I organised a trip through the Miss Ellie travel firm, based in Manchester, for a group of Cockney Reds. I'm glad I did because there were many forgeries flying around and it was always a good idea to avoid some of the travel firms with a poor reputation for ripping off fans. I was taking my son, then aged nine, and he saw this as a great adventure; so excited and feeling all grown-up, mixing with his dad's mates away from his mum for pretty much the first time. He was missing his sister's birthday party back home, but I hoped he could live with that. Little did we all know what lay ahead.*

We paid a bit over the odds, supposedly to stay in a posh hotel in Salou, but Miss Ellie had some well-off clients prepared to pay even more, so we were bumped to a crap place in Lloret de Mar. We relaxed in the warm sun by the beach and enjoyed a few beers, and had just toasted my daughter when we were joined in the bar by a couple of very pleasant black lads. They were over for the game from North London, a right couple of characters who we dubbed Dwight and Andy after Yorke and Cole. They joked with us and told tales that had us in fits. We went our separate ways as we left for the game and that was the last we saw of them; they didn't return that night. Later in the year we heard through the Cockney Reds' grapevine that one of them had been done by Old Bill after a dead body was found in the boot of his car. Apparently a dispute over nothing much had become heated and some minor punches were thrown, this bloke had suffered a heart attack, so matey put him in the boot and said nothing – well, not at first. He was done for manslaughter but apparently got off lightly. Anyway, we never saw him or his mate again.

We had a coach to take us into Barcelona and it was manic around the turnstiles, with crowds pushing to get in but thankfully no violence that I could see. As we stood there, Louis Van Gaal came up next to us – he was then the Barcelona coach – and told us to calm down and not to worry, as we would all get in OK. He was right, and what a ground it was too.

We all know what happened. I would like to think I'm a pretty hard sort of bloke but after we had won I was overcome. I cried and hugged my boy and anyone else near me. We stayed for ages to celebrate before having to rush back to our coach, fearful it might leave without us. It was strangely subdued on the journey back, as if we were in shock – it was quite amazing. We sat in a similar state back at the hotel bar. I would normally be downing lagers by the litre after something like that, but on this night I could only manage water, and not because I was acting the responsible dad. Our little group of Cockneys sat there long into the night talking endlessly of the game and how remarkable it had been. Bayern fans came and went in good humour, wishing us well. Sleep was difficult as excitement remained, and I just lay there on the bed watching my lad curled up in a deep sleep. He would never forget his first trip and missing his sister's party now seemed no bad thing.

By the next morning the thousands of Bayern fans had shipped out and Lloret was eerily quiet, a ghost town with only a hundred or so United remaining. Strangely, during the morning, hordes of Germans did turn up but they were all wearing 'Schumacher' tee-shirts, as they were booked in for the Spanish Grand Prix near Barcelona at the weekend. We left for the airport by taxi. At the check-in *desk I realised I'd left my boy's passport at the hotel. It took some time to sort out a taxi there and back and I was panicking all the time that I might miss the flight, but needn't have worried; there was a four-hour delay. No one can ever say travelling with United and the Cockneys is remotely dull.*

I was certainly not going to miss this game, but I was worried that I would have problems showing my passport, either at Gatwick or on arrival in Spain, in view of what had happened in Valencia in 1982. I was unsure if there was some sort of suspended sentence on me or something that would cause the Spanish police to either arrest me or put me on the next plane home, so I went to some lengths to find out what my position was. My wife had a friend who was a nanny in Spain to a real posh family; the dad was a lawyer and I heard back that he thought I would be fine. One of the police spotters at Old Trafford also told me there would be no problem.

Still I was not taking chances and decided to drive down with my mate Mike, who I had seen at the FA Cup final against Newcastle earlier in May. He had a friend over from the USA, an Irish-American bricklayer, and the three of us set off Sunday lunchtime for the car ferry at Dover. We then had a long drive through the night and neared the border between France and Spain the next morning. I still felt uneasy but we sailed through with no checks, and I was so relieved that once on the other side of the border I had to pull over and ring the missus, who had been convinced that I would end up in jail for months. We diverted to pick up a couple of Irish lads who had flown to an airport close to the same border, then headed towards Lloret.

Thousands of United were centred there. We had two snide tickets which we knew were fake, but we had paid peanuts for them back in the UK and only had them to try and get through any cordons near the ground, where inspection might not be too sharp; after that we would have to work out some way of gaining entrance. We found some rooms above a bar and booked in for three nights. We drank heavily as more and more United and Germans poured into town. There were minor skirmishes between the rival fans but nothing that serious, with loads of patriotic songs – and the odd anti-German ditty – to maintain a great atmosphere. I was quietly sipping my San Miguel outside a bar in the sunshine, making sure I kept away from any trouble, when Greater Manchester Police arrived with some Spanish counterparts, clearly looking for known troublemakers. This did not look good and I nearly fell off my chair in surprise, but although the coppers clocked me, they moved on.

Ahead of the match, thousands of us crowded onto trains into Barcelona. We headed to Los Ramblas, the popular touristy area, where we carried on drinking until it was time to move to the Nou Camp. I decided to keep fairly sober as I did not want to come so far only to be denied entry due to drunkenness and an invalid ticket. In the event the police did check our tickets and tore them up, but we managed to buy replacements from some Germans.

United had three-quarters of the stadium. We at first mixed with the Bayern fans, given that our tickets were from their allocation, but somehow ended up behind the goal where United would score those two late goals to win. What can I say about the game? After lifting the trophy, the team spent ages in front of us celebrating. I had never been so happy; we were almost delirious, as if on drugs. Eventually we left for the city centre but, whilst we stayed there all night, very few bars remained open, perhaps fearful of trouble. They needn't have been. Early Thursday morning we caught the packed train back to Lloret, where we had a relaxing day before the drive back on the Friday and overnight into the Saturday. Life didn't get much better.

No one will ever forget that final. Even now, almost every minute of that trip stays with me and I'm sure I'm not the only one who thinks like that.

* * *

The rise of the Champions League, contested by the best teams in the best stadia in Europe's finest cities, was not the end of football hooliganism. Once the Soviet Union had broken up, new faces appeared on the European scene, bringing their own brand of violence, mixed with a strong dose of ultra-nationalism and racism. Trips behind the former Iron Curtain could be a harrowing experience. Russia itself has a huge hooligan problem, and the world saw what their hyper-aggressive fans could do when they played England in the 2016 European Championships and rampaged through Marseille in an assault organised with military precision. Yet wherever we go worldwide, we always find friendly locals who support United – even in Russia. In Moscow for the Champions League final against Chelsea in 2008, we had a guy known as 'Fat Chelsea' with us, who is Fat Jack's mate. In almost every bar, Russians would come up and mix with us, seemingly happy to support United for the night. They also seemed to hate Chelsea, and poor old Fat Chelsea had to keep as low-profile as he could. The neutrals in the stadium didn't stay that way for long either, turning against Chelsea and roaring us on – with great success.

Another game in the East, in Kiev, the capital of the Ukraine, showed again how United's support extends far and wide. There was trouble during the day around the city's bars, and the heavy-handed police kettled United fans into a few narrow streets. The cops were suddenly thrown off guard, however, and had to rush off to deal with major trouble between Kiev fans and other Ukrainians, who were reported as being United followers and were brawling with their own kinsmen. Whoever they really were, their actions allowed our lads to escape the police cordon.

I might not make all of these trips personally, but the Cockney Reds are always represented. We may even, according to one account, have helped to trigger the Bosnian war!

BRIAN *Someone came up with the idea of a trip to watch a game in Hungary. 'Fly to Pula in Croatia and then it's a two-hour train ride – it's much cheaper doing it that way,' someone said. So a few Cockneys joined up with Tony O'Neill and some of the Mancs and off we went. As it happens the train ride was more like twenty hours and bloody uncomfortable. We were about thirty or so in total, and pissed out of our brains by the time we were halfway along the line at Ljubljana, where the train pulled over for a long stop. Glad to get some air, we piled out onto the platform. One lad, Banksy, fell on the track under the train and was so pissed he couldn't move. Some of us had to crawl under and pull him out. The locals hadn't seen anything like it, as we took over the station like some invading army out of control.*

As the journey went on, we mixed with scores of army conscripts in the buffet car. Half of them, we were told, were Croatian and the rest Bosnian. I wound them up a bit, not that they needed much, and they started arguing amongst themselves, before a full-scale set-to kicked off. Bottles and glasses flew, punches were thrown and windows were broken, but thankfully no bullets were fired. At first we thought it hilarious, but what stuck with us was the hatred in their eyes, and it became quite frightening. Two months later, the war started between the two countries, so perhaps this skirmish was just the foreplay and it was my provocation that fuelled the wheels towards the eventual conflict.

Anyone who thought extreme football violence was a thing of the past needed only to look at these former Soviet Bloc countries, where hooliganism seemed to be at the stage it had been in the UK thirty years earlier. The policing was equally crude, with strong-arm tactics, batons and tear gas a more common response than our own covert intelligence, ubiquitous CCTV and stewarding. In southern European countries such as Italy, meanwhile, well-organised groups of so-called 'ultras' seemed to control much of the sport, and even seemed able to influence to police.

Take the time United visited Rome to play Roma in 2007. For once we did not go looking for a row, but their ultras and the *carabinieri* had other ideas. There were differing views, as there always are, of who started the trouble or caused it to escalate. Many believe it was the local riot police, who stood only in the United section to start with and ignored the provocative behaviour of their home fans. When Roma scored, their ultras started to throw missiles over the barrier separating the two sets of supporters. The United fans were incensed and charged towards the barrier, throwing the missiles back at Roma. The police then took it upon themselves to hand out indiscriminate beatings to the visitors, some of whom were curled up on the floor begging for mercy. Some believe Roma deliberately provoked the United fans so that their police would wade in, a recognised tactic at that time. The fighting outside the ground was, if anything, even worse, and left pools of blood and scattered debris on a bridge to the stadium. Ten United fans were reported to have suffered stab wounds and more than fifty had to be patched up with bandages or plasters, many after random assaults by police.

The Independent Manchester United Supporters' Association (IMUSA) and even Amnesty International took up the case, producing footage that showed a female fan in her early twenties being attacked without provocation. She had been filming with her camera when a policeman snatched it and his colleagues beat her up: three of them hit her in the face, another struck her with his truncheon, and she was flung down a stairwell. While an Italian minister did subsequently admit his police might have been a tad excessive, the Italian FA argued it was a 'justified response'. IMUSA pushed for a full apology and compensation for the injured, and took legal action, but this was 'timed out' in the Italian courts, although UEFA did eventually fine Roma 47,700 euros, a puny amount.

The second leg against Roma, at Old Trafford, which United won 7–1, saw scuffles but nothing like Rome. Old Bill brought out dogs and mounted officers to separate rival fans throwing bottles outside the ground and arrested fourteen United and seven Roma, but the trouble was contained within five minutes. What a contrast in the way the two legs were handled. United, meanwhile, promised they would do everything to help the fans who had suffered in Rome, but in the event did nothing apart from make a verbal complaint and refused to communicate with IMUSA, even chucking them off the club's fan forum. 'This was an opportunity for Manchester United to work with us in helping fans who had been attacked,' an IMUSA official was reported as saying. 'As it is, the club stood to one side.' In 2010, the young woman who had been beaten up protested about the club's American owners, the Glazer family, and lifted a popular banner at a game saying, 'Love United, Hate Glazer'. She was thrown out and later banned from Old Trafford for life.

Of course, there were also plenty of good times on Italian trips, which over the years have grown in number. One, to Milan in February 2009, saw the debut of a particularly infamous garment that was seen by TV viewers all over the world.

GROOMY *A Euro away always brings a smile to travelling Reds, especially if 'the Chemist' is in your party, as he can supply any recreational substance you might want. Inter Milan at the San Siro was one of those occasions. It started off with our usual routine when we play in Milan, which is a room at the players' hotel, the Meliá Milano. Match-day dinner was in a very respectable restaurant with all the usual suspects. We also had with us the Prof, who is quite a legend amongst Italian university students, and who had arranged a meet with a few of them at this Latin drinking-and-fine-dining establishment. While the Prof was holding conversation with his idolising students, the rest of us Cockneys, along with the Grimsby boys, commenced drinking our way through copious amounts of wine. Enter the Chemist. Now it is well known that I do not partake in drugs of any sort, but at this point I was as pissed as fifty sailors. I was given/slipped a couple of pills and from somewhere the mankini appeared (truth be known, it was in my luggage at the start). The merriment continued, but I should point out that I am not responsible for any later actions, as it is all a blur. It is only through photos, conversations and TV coverage of the game that I know now that Borat is actually a Cockney Red and not from Kazakhstan. Needless to say, the topic of the*

mankini is one that is often regaled on our Euro exploits,
and I'm pleased, no doubt along with hundreds of others,
to say the green bathing costume ended its playing career
at the Giuseppe Meazza Stadium a good two years before
Andrea Pirlo did.

Fat Jack likes to put us up in smart hotels on his trips. Gone
are the days when we might be fifteen to a room, farting,
puking and snoring. Even in a luxury room, however, there
are some people you don't want to share with. Some have
quirky habits that take a bit of getting used to. One is Essex
Steve, an ex-military man who always dresses immaculately,
without a hair out of place. He is obsessed with personal security and so booby traps his hotel room, meaning any intruder
sets off alarms to alert him. It can be dangerous if you happen
to trigger these traps when arriving back in the room after he
has gone to sleep – you fear for your safety until he realises
who you are. Steve is big in business and always travels first-
class, and if we have been to a European game he is always up,
out and away home before we would even think of waking.
His military training means he leaves the room cleaner than
when he arrived. But he fears no-one, and if we have a spot of
bother we can count on him, make no mistake.

My own foreign travelling is selective these days and usually
reserved for big matches like finals. Many United see these
trips as a jolly but that's not to say there aren't some hairy
moments, whether involving foreign police or the local head-
cases. What amazes me is the travel hours and effort some
people will put in. Groomy rarely misses any match. At the
time of the sixtieth anniversary of the Munich air disaster,
he flew to Belgrade, from where the Busby Babes had been
returning in 1958 when their plane crashed, to watch our
Under-19s play in a goodwill game. He has been to nearly

forty different countries to watch United. Others travel from the USA and even Australia for as many games as they can, partly to ensure they can qualify for tickets for the biggest matches via any ballot. Following the team takes much more commitment than it did forty years ago.

CHAPTER 16

FACES AND FOES

The old stagers like me and The Ghost, Griff (before he was thrown out and went into hiding), Tony, Tooting Steve (not seen much these days), the violent Peckham brothers and the younger Joe and his mates, Brian, Micky W, Big K; these to me are the 'real' Cockney Reds, mates with history, the core of the group. Many go back together to the Sixties. Nowadays, however, we have others in our ranks. They are just as committed to United and see themselves, quite rightly, as Cockney Reds, but they are different. Yes, they have had their moments and been caught up in trouble, but do not look for it in the way we did and are happy to walk away. They include Fat Jack, our ticket and trip organiser, the Prof, Essex Steve, 'Mankini Man' Groomy and many more. Most have their own little clique but we all come together, as many as a hundred of us at times, before games. Then we're off to our seats, nothing like those days when we stood together as a force on the terraces.

There have been other main faces in the past. One was Tank, a true Cockney Red despite living in Northampton. I'm not sure I ever knew his real name, but he was an out-and-out criminal who built his life outside the law. I went to his wedding in the early Nineties and afterwards drove to Billing Aquadrome, near Northampton, for the reception. Tank

246

worked at the time as a bouncer on the door of a club, and had been pummelled in a fight the night before. He looked a right mess when I met him at the reception; God knows what his wedding photos came out like.

I had gone there with the Peckham brothers to join over a hundred guests including a fair number of Cockney Reds. When we came to leave, I found that only the sidelights would work on my car. I did not want to drive a long way home at night without headlamps, especially when I'd had a lot to drink, but was not sure what to do. We went back into the reception and soon afterwards a car turned up to take Tank and his wife to their honeymoon hotel. However he didn't want to leave me and the brothers with nowhere to stay. Not many blokes would have bothered with our predicament, especially on their wedding night, but this was Tank. His wife was keen to get going and went into a strop when Tank ignored her, so much so she threw her bouquet of flowers at him, followed by her wedding ring. Then she got into the car and told the driver to drive off.

Tank just shrugged and told us to get into my car and drive into Northampton. We thought he wanted us to follow his wife but instead he took us to a pub owned by a mate who had been at the wedding. Tank rattled on the pub door until his mate came down in his pyjamas and agreed to let us stay in the bar until after dawn, when I would no longer need lights to drive. Tank then ordered a taxi and went off to find his wife. The landlord told us to help ourselves to any drinks and returned to bed.

Tank was typical Cockney Red – do anything for a mate. That night he did eventually find his wife and it was all smoothed over, although in later years they split up. He eventually killed himself after a period of ill-health. Amongst other things he suffered from Bell's palsy, which made his face drop on one side. The turnout of Cockney Reds for his funeral was amazing, and the Mancs were there in force too, with men like Tony O'Neill showing typical Reds camaraderie. I was delayed by traffic and missed the service but the wake was some occasion.

Tank had helped me out with cash at times when I was struggling, but I am not sure the money ever came from a legitimate source. What I do know is that on one occasion he and I were in a supermarket, and on paying for his goods he asked for 'cash back'. He gave me the shopping, but I knew he was using a stolen or fake credit card to draw the cash. We moved on to more than one supermarket the same day. That was him all over, a sort of Robin Hood although I doubt the Law would have seen it that way.

He drifted away from attending games in the period before his death. Then one day I was driving along with my wife when we heard a newsflash that an armed gunman was believed to be holding a priest hostage in a church, surrounded by police. It turned out to be Tank. He had been driving near his home when he realised he was being followed by police, so he pulled over outside this church, took a shotgun from the back seat, grabbed some cartridges of shot and ran inside, where he held the priest at gunpoint. I'm sure he wouldn't have hurt a terrified cleric, but this was serious stuff. The police knew him and told him not to be so stupid and to empty the shotgun and put the cartridges and any spares to one side, as being captured with a loaded gun would mean a longer prison sentence. Tank saw the light, dropped the ammo into the church organ pipes and surrendered. He was charged with the lesser firearm offence, although he did have to serve time.

* * *

I am now officially a state pensioner, with a dodgy back and none of the nimbleness of youth. I could not be as active or effective in a fight even if there were any, but generally they are rare. I'm still handy if it comes to it, as a few incidents in recent years show, but it is tame stuff now by comparison to the past. The young United today are nothing like we were – well, maybe a few are, from the sink estates around Manchester, London and the bigger inner cities. The Government and police, with cameras everywhere, have won the battle to control hooliganism in our national game. It is still there, simmering, but nothing like it was.

The generation after mine were the boys born in the Sixties, and by the time they were teenagers the hooligan era was well underway. They joined it rather than created it, which is a lot different. Take Fat Jack, and his rise to become a well-known face among the Cockneys (although he never claims to be a true Cockney Red). Born in 1962, he is now seen as a leader, certainly for our little firm-within-the-firm, not for any fighting prowess but because he organises all our trips and sorts out the tickets. This might not seem much, but you can no longer go to games without a ticket. In the old days you would just pitch up and pay, or get in somehow, often in the other team's end, but with Old Trafford season tickets now at a premium, we often share a number around our group. Fat Jack has had his moments, but he doesn't go looking for trouble. Yet his upbringing was similar to mine.

He was born into a family living on one of the posher council estates in Tooting, the Ansell Road area, but this was directly opposite one of the worst housing estates in South London , a place where all the problem juveniles hung out – such boys as Joe, who is a few years older than Fat Jack and, like him, went to Battersea Grammar School. They didn't know each other then but whilst Fat Jack got five proper 'O' levels despite being in constant trouble and not doing much in his final year, Joe was suspended from the school for such long periods that he never got as far as doing a GCE! Fat Jack was in a street gang of a few faces, mainly Chelsea fans. He attended his first game when aged eleven, in a period when United were not at their best and not many youths from his part of London thought of supporting them.

He was from the short-lived Bay City Roller/glam era, as opposed to my semi-rocker/biker background, and would go off to games in his mid-teens with a United scarf tied around his wrist or his waist. Later he and his mates adopted cropped hair and Harrington jackets to look the business. They were a little gang of no more than ten and included some Chelsea lads, who were happy to tag along to United for some action. As spotty sixteen-year-olds they would often try getting into pubs before games but were invariably thrown out for being under-age, something that had rarely happened to us at that same age, as we had moved in a much bigger mob and few landlords or bouncers would confront thirty or forty hooligans. Once he had starred with his GCEs, Jack went into the wide world to work in wholesale book and magazine distribution.

FAT JACK *I do not consider myself a Cockney Red. Despite coming from the Wandsworth borough of South London, Tooting to be precise, I have never thought of myself as a member of that recognised firm drawn from London and the Home Counties, whose byword was often violence and hooliganism. I started to 'support' United at primary school, and when asked who I wanted to be in the playground it was always George Best. My first United game was Bobby Charlton's last, at Stamford Bridge in 1973, and we lost 1–0. A kid from my road who was a couple of years* *older took me in the Shed. All I can remember is plenty of shoving and constantly looking around the stand rather than at the pitch.*

The first home game I went to was in the same season, with a kid from my class and his old man who had season tickets in the Railway stand. We drew 0–0 with Everton and once again it was the noise and chants which were mesmerising. My first real contact with the Cockney Reds was after a midweek game at Southampton, not long before the Cup final in 1979 against Arsenal. By then I had become a proper nuisance at school and was always fighting with lads from other schools. To be fair our uniform up until the third-year was a black-and-white striped blazer, which might as well have said, 'Kick my head in.' We got off the train from Waterloo after a journey where Fat Chester, a skinhead with a lion tattoo on his forearm, was passing the slops of his finished beer cans to younger lads. I overheard one of the lads saying West Ham would be waiting, and tried to tag along. This Greek-looking fella turned round and said, 'Fuck off, kid.' I was taken aback and embarrassed. That was it for me; I decided I wanted very little to do with this type of fan and what they stood for (although I later got to know the guy, called Mick). I had by then been to St Etienne on my own, a semi-final at Maine Road and loads of other trouble games.

On top of football, violent gang culture was alive and kicking. A casual glance in someone's direction could earn a headbutt, a right-hander, or even a chiv or bottle round the face. A group of us skinheads, as many were, going to different areas of London was very dangerous. You were unable to just stroll into another mob's territory without mass brawls. A lot was made in the papers about 'Paki-bashing' and 'queer-bashing' but any group at the time was a target for being bashed: lads from rival schools, different areas, Mods, rockers, teddy boys, whoever you came into contact with first.

Fighting at football for me was more of a random thing, and despite great success when fighting rival skinhead gangs, I often came a cropper at football. For the infamous Norwich game, I went with three pals from school: a Yid, a Gooner and a Palace fan who is still one of my best mates. All dressed in black Harringtons, we must have been the only United fans who got chased and bashed that day. At a later game at QPR, normally easy pickings for the Red hordes, me and Joe Cassar from school cut through the White City estate, only to be accosted by a group who lived there. They took Joe's scarf and gave us a good hiding.

Tottenham away saw me and a big lump called Dave being followed by a couple of Yids down the Seven Sisters Road from the Corner Pin. By the time we were halfway down, towards the tube, the group had grown, and started singing, 'You two fat bastards are gonna die,' to the melody of the Piranhas tune 'Tom Hark'. When we got to the tube they duly set upon us in the corridor leading to the platforms. Thank fuck there were so many, as most of the kicks and punches landed on their own. We had almost made it to our platform when someone pulled across an accordion-type metal gate used to prevent overcrowding, leaving me on one side with the Spurs yobs and Dave on the other with the police. Dave berated Plod in no uncertain terms, shouting, 'My mate's getting killed!' So what do they do? Nick him, and he ends up getting six months' youth custody in Feltham. Once the Yids thought I had taken enough of a kicking, they left me, nursing more than a few cuts and bruises but able to walk away to a waiting train.

My best pal and godfather to my two oldest girls is a Chelsea lad. After we beat them 2–1 in 1986, their firm were none too pleased and rampaged around the Kings Road area. Someone was glassed very badly, and the police put out a public alert for a heavily-built and dangerous Chelsea fan known only as the 'Fat Man'. My mate was arrested and ended up being falsely accused. Half a dozen of us stood on a police line-up for him, as the Filth had originally picked five anorexic-looking fuckers to stand next to him and make him look guilty. Justice was done at court and he got off – the real Fat Man was identified and received one of the longest-ever jail sentences for football-related violence. After that salutary episode, I had my third kid in quick succession and football became low on my priorities. I also developed a severe gambling habit. I did not start going to games again until 1990.

I now live just off the M40 and run trips up to Old Trafford and to games in the North. Our group started booking their tickets with me as long ago as 1994 and we often meet up near my place before moving on to the game. There is never any spivving or selling at above face value. I eventually managed, over a number of years, to sort out a raft of tickets for about twenty of us in the old Scoreboard End, which used to house the away fans. I also manage to trade some of our home tickets to the Mancs for away ones, but I insist it must be at face value, whereas the touts will always have a mark-up. Obtaining tickets for away games is so much harder than it used to be. When we played Leicester City away in 2016, we had to turn up at the Leicester Tigers rugby ground with our passports to pick up the tickets. Passports, for a domestic game! Imagine the intelligence that provides to the Old Bill, should there be any trouble.

We often mix with players, former and current, and meet them on away trips in hotels (we never go less than four-star) or sometimes in bars. It's true what they say though: it is not always a good idea to meet your heroes in the flesh. I met my idol, Bryan Robson, in Transylvania for a game against Cluj in 2012. With him were a couple of other United club 'ambassadors', Mickey Thomas and Alex Stepney. I was enjoying a drink and chatting with our mate Joe and Alex Stepney about old times in Tooting, where they both come from. I then started up a conversation with Robbo. Admittedly we had both had a few drinks, and Robbo had a reputation even in his playing days of being a drinker. United had just sold the young Paul Pogba and brought Paul Scholes back into the team. I thought this was a short-term, short-sighted fix and that Pogba would be a star one day, and said so. 'What do you know?' said Robbo curtly. I replied, 'I can see what I see.' I then pointed out that he had been dropped for the 1994 cup final by Fergie because he had run his course, like Scholesey had. Well, that set him off. He said I was not even from Manchester and commented on how fat I was (then!). 'Fat as I might be,' I said, 'I could still sort out a Geordie cunt like you – and you're not even a Geordie!'

Someone overheard our 'chat' and it later appeared in the Daily Mirror and the fanzine Red Issue. I don't suppose Robbo thought much of that, and when I bumped into him in Braga at the next European game he blanked me. He did talk to Joe in the bar, but when he later saw The Ghost in the lift at the hotel he had a go about me, knowing The Ghost was my mate. Our next game was in Donetsk, where I came across Robbo again at the Under-23s match the night before the main game. He saw me coming and quickly started talking on his mobile phone. I couldn't hear what he was saying but I was there for ages and he still held the phone to his ear. Do calls ever last that long? It seems he was upset because the Mirror claimed he had been drunk, and he perhaps assumed that came from me, but it didn't.

I've had some adventures abroad. In Tokyo for the 1999 Intercontinental Cup against Big Phil Scolari's Palmeiras, I was out on the town after the game until about five in the morning. When I finally tried to get into the hotel lift, paralytic drunk, I was told it was full. I wasn't having that and barged in, only for this Brazilian to draw a knife on me. Drunk as I was, I quickly backed down. Another time I was again in Tokyo, for a pre-season tournament called the Japan Cup and was travelling with my mate, the former player Ashley Grimes. We decided to kill time by going to the races and by chance ran into Fergie, whose horse Montjeu was running and was a likely favourite. 'What the fuck are you doing here?' he asked Ash, which I guess is Glaswegian for 'hello'. We chatted about his horse and he said he felt it wasn't one hundred per cent, and for a punt we should go each-way on Indigenous. I asked Fergie if he'd do a photo and he said, 'Sure', expecting us to take one of him. Instead I handed the camera to him and asked him to do one of me and Ash. 'You cheeky buggers,' he said, but took the photo anyway and off he went with a laugh. We had the last laugh when Indigenous romped in second and the each-way paid 33-1. Fergie's tip covered our whole trip.

Another relative newcomer to the firm is Budgie. I first met him in 2008. I was up in Manchester for a game when I had a call on my mobile from Joe telling me to join him and some mates in a tapas bar in the Deansgate area. Joe must have briefed Budgie on who I was, or perhaps he already knew, and he seemed very interested in me and how I had gained my reputation. I took to him straightaway. He was a tall, quiet bloke in his late forties, and reminded me of the young Michael Caine from the *Get Carter* films, with his spectacles, a certain way of speaking and an understated charm. I was later to find out that he was more than just a face from South London, and had a reputation in the criminal world that was second to none. He seemed to be a regular bloke who liked football, but came from a tough Irish family and was involved in some major crimes. I'm glad he never asked me to work for him, as I might not have been able to refuse, which could have led to some serious time behind bars, something he is now having to deal with himself. We miss him.

A staunch Cockney Red of much earlier vintage is J-Stander, who has contributed much to this story. Born in the early Sixties, he was at many of the major incidents and events I have covered.

J-STANDER *I went to my first game in 1973 at Tottenham with a friend and his mum. I was twelve. The first time I remember feeling both frightened yet excited at a game was against West Ham soon after, as I watched both sets of fans run riot, and the game was stopped. I witnessed some awful fighting under the stands and was glad to get away unscathed. I also vividly recall a later game at West Ham in May 1977, the last game of the season. United were banned from attending in view of the violence of their fans since the 1974/75 season. I was able to go along with my dad because a friend's mum had a contact at Upton Park who was able to secure a load of tokens from the Hammers' match-day programmes, which gave access to tickets. She got us into the West Ham end. That was quite* *an experience of how hostile a crowd could be, despite there being no away supporters.*

The following year I walked from Stratford to Upton Park for the game and witnessed violence as extreme and frightening as I would have thought possible. I did not really want to become involved in any of this, but was later sucked into it alongside Bob and the others, more for the protection they could provide than anything else, but also due to the extreme provocation from opposition fans and, to an extent, the police's heavy-handedness.

Going to Upton Park was always special, not least the occasion when Tony O'Neill and the Mancs joined the Cockney Reds to put the fear of God up West Ham. The usual Euston meet up was changed by O'Neill so that United weren't in the normal haunts they would frequent before travelling to the East End. This was done to confuse Old Bill, mainly because there was paranoia in our ranks that someone would tell the police what was planned. My small group were caught out by this secrecy hence were not able to join up with O'Neill's group. He had passed word round for all to come with black balaclavas and everyone did. As they assembled close to Upton Park in front of the masses of West Ham, he shouted, 'Balaclavas on!', and United charged forward with a mighty roar. Apparently it was the most fearsome sight ever and West Ham were scared witless.

* * *

Just as we had our faces, so other firms had theirs. 'Honour amongst thieves' is a well-worn phrase, and there exists in many criminal organisations a kind of brotherhood both within and outside the group. Faces become known, gain a reputation and earn a certain level of respect, even from their enemies. Football hooliganism is not dissimilar. Many 'top boys' become renowned in their own world, and earn the acknowledgment of their peers.

One day in the Eighties we had a run-in with Chelsea in West London. A hundred or so United had been locked out of Stamford Bridge and went along Fulham Palace Road looking for someone to take on. The police would not allow us into any pubs, which didn't help our mood. Suddenly a load of Chelsea poured out of a boozer up the road, and tore into the United who were walking ahead at the front of our mob. I soon caught up and was just about to steam in when I found one of Chelsea's major faces, Martin King, standing next to me. I looked at him and nodded; he did the same. We had known of each other for some years, from going to the same pubs and clubs in South London.

'You've got a good group of lads there,' said Martin.

'Thanks. Yours are a bit tasty too,' I replied.

The police split up the fighting groups and Martin and I went our separate ways, mutual respect intact. As I have said, I knew a lot of Chelsea, many of them hard lads who lived near me, and always gave them more respect than those from other clubs. Sometimes, when outnumbered, it was sensible to do so.

I had first run into Martin at Tiffany's nightclub in Wimbledon in the early Seventies, in an incident he later mentioned in the excellent book *Hoolifan*, written with Martin Knight. The club doormen had been forced to intervene to break up a scuffle between my Cockney Reds and his Chelsea crew. The two chief protagonists were what he calls 'an Indian-looking fella' – that would be me – and one of their main chaps, known as Eccles. 'Come on, Bob, save it for the terraces, not here' one of the bouncers pleaded. The situation was defused, and I walked over to a couple of the Chelsea chaps I knew at the bar and shook their hands. One of them introduced me to Martin King, as he recalls in his book:

'Martin, this is Bob, or Banana Bob to his friends.'

Banana Bob smiled and shook my hand. I found out later that he was probably better known as Bob the Wog, although I don't think his family called him that. Bob's main haunt was Scamps, a night-club in Sutton, and he was fast establishing himself as the main man among the United following in London.

Even back then, King and I knew about each other and had a mutual respect. Another Chelsea face I respected was Babs, who famously had one arm – it was remarkable that he was able to stand and fight so well. The same went for Johnny Hoy at Arsenal, Tanner at Spurs, and Tiny and Harry the Dog at Millwall. Another stand-out figure was Dainton Connell, the main face of Arsenal's firm from the Seventies onwards and highly rated by us all. The Cockney Reds had countless run-ins with him and his Gooners firm, and he was up there amongst the top names. Dainton was a major factor in keeping the right-wing British National Party from getting a foothold among the firms at Arsenal, and this then extended to United and elsewhere – we certainly took a cue from what he did to keep political movements out of football. He was killed in a car crash in Moscow in 2007 and his funeral was something else, with over 3,000 in attendance, including lads from many other clubs, even Tottenham. Arsenal players attended the wake at Alexandra Palace and fans erected a plaque outside the Emirates in his memory before the council removed it.

With Euston being such a hub for travel to games in the Midlands and North, there was much mingling of the firms from the various clubs. Over the years we came to recognise all of the top London faces. In many ways the main heads in the various firms formed a sort of (low!) society elite, who all knew each other. Being a known face also had its pitfalls, of course. West Ham were top-notch, one of the few firms who held their own in Manchester, and you had to rate them for that. In the mid-Seventies a guy called Bill Gardner emerged as their leading face and became a legend in the East End. Later the likes of Cass Pennant took up the mantle, and the Inter-City Firm became known and feared up and down the country.

My first run-in with Gardner came about by chance while returning from a game in the Midlands in the early Seventies with my mentor, Snowy. We were waiting for a train to London from Birmingham New Street and as it pulled in, a large group of West Ham fans arrived on our platform and piled on board. We probably shouldn't have got on, as there were only the two of us and as I knew there might be trouble, but I wanted to get back, having arranged to meet my girl-friend at the time. Our carriage was taken over by the West Ham fans. Snowy and I started up a friendly chat with two of them sitting across the table from us, and it all seemed pretty amicable. But as the train passed Coventry, this big bloke, who I later found out to be Gardner, came up and said, 'Your name's Bob, ain't it?' I said nothing. At the time I had heard the name Bill Gardner but never seen him, so did not know this was him. I instinctively knew, however, that he was not a bloke to be messed with, especially with only Snowy for support in a carriage full of Hammers.

Gardner went for me as I sat at the table. I protected my face as best I could, but he landed a few blows on the top of my head and on my arms. I just took it, until finally he decided he'd had enough. I was pretty annoyed, but the outcome could have been very nasty if I had fought back, and it was still a long way to London. Shortly after, another West Ham thug called

Bunter came along and took a few more digs at me. I wasn't really hurt but, looking back, it was probably the worst situation I have been in among rival fans, as some of the mob might have had weapons and done me really badly. There were even cases of people being thrown from trains back in those days.

I would gladly have tried to serve Gardner a taste of his own medicine had we met again, but the opportunity never arose. I don't bear him any animosity. On that day I respected who he was and what he stood for, and might well have done the same as him had our roles been reversed. We each had reputations to maintain. I still feel I was right not to react at the time: some years later two Cockney Reds, Roy Downes and Tony Cornish, got badly done over by West Ham in similar circumstances. Roy had abused some West Ham fans early in the day at Euston, when he was on his way to Old Trafford and the Hammers were going to Stoke City. By chance his train on the way back stopped at Stoke and the same West Ham stormed on, recognised him from earlier and attacked him and Cornish. They fought back but both ended up being slashed, with Downes the more seriously stabbed. They both staggered off the train at the next stop and were rushed to hospital.

Sometimes situations arise when you have to back off even in a large group. At one game against Birmingham City in the Eighties, their Zulus firm seriously outnumbered us on the streets near St Andrew's. Not only that, the police were out in force and I could see the only outcome if we took them on was an arrest. One Manc made a big deal out of the Cockneys walking away and used me as a scapegoat, until I forcibly told him, 'Don't you ever accuse me of backing down or not confronting the opposition. You should always remember there are times when it is just not worth getting nicked.' He got the message.

West Ham even developed a chant about me and Tooting Steve, linked to a popular hit of the time. I took it as a compliment, that they saw me as a major target. I can't remember the words after all these years, but they were not flattering.

* * *

We knew a fair few of Tottenham Hotspur's boys and I held a soft spot for their great team of the early Sixties when I was a kid, but I came to dislike the club and their fans. I have heard some Spurs mouthing off in recent years about the Cockney Reds being all talk and no do. They have short memories. When did Spurs ever put in a show in Manchester? I do have some respect for them on their own patch, but not in Manchester.

At a game against them in the Seventies, about two hundred Reds infiltrated the Shelf, where their main lads congregated. It kicked off with them underneath the stand and a mate, Stevie Wright, a handy Tottenham fan who had worked the door at Scamps, came over and warned me to watch out for certain faces, pointing out a few. We were well on top of them at the time, so to me it didn't matter. The fighting died down as Old Bill waded in and slung people out or arrested them, and our numbers dwindled. We had done what we came for – made a good show – and I went into the stand and started to climb over a fence into the neutral terrace. This fat Spurs fan, a face pointed out earlier by Stevie, tried to grab me but I wriggled clear and gave him a mouthful, gloating that we had done them over. He shouted angrily back that he had my number and would get me another day.

Months later, I was in Scamps with my girlfriend when Stevie came over with two mates. One was this fat bloke from the Shelf. Taken by surprise, I was aggressive right away. He recognised me too and didn't need Stevie to tell me I was

Banana Bob. He went to shake my hand, perhaps as a mark of respect from one hooligan to another, but I ignored it and said, 'If you want to carry on the fight, then let's start it outside, right now.' He shrugged and walked off. Later I felt I had been disrespectful, but back then it took very little for me to get into a fight; I was often all aggression without engaging the brain. I regret it still.

But I knew that even away from football, opposition fans might see an opportunity to get one over on me. 'Respect' was no guarantee that people would behave properly, especially if they had a numerical advantage over me and any mates I might be with. I had another close encounter with Tottenham when a load of them in a stag party turned up at Scamps and recognised me. As they drank through the evening, some of them occasionally looked over and I could see they were talking about me. I evaluated the situation. They might not have been planning trouble, but I didn't want to take the chance that they might follow me out or be waiting outside later. There could also be some Chelsea or Millwall in the club who might be prepared to make common cause with them against the hated Man United. I spoke to the mates I was with and we decided to go to our cars to arm ourselves and to see if these Spurs lads followed. We found the usual work tools like pickaxe handles and hammers, and I had a baseball bat. We then waited outside, hidden but able to see the club's front entrance. We could have just legged it but that was not something we would ever do – we would put up a fight if we had to, despite the fact we were outnumbered and had no way of calling reinforcements. We were mad to stay but something in us made us do so. It was probably the best thing all round when the Scamps bouncers, having sensed trouble brewing, made sure the stag party left by a different exit. This was hardly an isolated case. I have faced many similar over the years, an occupational hazard of being a prominent Cockney Red in a city full of rivals.

Some might say the oldest foes should be Man City, but if I was to put them in order of which I detest the most, it would be Liverpool, City and then Leeds United. In recent times we have only played Leeds in cups but war against the other two still rages. Their Munich songs, often with varying words, rankle with us as I am sure some of ours do with them. Now that City have a half-decent team and can at least compete with us, the next few seasons will be interesting. I am convinced we'll see unprecedented violence at times as we saw at Wembley a few years back. What will the media make of that? What will the police do? Some parts of Manchester are violent places, with increasing street crime. It might only take a spark and we'd be back to the Seventies, especially if an economic downturn throws masses out of work and people become desperate. Who knows?

STILL NAUGHTY IN THE NOUGHTIES

By the advent of the twenty-first century, the main faces in the Cockney Reds were all in their fifties. I had certainly calmed down from my wildest days and so had most others, although we still had our moments. On a personal level, my wife and I and our daughter decided we had had enough of the UK, and in September 2001 we shipped out to Spain to try our luck there. Building jobs would be plentiful, my wife could seek work, and we knew of schools on the Costa Blanca that had a mix of English and Spanish pupils, suitable for our teenage daughter. We would rent accommodation at first, then look to buy if we managed to settle.

I spent two grand on getting our possessions out there and flew out, as chance would have it, on the day of 9/11. Things went fine for a while, the wife secured work in a friend's restaurant and I installed wall safes and security windows, plus drove a taxi. The problem was our daughter: she just couldn't fit in at the school and make friends. We were concerned, and matters came to a head at Christmas 2001, after just four months. Realising our daughter's education was most important, we drove home and stayed with the in-laws so she could return to her old school. I worked on a building site for a couple of months before the wife and I returned to Spain to give it another go, leaving our daughter with some close friends.

We travelled back and forward to the UK throughout 2002 and beyond, spending most of our time in Spain. In the summer of 2003, I took myself off to New York and Philadelphia for United's pre-season tour. In New York, a Cockney Red called Gene, who came from Reading and whose dad I had worked for in the past, persuaded me there was loads of work out there, and I thought it would be a good idea to stay and make some serious money. After a quick return to Spain, I went back to the States and was offered a steady job by an Irish firm, via the Irish lad we had picked up on our way to Barcelona in 1999. I had no green card, so was working illegally. I loved the US, but eventually decided that my absence was unfair on my family, so I gave up and returned to Spain. Looking back, I should have moved my unhappy wife back to live with her parents in the UK and stayed for as long as I could in the US, enabling me to return home with a tidy sum. Instead we all settled back in the UK in late summer 2003.

Through all of this, I missed out on following the Reds, although there was plenty of football on TV abroad (and United seemed to be on every week). What I did notice when I re-joined the Cockneys after a couple of years' absence was how much change had taken place around the game. Certainly the judicial sentences seemed stiffer if you were caught causing trouble. The hardcore, all of us mates from way back, remained solid but ours was just one of many Cockney Red groups dotted around the south. There were no more regular meetings at Euston, no getting in opposition ends, no taking on the Old Bill. Sure, there were still kick-offs, but nothing like the old days, and any action tended to be well away from the ground. More women and kids were going to games too, which changed the atmosphere.

New faces came along, but they were different somehow, nothing like the head-the-balls of my generation. Perhaps they were the product of a changed country: more affluent, less working-class, with a less edgy social life that revolved more around weed, ecstasy and dance music than booze, whizz and fighting. The new breed, mates like the Prof and Fat Jack, were content to enjoy the company of the older Cockneys without being drawn into violence unless seriously provoked. Sometimes, however, our newer additions were sucked into trouble by circumstance. Sometimes the strife even arose within our own ranks, culminating in a clash between United fans at an evening game at Selhurst Park in 2016 – more of which later. There were others too.

SCOREBOARDER *Not long ago we were coming out of Old Trafford at the end of the game and wanted to get quickly out to the motorway. We arrived at the car but there was no Banana, so we had to wait. He finally turned up, puffing and panting. This mate, Paul, says to him, 'Look, Bob you're taking the piss.'*

'Yeah, yeah, look I'm sorry I'm late,' says Bob, as we got into the car. But the traffic had now built up, and every time we hit a hold-up, Paul kept saying, 'This is all your fucking fault, Bob.'

Bob was saying, 'Look, Paul, I said sorry and that's all I'm gonna say.'

This carried on and they ended up having a tussle on the back seat, until we calmed them down.

THE GHOST *Everyone thought that was the end of it, although Bob kept asking me about this Paul, a feller in his forties. He was almost twenty years younger than Bob, who was clearly not backing down on this point of* *principle whirling round in his brain. It must have gone on for months and resurfaced when we went to Wembley for the Charity Shield. Pre-match we were in Canon's Park at Morano's, a sort of Irish brasserie. Two brothers who live locally, proper well-respected Cockney Reds, arranged the meet. Paul goes up to the bar and Bob follows, grabs Paul and ends up chinning him. The Cockneys seemed to line up with one or the other of them and it was only me and Fat Jack that stopped things kicking off. Old Bill did come in and break it up when it was almost over, while the whole room went silent. It had all gone too far between the United groups and all because Bob was late getting back to the car months before. Paul should have known better, or perhaps we should have told him that you don't mess with Banana Bob.*

This wasn't quite how I saw it. Paul, who is not everyone's cup of tea, was out of order having a go at me for being late. I was in no rush to come out of the ground, as I wanted to celebrate us beating City over two legs 4–3 in the League Cup, and I was pissed off that he took exception. This festered with me for some time and after I had hit him I did say, 'And don't you ever talk to me like that again.' I thought I deserved some respect from a bloke many years younger than me. I did later apologise, and I think he was sorry too. As for setting off two groups in the bar when I chinned him, I didn't notice that at the time or that there was the threat of a fight between us. It's all water under the bridge now.

FAT JACK *As the ticket and travel organiser for Bob's small band of Cockneys, I had to ban him for six months after he had whacked Paul. It was not a nasty thing I did, it was done in a friendly way and Bob accepted the 'sentence'. He* *knew he was out of order nearly setting off a war between different firms within the Cockneys and took my decision well. But we look up to Banana Bob and all the older Cockney Reds, and respect them for what they've done.*

I missed out on a few major incidents due to not being able to go to as many games as I would like, as times have often been hard for me money-wise. One was in the 2003/04 season, when the Cockneys were travelling by train back to Marylebone Station.

THE GHOST *Arsenal were the 'Invincibles', and we had to go up to Villa Park for the FA Cup semi-final against them. There were no trains from Euston that weekend, so we had to travel from Marylebone to Snow Hill Birmingham. Word went around at the game that we should all try to catch so-and-so train back to London. 'Why?' we asked. 'Just do it,' we were told. So about a hundred Cockneys were on this train, asking what the hell was going on. It turned out that Arsenal had decided this was to be their train too. The North London Reds had heard of this the week before, and with their hatred for the Gooners they made sure we had good numbers to see just how invincible they were. A lot of Wolves fans from London were also on board and it kicked off all along the train. Me and my mates couldn't be arsed to go chasing up and down the carriages but many of our crowd did and came back with split heads and bloody noses. The trouble was, women and children were caught up in all this, with bottles being thrown and so on.*

The train stopped at Princes Risborough and me and a mate, Brian, had had enough, so we got off and started walking along the platform. We passed one carriage, looked in through the window and all we could see was fighting, with objects flying through the air. Brian opened a door and we started pulling blokes out of this real heavy fight and, making sure we had not hauled out any Mancs by mistake, pushed their heads down between the edge of the train and the platform, threatening to keep them there when the train pulled out. An off-duty copper got on his mobile so we released them, and the next thing we knew a helicopter was circling above. One of the people badly hurt in the fighting was a mate we knew as Pat. He was done over on the train, then went into the buffet at the station, where he was attacked again. I can see him now, staggering out, covered in blood from head to foot.

We hopped back on the train as it left, and when it arrived at Marylebone I shot out through the back of a carriage with Brian and our mate, Ads, to avoid arrest. But the Old Bill were lined up along the platform. It was like they were expecting a terrorist attack, the way they were tooled up. The other doors of the train remained locked so that those inside could be let out in stages, which they were. We three got through the barrier okay, only to run into Birmingham City on the concourse, coming from a game in London. It looked like it might kick off again, but Old Bill were mob-handed and saw us out of the station and away.

We later heard that the police videoed every single football fan on the train as they gradually opened the doors back on the platform. One Cockney Red was sitting next to an American and another guy wearing a huge turban, who was a solicitor. Neither of them had anything to do with football. Our lad thought he could squirm out of being filmed if he stuck with these two geezers but it wasn't to be, as all three were videoed. The American and the turban chap demanded to know what the hell was going on, with the police responding that they had been involved in the violence. They both took grave exception!

Another memorable trip I missed was to Scotland, a place we did not visit that often, to play Rangers in the Champions League in 2003. It turned into an invasion. Mancs, Cockneys and many other groups arrived in Glasgow by air, train and car. We had never played Rangers in a competitive game before, although we had met them in a 'friendly' at Old Trafford in 1974, when there was a near-riot. Expectations were high as United took over the city centre.

THE GHOST *I met up with Brian, a few other Cockneys and some Mancs from south Manchester. Some of the lads were staying in Sauchiehall Street and I joined them as we settled into pubs on the Celtic side of the city. Celtic fans were out in force, with many just having arrived back from a Champions League trip the day before. We got on all right with them – they seemed on our side and I suppose that was partly due to the fact we were there to turn over Rangers. As we were told that day, they also saw us as a Catholic club with strong links to Ireland, despite the fact that we had a Protestant manager who had played for Rangers. That old crap about religion seemed outdated to us but clearly not to them. Later, we headed for the infamous Bairds bar, near Celtic Park, which was the Celtic pub and, although a dump, was crammed with green-and-white memorabilia. It has now been permanently closed due to violence.*

Some Celtic fans and a doorman had warned us not to go over to the Rangers part of the city, as their fans also saw us as this Catholic club. We were having none of it and took over almost every Rangers pub. Even Celtic have never managed that. Rangers didn't like it one little bit. We also travelled across the city by underground, despite having been warned not to, as Rangers would be waiting to attack us. They might have been, but our numbers were so great that they thought better of it.

BRIAN *In the late afternoon I was in this pub not far from Ibrox with a mate, and it was eighty per cent Rangers and twenty per cent United. The tension was high, with anti-Catholic chants and anti-English or pro-Scottish Nationalist songs aimed at us. However, they didn't make a move, perhaps fearing our reputation. We did have some maniacs amongst us, so it was just as well. Looking back, they bottled it. We were too much for them, Mancs and Cockneys coming together and holding firm.*

We moved on to the ground, where my mate had bought a ticket in the Rangers end off some tout. That seemed like taking your life in your hands but he managed to get through the game, with Rangers not having much to shout about and my mate hiding his celebration when we scored the only goal. Not only was it a victory on the pitch it was the same off it, although there was little violence near the ground, with Old Bill well organised. The flashpoints occurred some way across the city, with not one big flare-up but a number of isolated incidents.

THE GHOST *I have Scottish roots myself, but as we approached the ground some tartan lemon was giving it all mouth, so I went straight over. He mumbled something and sneered, so I decked him. He collapsed to the ground with blood spurting from his face. Before any of his mates could help him, or get me, I was off, diving into the United crowd. The funny thing was, two weeks later at the return*

272

game I was walking down Warwick Road when I saw this wanker with some mates. The temptation was too much, so I went over, stood in front of him and said, 'Remember me?' and planted a well-directed Glasgow kiss close to the scar from the previous time we had met.

There were twenty-six arrests up in Glasgow, mainly our so-called 'Men in Black', while a couple of Cockney Reds were fined for fighting with the police.

* * *

From the mid-Nineties onwards the police have had the power to dish out Section 60 notices on match days to football fans they think might cause public disorder, and could detain you for long enough to miss the game. This was the stop-and-search initiative some clever dick dreamed up that caused so many problems, particularly with its overuse against black youths in certain areas. The use of Section 60s didn't last long at football, but was annoying and showed the pathetic way the police sometimes dealt with us. Their other ploy was to arrive at pubs before matches and lock us in, causing maximum inconvenience.

BRIAN *A group of us headed for this pub near Euston once and Old Bill were there frisking us and serving out their Section 60s. Suddenly the pub doors were all locked and some inspector announced we weren't going anywhere until after the game. The boys were in a rage and the inspector decided on a hasty retreat before he came to grief, leaving some of his men inside the pub. I went up to one and said, 'Look, mate, I'm an alcoholic and I shouldn't be left in here for all that time with temptation all around me.' Of course, I was lying but he didn't know that, and it looked* *like I had blagged my way out. He told me to hang on while he spoke to his sergeant. Over the two came and the sergeant said, 'Hello Brian, since when have you been an alcoholic, five minutes ago?' The bugger knew me.*

STATUS QUO TONY *Although we were locked in this pub, it was one of the best days out that I can remember with the Cockney Reds. It was 2003 and we had been up to Watford for an 11am kick-off and after the game came back to Euston, where we went into the Euston Flyer pub across the road. Old Bill followed us from the station and were heavy handed even for them. What we didn't know was that there was a demonstration planned for that part of London in the afternoon over Iraq, while Derby County were at Tottenham, West Brom at QPR, and the Birmingham Zulus were also in town for a game. So Old Bill had their hands full.*

They surrounded the Euston Flyer and wouldn't let us out. We were about two hundred strong. I went to the back of the pub, where there was a fire exit with no-one outside, and about a hundred got out before anyone was stopped. I stayed behind drinking with Brian and his mates, but had to take refuge in a corner when some of those inside started taking the place apart in protest, after being told we would be kept there for five hours. Old Bill beat a hasty retreat outside and thereafter communicated with us by a loudspeaker through the pub's letter box.

I thought I had better phone the missus and tell her I would be home late, as I was locked in a pub. She didn't believe me. Our mate Mick phoned his missus too, with the same outcome. The bar stayed open for a while, until the damage became too much. Looking out through the windows we could see local Plod replaced by those with the tall shields to protect them from missiles. I decided to keep out of the way. A little later those with the tall shields were replaced by the smaller shields and bigger batons of the Riot Squad, and we feared this might get nasty.

Suddenly the front door opened and we were invited out. 'Not likely, you're gonna smash us,' someone shouted. 'No, come out, you can go,' was the reply. Gingerly we stepped outside, and in front of us the Riot Squad parted like the Red Sea. We were still suspicious and were right to be so: Old Bill wanted to put us all on a train to Manchester. 'But we aren't all from there' we chimed in. They were not offering a choice, however, so I turned back into the pub, walked to the back and made an escape through a window, along with a few others. Others managed to escape while being escorted to the station but some poor Aussie, who had nothing to do with United and was just enjoying a few beers in the bar, did end up in Manchester – even though he lived around the corner from Euston Station!

The upshot of the day was that it appeared much of what had gone on in the pub had been secretly filmed by Old Bill. My mate Seamus was arrested after he was caught throwing something on the floor whilst talking into his phone. The police interpreted this as causing an affray, or similar, but poor old Seamus was having a right old argument with his girlfriend, she upset him over something and, in anger, he threw this glass onto the floor. Apparently, I was caught on camera going over to Seamus, saying something and laughing. The police said this showed we were conspiring, but I was laughing at what Seamus was saying to this girl and had said to him, 'Don't smash anything.' When Seamus was asked about this and told the cops, they said, 'Can't you come up with something better than that?' They took him to court and he got a £500 fine.

Something similar happened in 2007, when there was another top turnout before a game against Arsenal at their place. On this occasion, many did not even intend going to the game.

THE GHOST *More than a hundred of us met up in the Chalk Farm/Kentish Town area before the match to search out a few Gooners, take over a few pubs and watch the game on TV, with only a few going on to the Emirates. The Old Bill are canny by now and have spotters, probably some infiltrators reporting back, and all sorts of intelligence, giving them a good idea of what we're up to. True to form, as soon as United were in the pubs, Old Bill was there. No Arsenal put in an appearance. Many of the Reds were shitting themselves because they were banned from being near grounds and should not have been there, so they legged it as soon as the coppers started taking photos of the crowd to check faces.*

Not only was there Met Police but also some from an elite group, plus the City of London Police and Greater Manchester too, showing how organised they had become and how difficult it was for us. There was some trouble in the pubs due to the drinking, but only against the police. Bottles were thrown and a few things were smashed during a game of high drama which saw United took the lead when Ronaldo scored in the eighty-second minute, only for a scrambled goal by William Gallas in stoppage time to make it 2-2 and deny us all three points. There was some doubt if the ball had crossed the line – in fact it was well over – and that didn't help the atmosphere.

Cue mayhem, with some fighting amongst the United themselves, but mainly with the coppers. By now this one pub was jam-packed with United, with texting ensuring that all came to this one place, and there was so much trouble that the police closed the pub. The message went around to move on to Camden, but the Old Bill were able to follow. They were attacked in the streets, and this continued when everyone moved on again to the King's Cross/Euston area. All this was not helped with the police taking photos of as many as they could, including those not involved in the violence. Many United were nicked for all sorts of offences. All through that day the violence was as bad as at any time in the past forty years, but it largely went unreported – it was, after all, away from the game itself, and shows the new chapter in hooliganism, how it now occurs and how it is dealt with.

In 2008 some United arranged to 'meet up' with Stoke City fans for a ruck, all set up on the mobile phones. Stoke were to meet in one pub while we would go to the Flat Iron in Salford, from where we would arrange a face-off somewhere between the two. I travelled up from London, was dropped off at the ground and caught a taxi to the Flat Iron, but when I arrived the police were already filming and taking photos of the two hundred or so Reds inside and outside the pub. Those banned from games were forced to hide in the toilets or out the back amongst the empties, so as not to be recognised. I also discovered that once you had gone in the pub, the police would not let you leave, much to my annoyance.

After about an hour I managed to get outside and, not wanting to miss the match, approached this officer who looked in charge. 'Look,' I said, 'I'm only here to pick up my season ticket and came for a swift pint. I'm nothing to do with any of this.' He eyed me up and down suspiciously, but clearly had more important things to worry about than some middle-aged whinger. 'You'd better bugger off then,' he said, and I did. I heard later that Stoke were corralled in another pub and then put back on their coaches, having all been given daily banning order certificates. They were up in arms about it, took the matter to court for compensation from the police, and won. As for the Flat Iron, like many old pubs it was bulldozed to make way for a shopping centre.

The media largely appears to have lost interest in reporting serious domestic hooliganism, apart from the occasional incident such as the United coach being stoned at the last ever game at Upton Park. The Wembley Cup semi-final against City in 2011 was an example of how little interest there is now. There was some serious, old-style hostility, yet I couldn't believe so little was reported about it. I even rushed home to catch the news, as the disturbances were as bad as any in the Seventies, but nothing appeared. Could this be a deliberate policy not to report on such violence and thereby avoid glorifying it?

United fans had been given the Wembley Park Station and the nearby pub area before the game. City would never come into there. We heard later that their main firm went to Watford to drink, chickening out of any potential confrontation, after their coaches had been attacked by Mancs at service stations all the way down the motorway. The Cockney Reds had arranged to meet from opening time at a designated City pub in the area around Wembley Central. Over four hundred of us were there by 1pm, wearing no colours, as usual. This caught the police on the hop and only when they sent in spotters did they realise we were United and call up reinforcements. The occasional City came in, saw us, and quickly turned on their heels. To confuse the cops, we even sang 'Blue Moon'. That threw them completely.

We were there for about two hours, while the police grew in number. Some City came out of pubs along the way, but Old Bill kept them at bay – City weren't really that keen as usual. The police then escorted us the mile or so to an open area forming the grounds of a pub, at the end of this driveway with only one way in and out. Coppers on horses and with dogs remained at the end of this driveway to keep an eye on us and we were not allowed to leave until twenty minutes before kick-off. As we finally came out and made our way across the forecourt onto Wembley Way, there was some fighting in small groups, but by then it was eighty per cent United, as City had already gone to their seats.

After losing the game, we came down the ramps to where the road levels out. Hundreds of United were waiting to get at City, but they had mainly been smart enough to avoid us. Mounted cops, dog units and riot police with shields kept us apart from what City fans were there, so we attacked them instead. It turned into an all-out battle, mainly with the police. The whole of Wembley Way was a seething mass of angry Red Devils. Crowd barriers were knocked over and this freaked out the horses, who wouldn't step on to them. Some reared up, almost throwing their riders, and had to be turned and ridden away. Helicopters hovering overhead must have called up reinforcements, as more coppers poured out of police vans all along Wembley Way.

It was mayhem, and all caught on video for the world to see, which makes it even more surprising that there was nothing in the media to speak of. I had not seen Old Bill so wound up for years. They weren't afraid to use their boots on some United who were knocked to the ground. I can still see those fans curled up to protect themselves, heads being whacked with truncheons, and blood-splattered blokes stumbling towards the underground station. My little firm joined them, as we had pre-arranged a meet with a few mates at Euston. The police were there waiting with enough numbers to keep the lid on everything, and with CCTV everywhere it was not worth risking an arrest. We did come across some Millwall numpties on their way home, but they were so pissed that they wouldn't have been capable of a fight, so we let them go.

We thought about hanging around to wait for any City heading back to Manchester, but Old Bill was getting busy, so we left. Poor Mick C from Peckham somehow became separated from the rest of us and ran into some mouthy Bolton fans, who were in town for the other semi-final the next day. They attacked him and one hit him with a traffic bollard: he was badly injured and taken off to hospital with possible life-threatening injuries. I'm glad to say he did recover. When I finally arrived home, there was nothing of the violence on the TV news, radio and very little in the Sunday papers. It was like it never happened, although much of it was filmed and is still available on YouTube. For me what happened was a great reminder of the old days and it certainly rekindled my fire, although such times are few and far between – more's the pity.

Now when my Cockney Red mates meet up it is like a reunion for campaign veterans, reminiscing about the good old days. We might not even make the game but are often content to stay in a pub, enjoy a few pints and watch on TV. Tickets for the biggest matches are hard to obtain anyway, although we can still pull off the scams of yesteryear when required, as the 2011 Wembley Champions League final against Barcelona was to prove. I loved the old Wembley and hate the new one, but both have seen many United successes. This Barcelona game was not to be one, as it turned into a right drubbing from Lionel Messi and his mates.

Before the game we met up in the West End, the cream of the old Cockney Reds. Few of us had tickets and the black market was outrageous – we had been offered some at £1,000 a crack. Fuck that. We found some Barcelona fans dotted around the streets and tried to isolate a few we could intimidate and relieve of their tickets, with no success. After a few drinks, hundreds of us left the West End and headed to the ground, earlier than usual at about 5.30pm. As we walked down Wembley Way, a few of us stopped to have a piss alongside a hotdog stall. Some Barca stood around nearby. I shouted over and one said something back, so I gave him a slap – or at least tried to, but I was stumbling about, flailing my fists and barely making contact due to too much drink. They just walked off. Further on a larger Barca group were having their photo taken with a huge flag draped across them and the stadium behind. I jumped into the middle of them, grabbed the flag and stamped it into the ground. They looked at me in surprise and probably thought I was nuts. I stared back threateningly but they just laughed and turned away, and to be honest I felt a bit stupid.

My group, including Micky W, Big K and one of the two Peckham brothers, continued towards Wembley Stadium, and at one of the entrances we heard a commotion. The security staff had opened the doors to throw out some jibbers, leaving a gap about six feet wide. We all set off at a sprint and burst through it, along with a couple of dozen more, with stewards desperately trying to stop us with rugby tackles and trips. My little group managed to hurdle the fallen bodies and were in. We still had an hour and a half to kick-off, so we hung about the concourse, eating and drinking. The security team knew that loads of us had got in through that door and would not have seats, so they were on the lookout for anyone without a valid ticket. One even came right up to me and asked if I had a ticket. Quick as a flash I said, 'Mi amigo, ticket,' and pointed towards some Barca fans a few yards away. He clocked my swarthy, Mediterranean look, shrugged and walked off.

The problem was to get into the seated area, which meant negotiating another ticket check. Over the years we have developed various ways of using a single ticket multiple times, jumping over and crawling under turnstiles, crowding through with a paying customer, saying a mate had our ticket, slipping the gateman twenty quid, and so on. This time a used ticket belonging to a mate was passed back to me and in I went. Once into the seated area, I decided it would be too conspicuous to make people move, so I climbed over some seats to get near the back, re-joined the Peckham boy and found a spot above one of the exits, where six rows extended in front of the executive boxes. We stood with a few others we knew, with more of us there than actual seats and some standing in the gangway. Most of us had jibbed in one way or another. We had to keep moving around during the game to avoid the suspicious security staff, and with about ten minutes left – and United getting stuffed – finally managed to bag some seats, as a number of disgruntled fans had left. The only thing pleasing about that night was that we still had ways of jibbing into grounds despite the stricter security. It felt like old times.

The memories also flooded back at the Community Shield against Leicester City in August 2016. Our group of about twenty, including some northerners, met in Shepherd Market, a little area tucked away in Mayfair. After a few drinks we caught the tube to Wembley about forty minutes before kick-off – we still never like to arrive early – and spread out along the carriage. At Baker Street about a dozen young Leicester lads got on, singing loudly, none of them wearing colours. We also wore no colours and to these lads we must have looked like a bunch of old men. They told us they called themselves the 'Fosse Babies' – Leicester's main firm was known as the Baby Squad – and obviously fancied themselves.

We did have a little lad with us who was wearing his United shirt, and one of the Leicester spotted this and started abusing us with the usual hilarious comments, like, 'I bet you're from somewhere miles away like Cornwall.' That didn't go down well, especially as it was mainly directed towards 'Nice Paul', who happens to come from Salford. Paul, who normally wouldn't hurt a fly, took great exception and threw a right-hander, sparking a full-scale ruck. I don't think the Leicester had realised how many of us there were, and when the train stopped at Dollis Hill we threw them all off. Those young bucks probably remain upset to this day that they were chucked off a train by a group of OAPs.

RESPECTABLE - ALMOST

A hardcore group remains within the Cockney Reds, many with a hooligan past. There are also many others who have become friends along the way, and some who tag along. They are not what I call true Cockney Reds because to me that name only belongs to that elite with a reputation stretching back over many years. We welcome in these others and mix with them but know that if anything kicks off, some are not to be counted on. Such is life.

With United's universal support, we also come across fans of different nationalities wherever we travel. They have latched onto us as in Russia, Macedonia, Holland and many other countries in recent times. Most are passing acquaintances but some keep in contact and meet up with us if they come to any games in England or when we play in their neck of the woods. One such is Jeremy, a Frenchman from Lyon whose family run a food business. If we are playing in France he will sort us out a top hotel and restaurant and we will do the same for him when he comes over here. He is a real gentleman and looks like Eric Cantona in his prime, all dark eyes, tall and straight-backed with that sort of imposing strut. This goes down well with the ladies. Some of our lads took their wives out to Lyon for a weekend and he had the girls swooning at his good looks and immaculate charm, complimented by the fancy box of macaroons he bought them – the way to an English girl's heart! Yet his first trip to London, at White Hart Lane, was nearly disastrous.

JOE *I was with Fat Jack outside Tottenham's ground when we spotted this geezer, Jeremy, who we had met in Milan on a Euro away trip, holding a sign. On it was scrawled 'Man U ticket wanted'. Given the reputation of Spurs, it was a foolish thing to do and Fat Jack went up to him and said, 'What the fuck are you doing? You'll get killed, put that bloody thing down and come with me, I'll give you a ticket.' Fat Jack is never short of a spare. From that point on a lasting friendship was created. We usually meet up with Jeremy and his firm when playing anywhere near Lyon.*

At one such game, Fat Jack's tickets were for the Lyon corporate area. There were some harsh glances at us in there, but everything was OK until United scored. Me, Budgie and Fat Jack jumped up, only to be subjected to verbal abuse and spitting. We just had to take it as we didn't want to be arrested by the French police, not with their reputation. Anyway United won, so we quietly gloated as these fans quickly left when the game ended. Out on the streets after the game, we joined a group of United to walk back to our hotel. We were in this sort of council estate, rundown and moody. From round one corner a gang of local thugs appeared, and these were not a bunch of kids either, more like local mafia. There must have been over a hundred of them. We took a deep breath and walked towards them. This was no time to be heroes as we were well outnumbered. They stood, many with arms folded, as we neared them, and we couldn't see if they were tooled up, but assumed they were. We were later to learn that even the Lyon fans won't go down onto this estate and it wasn't unusual for its gangs to use CS gas, knives and even guns. You could hear a pin drop as we kept moving forward and some Reds hesitated behind me, thinking it might be better to turn and run.

Those at the front brazened it out and these French stood to one side and let us through. It was unreal – and unexpected. Were they just looking for Lyon fans? Did they like what we'd done in 1977 to St Etienne, their fierce rivals less than an hour away? I would like to think they showed us respect, given the reputation we had. Once past them we quickened our pace and soon arrived at our rather posh hotel beyond this rough estate. The contrast between the two places was remarkable – and a welcome relief.

We played St Etienne in France in 2016 and met up with Jeremy and his firm at the Smoking Dog bar, run by Forest fan Dave. They are both now honorary Cockney Reds. Jeremy and his mates were due to meet up with us at the ground, but he was recognised by a group of St Etienne ultras, who attacked him with knives and bottles. He had to take refuge inside a nearby food stall and was only spared when the police arrived. We now realised the reputation he had in Lyon, and that he was a figure of hate for rival ultras.

Another popular lad was Kilburn John, who was born in England but was of Greek parentage. He died very suddenly of a heart attack in 2012. He was only in his forties, and we were all shocked and upset to lose a good mate so young. In a fight John would always be at your shoulder, lending a hand when called on. More than three hundred United lads attended his Greek Orthodox funeral in Shepherd's Bush, with a large turnout of Cockneys. It was a two-hour service, followed by a burial, and United flags and colours were everywhere. We returned to a pub in Shepherd's Bush for the wake and gave John a great send-off. A few weeks later a few of us met up at Dulwich Hamlet's ground to hold a fund-raising memorial gathering for John. There were items auctioned, raffles and collections and we raised over £7,000 in his memory. I felt so proud of the Cockney Reds that day, coming together to support a mate's family shattered by loss. Pulling together and socialising is now a feature of the Cockneys.

Three years later, I celebrated my sixty-fifth birthday in some style, with many of the thugs from days gone by and the new breed joining in. We were playing Palace at Selhurst Park, so we started off at the Greyhound on Streatham Common, with more than four hundred there. Half went to the game, the rest stayed to watch it on TV. From there we moved on to Wimbledon Hill where we met up with Budgie, Fat Jack and some Irish lads in a late bar with music in the back room. By then I was well and truly drunk. Budgie provided a chauffeur to take me to Morden to be picked up by my wife, by which time I could hardly stand. I was proud so many came along and would like to think it was to show what I meant to them – but then it might have been just to get a free drink!

In 2014 we were all reunited again on a trip to Magaluf for the stag party of St Albans Steve. I booked for five days and travelled with Tank. We all stayed in a selection of hotels, most of us Cockney Reds plus a few of Steve's friends from St Albans and a group of United from Cheltenham. I roomed with this St Albans nutter called Micky Mac who, I suspect, no-one else wanted to share with. He insisted on having his music on full blast – and I mean deafening. Everyone in the group was aged over forty, with some of us in our sixties, but we enjoyed each other's company as if we were teenagers on a jaunt. Our first full day saw us hit the Strip, but I started drinking too early and was in bed before lights out. Most of the lads stayed behind in a bar where one was picked on by a Leeds fan, who recognised his Manc accent. Some other Leeds joined in, not realising the whole bar was full of United. It was typical Leeds bullying, but they came unstuck and were thrown out of the bar and told to do one. They were not seen for the next four days and nights.

Most of the days were spent drinking, taking the piss out of each other and recalling past battles, all in good humour and avoiding trouble – although when passing a Newcastle United themed bar we couldn't resist mocking them in song. There was no reaction from those inside. On the Saturday night we wanted to watch the Carl Froch–George Groves boxing bout. With there being so many of us, we decided to move away from the Strip and take over a bar with a TV showing the fight. We had this Romanian with us, a right villain, who suggested a bar he knew twenty minutes away. That seemed ideal but the more violent in our group said they would rather have their own fight and wanted to scour the Strip to chase down those Leeds. It seemed pointless to me, a hundred of us making a nuisance just to have a ruck with some arseholes who would probably wet themselves and run off. I got my way and we took over this bar, cheering on Froch, as Groves was a Chelsea fan who entered the ring wearing Chelsea colours. We were jumping up and down when Froch won by a knockout in the eighth round.

Soon after, Tank returned from the gents' toilet and started an argument with this northerner, who it turned out was another Leeds numpty. Apparently something derogatory had been said in the bogs, and Tank was never one to let that pass. When the Leeds fan realised the bar was packed with United, he swiftly backed down. I even stepped in as peacemaker, for once. Although they looked older, greyer and slower, I still saw these lads as what they had been so many years ago, as if teen-agers in a bar: lively, lairy, up for trouble and still all United. It was as if nothing had changed and we were as we used to be. I knew it was an illusion, yet there was still that some-thing about the group, a certain menace, an air of still seeking action. It felt like the old days. Do old hoolies ever change?

Increasingly, however, the chaps go to games with their off-spring – many of them now adults themselves – and even their grandchildren. The next generation are not the same as us, which is probably for the best, although they do have their moments. I recall a game some years ago when we played Liverpool in the League Cup final at the Millennium Stadium in Cardiff, as Wembley was being rebuilt. As if the Mickeys weren't enough, we were likely to run into the Cardiff Soul Crew, a tidy firm in their own right. True to form, when we arrived by train a few Cardiff City were there, but we saw them off, then turned our attention to the Scousers. Our little group comprised between fifteen and twenty, all quite handy if a little long in the tooth. There was the usual stand-off and verbal abuse before the Taff police sent us all on our way. We then took taxis from Cardiff to our hotel in St Mellons, out on the road to Newport. When we arrived we found some Liverpool were staying in the same hotel and had hung flags outside the bedroom windows on the first floor. One was no ordinary flag, as it contained autographs of players past and present, plus that of Bill Shankly, which shows how old and, no doubt, treasured it was. Someone said, 'We'll have that.'

There is only one notable pub in St Mellons and we were in it the night before the game. It was an odd place and we were told by the landlord how witchcraft had been practised there over centuries, and indeed still is today. Maybe that explains the two strange things that were to happen that evening. There was an ancient soldier in the bar in jacket and tie, with a host of shining medals from his army service. One lad, being polite and keen to make an impression, went over to the old boy and complimented him on his medals. The old boy stood up, grabbed him by the throat and threatened him. Funny lot, the Taffs. The lad apologised, although he was not sure what for, and the old boy let him go.

Status Quo Tony, meanwhile, fell into deep conversation with another local. Someone had made a comment earlier at the hotel about the village being known for wife swapping, and we all laughed it off as a joke. However in this pub it had not gone unnoticed that Tony was Rick Parfitt's double, and this bloke suggested Tony join him back at his place.

'What are you,' said Tony, 'some bleeding poofter?'

'No, no!' the bloke said, 'I want you to come back and meet the wife.'

Tony twigged this was an offer of a threesome. He politely declined.

We were up early for breakfast the next morning, well before any of the Scousers. Some of our group had arranged a taxi into Cardiff, including two lads from Manchester, the sons of a Cockney Red. Just as their cab was about to leave, the doors were flung open and these two leapt out, told the driver to wait, ran over to the hotel, jumped up and grabbed the autographed flag, which was hanging from a second-floor window. They then hauled it into the taxi, which drove off. It turned out the Manc lads had had trouble with the Scousers in St Mellons the previous night and were looking for payback. They later tied the flag to a fence near the stadium and set it alight, in full view of a large group of Scousers.

Of course, in any group there are tensions, be it around sport, work or social life. In football it is not unknown for fans of the same club to fall out and end up fighting. It has not happened much at United, but we have had occasional run-ins with the Mancs and others, such as those Reds in Chesterfield years ago. One cold December evening in 2016 saw a row between various United fans at a night match at Crystal Palace. There's always an edge when we play Palace, what with the Cantona kung fu kick and the death of that lad before the semi-final in the Nineties. Selhurst Park is also relatively local for many of us, and so is not a game the Cockney Reds ever miss.

On this day I started off from leafy Surrey in mid-afternoon, due to the bloody train drivers on Southern Rail being out on strike. Jason picked me up in his Bentley Continental – hence his nickname, 'Bentley Bitch' – for a comfortable trip up to the Croydon area and on to a tapas bar near Selhurst Park. There we met a few others, helped clean up some of the food they had ordered and had a few drinks to get warmed up. Me and Jason, who works in recruitment and has got a few bob, started off on some Budweisers before moving on to shots of sambuca. Fat Jack was with us for a while, but he was due in one of the corporate boxes, which are little more than an excuse for a piss-up (we saw him later and he was completely off his head). Fairly tanked up ourselves by 7.30, we went into the ground and met up with a few of the other Cockney Reds in a bar under the stand. Some went up into the stand to watch the game but a few of us stayed at the bar, which kept serving and had a TV screen on the wall with a live feed of the action. It was noisy and crowded, all United, and, to be honest, I'd had a few and can't remember much, but days after the game I was shown a phone video of a fight that someone sent to Joe. I hardly appear in it but could pick out Joe and Jason and recognised nearly all the other faces, some of whom were Mancs.

What happened was that shortly before half-time the bar started filling up. Then Paul Pogba scored and everyone jumped up and down, hugging and cheering, and the Mancs started their 'Manchester! Manchester!' chant. For some reason this set off some pushing and shoving, beer was spilt, and an argument kicked off. Out of nowhere the contents of one of those large plastic mustard bottles was splattered across the heads of people packed into this small area. It went all over Joe, Jason and another mate, a Chelsea fan, who was with us. They were none too pleased and one of them went for the bloke who had squirted the mustard. Threats were shouted and more beer was thrown, drenching many nearby. An older Manc, a nasty piece of work, was identified as the mustard culprit and cowered away, knowing he was in for a kicking.

Joe decided to go to the toilets to clean up and called for Jason to follow him, but Jason was having words with a younger Manc who was with his wife. Jason threw a punch, the wife screamed and the Manc staggered away with blood pouring from his nose, shouting, 'What the fuck was that for?' Someone else then went for the mustard thrower and Joe had to rush back and step in to keep them apart, with help from others. It was an all-in between United and bedlam. One of the crowd on the video turned out to be a young undercover cop, who got involved as it all kicked off and signalled to the bar staff to close their shutters. At that point the video ends. Later I saw a still from the club CCTV – I'm not sure who procured it – showing Joe keeping these younger lads apart.

When it all settled down, we split up. I left to find my seat, passing the lad with the bloodied nose and his wife, who were leaving by the nearest exit. A few remained to watch the game on TV, including Jason, before deciding they had had enough as the second half got underway. As I found out later, they went to a pub down the end of Whitehorse Lane. I stayed up in my seat but, to be honest, was out of it through the drink. I just about followed that we won 2–1. The whole incident was over in a couple of minutes – no stewards arrived, no police and no arrests. Some of the CCTV somehow appeared on social media later, and I'm sure the Old Bill would have picked out a few faces to add to their intelligence gathering, but there was no comeback.

I staggered out of the ground at the end of the game and tried Jason's phone but got no answer. I vaguely remembered where he had left the Bentley, but when I eventually found it, he wasn't there. I phoned and texted again, but he didn't hear as he was in a crowded pub. The upshot was that I had no driver to take me home and no trains were running. I had no choice but to go for Plan B, which was to ring my daughter, who just happened to be working on someone's nails in Croydon, down the road. She wasn't over-pleased, but said she'd be there in about half an hour. By then I was well and truly stressed. I eventually arrived home at about midnight, to face some grief from my wife, which didn't improve my mood. Jason then rang to say he had arrived back at the car soon after I had left and wondered where the hell I was. He did apologise.

* * *

There are other times when, for whatever reason an event brings out all the old faces from the Cockney Reds. Many of us mix socially, sometimes for a meal or barbecue with wives and families included. Funerals bring us together all too often these days, but there are also the occasional significant birthdays or the odd wedding to celebrate. They become a sort of 'Thugs Reunited' to help everyone keep in contact. Foreign trips to follow United are also as much social and even cultural as they are about football – we even visit museums and the tourist sights, something I never thought would happen. We organise mainly through Fat Jack for flights, tickets and hotels.

My most recent excursion was to the Europa League final in Stockholm in 2017, against Ajax. In the old days this would have promised one helluva scrap with the Dutch, but what transpired as a good example of just how much football has changed off the field. I did not originally intend to go, despite having access to a match ticket, but someone dropped out of Fat Jack's trip and I was offered a last-minute place for a bargain total cost of £500. The disadvantage of budget airlines, in this case Ryanair, is that they often fly to and from smaller, less convenient airports: for Stockholm, United fans arrived at five different airfields, not including those who caught cheaper flights to Denmark and travelled on by boat and train. All this meant we were split up from the start and not all rolling into the city centre together like those good old days. Many fans were loaded onto coaches under police escort straight from their airport.

I travelled with Henry, the Prof's brother, while the Prof flew in from Chicago. We arrived at our hotel to find we needed to pay a thousand-euro deposit by credit card. I didn't have one and Henry didn't have enough credit on his to pay so we would have to wait for the Prof. Whilst doing so I enjoyed a complimentary drink when a friend, Stoneleigh Mark, turns up, so I leave my bag with Henry who's brought his own bottle of vodka and head off with Mark to a bar where I find some Reds, including St Albans Steve. This was lunchtime. Word was that Ajax were mainly coming in by coach and most of their fans had not yet arrived. However four flash young punks appeared and seemed to be looking at us. We guessed they were Ajax lads and might be sussing us out. A Manc called Joe went over to one of them and initiated a lively 'discussion'. Others got up from their seats and confronted them thinking 'we're not having this'. Two of the Dutch lads suddenly pulled out weapons, including an extendable truncheon, and the other two threw bottles and glasses at us. One hit St Albans Steve, striking him a painful blow to his side, while a bottle hit above some windows and shattered around us. We moved towards them but they legged it.

We were joined by some Dutch friends, who said that about 1,000 hardcore Ajax were due in. I suspected there would be more trouble but reluctantly decided that, with my decidedly dodgy back, there was not much chance of me chasing after anyone. We settled down for the afternoon session. The beer was bloody expensive, but we were told it was cheaper here than some places where it was £8 a pint. I eventually returned to the hotel and met up with the Prof and after a change and wash we went down to the old town full of bars in the late evening, where groups of Ajax were hanging around. They largely ignored us. The now-pissed Henry (who got a right earful from his brother for being drunk) had emptied his vodka bottle and wasn't allowed into this other bar, so the Prof took him back to the hotel to sleep it off. I ended up at the bar I had been in at lunchtime.

Late the next morning I was in touch with Joe, who was at a different hotel with Fat Jack, and we met up with around twenty other friends drinking by the canal side. We went on to eat in the most expensive Italian restaurant you can imagine: the bill came to £140 a head, but one of the group, Matthew, very kindly treated me. From there most of us met up with another group at a bar nearby, then headed to the station for the train to the stadium. The police were out in force but were friendly and tolerant, ushering United onto an overground train and Ajax onto the underground to keep us apart. Many main faces in the Cockney Reds had turned out but we saw no trouble at the game, with the segregation working just fine. On the way back into the city some of the lads chose to gate-crash the underground and mingle with Ajax, looking for trouble, but none came. If I had said back in 1980 that this would become the norm, no-one would have believed me.

Our group returned to celebrate at a hotel with more than a few drinks. By 2am I'd had enough and I wandered through the streets back towards my own hotel. I noticed a bar with some lads outside who I knew, and stopped to chat. Inside I found a large group of what I call 'proper lads'. I stayed for about twenty minutes catching up with some of these old mates: Mancs, Cockneys and others. Talking to them about the old days gave me food for thought about how different things were from then. Part of me felt disappointed at how staid it all was, but then I took a hard look at myself. An old boy with a dodgy back would be sod-all use to anyone in a row. Then again, you never know.

Another example of changed times came when we played Huddersfield Town in 2017, for the first time in donkey's years, at a stadium few of us had been to. We began with our usual gathering of the troops at Fat Jack's, just off the M40. One of those with us, Billy, couldn't attend the actual game, as he had to get to his son's football presentation that evening, but to keep up his priority booking status he had to collect the match ticket. Unfortunately the only way to do this was to pick it up from Huddersfield's ticket office! So he would have to leave early to get back to Wakefield Station to catch his train home. The Prof also came all the way over from Chicago, mainly to keep his priority status for future tickets. Mad, but that is what football has become.

From Wakefield we went to a posh bar-restaurant recom- mended by a mate who lived locally. It was very grand and, well fed and watered, we rocked up at the ground – to find pandemonium. Perhaps Huddersfield had forgotten what hosting United was like. There were only a few turnstiles and, more importantly, no modern scanning of tickets; each ticket had to be given to a gateman, who tore off one part. We had been given about 2,000 tickets but there must have been closer to 4,000 United there, a turnout that included many old Cockney faces. Intelligence had been passed around that forged tickets could be used, due to the lack of scanning, and these were plentiful. Long queues breed trouble and the police were struggling to cope, although as usual some of our lads stayed in the local pubs with no intention of going to the game. In one, packed with United, a lone Huddersfield fan came in and said he had a hundred mates waiting down the road ready for a fight. United just laughed at him and told him to do one for his own safety.

A well-known Cockney Red had spent days trying to get a ticket through contacts on social media, without success. At the ground he bumped into none other than the great Denis Law and shared a selfie, but still had no ticket – until he saw an opportunity and befriended a young Huddersfield fan in a wheelchair. The lad agreed to take on a new carer for the day, so with job done the two enjoyed the game from the disabled section – particularly the young lad, who saw his team win and celebrated with a selfie on one Cockney's Facebook page. That's modern-day football for you.

CHAPTER 18

THE FUTURE

O ld hoolies never die but they certainly age. The onset of Type 2 diabetes has meant I have had to make some lifestyle concessions, particularly where drink is concerned. My work also came to a dramatic halt when I fell off a ladder in May 2016 and suffered serious back problems. I was on crutches for a couple of months, then could only walk with the aid of a stick for some time after that. The mornings were the worst time and trying to get the body moving was an ordeal, despite a regime of strong painkillers and anti-inflammatories. I had NHS physio and did my own stuff at home on my bike, bench and weights. My justifiable compensation claim for industrial injury proved to be a drawn-out process and ultimately failed due to lack of suitable evidence, leaving me out of pocket due to the period that I was unable to work.

With money being put to better use elsewhere, my priorities have changed. I still go to games but fewer than before; it's the same with trips abroad. The lads rib me about being careful with my money but some of them are bloody millionaires. They should try being me!

JOE *There was this time at the Melia Hotel in Madrid before a game. We always stay 'red' grade, meaning you get free drinks and free food, sort of all-inclusive. But*

Bob, being Bob, didn't want any extra cost and just paid for an ordinary room. So what does he do? Sit in the red lounge with us and enjoy everything on offer, loving it: 'Yeah, I've paid less than you mugs and still getting all this, blah, blah, blah.' But when he came to check out, they did him like a kipper. The manager called him over and said, 'We've got you in the red lounge enjoying it all when you shouldn't have been, so you owe us a hundred euros.'

'A hundred euros! Bollocks to that, I wasn't even in there!' said Bob.

'We have you on CCTV, sir,' said the manager. 'You were enjoying it more than most.'

Grumbling at being rumbled, Bob had to cough up more than we had paid for the red upgrade.

Bob carries this burden of having short arms and long pockets, and we pull his leg about it. In Rome one night there were a load of moths flying around the stands in the warm weather, and someone shouted out, 'Hello, Banana's opened his wallet at last.' On another occasion, Bob was seen taking a £50 note out of his wallet. Someone spotted it and said, 'Bloody hell, Bob, you robbed a bank or something?' Another lad took a photo to record it for posterity. None of us had spotted him with a twenty-quid note before, let alone a fifty.

Of course, this is all a load of bollocks. I was not the only one trying it on at the hotel in Madrid and then had to pay. Anyway, you must give jibbing a go or it's no fun. Look, I'm as generous as the next man!

* * *

299

So, what of now and the future? I try and tell myself I don't want, or look for, trouble any more. In the old days if you were arrested or charged it was like a campaign medal, an honour: to get into the other team's 'end', to make a point, to rule the terrace, to give Old Bill a run for their money, to be feared by the locals as we hit town and to give visiting firms a welcome in Manchester they would not forget in a hurry. Those days are gone. But United and the Cockney Reds remains a passion for me, one that deep inside burns as fiercely as ever.

I was on holiday with the missus and some friends in Spain a couple of years ago, staying in the same all-inclusive place as used in the TV comedy *Benidorm*, the Solana. There weren't many days when we didn't fill our boots with the booze on tap all day. One day I went with my wife and friends to a bar across the road, where I struck up a conversation with a northerner. He was a Leeds fan but was OK and bought me and the wife a drink. There was a group of thirtysomethings in there on a stag do, some wearing football shirts, including Southampton, Tottenham and Liverpool. United had just signed Morgan Schneiderlin, so I tried to chat to this drunken Southampton fan about it, but he was off-hand and didn't want to know, which pissed me off. I'd had a few and was wound up, and the sight of his mate in a Liverpool shirt didn't help. Some comment was made that I didn't like, so I took off my tee-shirt, handed it to the wife and walked towards them. I saw this Liverpool shirt in front of me and just whacked the bloke. My ring scraped a gouge across his nose, cheek and mouth and he staggered back, nearly falling over the bar – it was a classic right hook and one of my best. The bar's bouncers moved in and escorted me out as I continued abusing the fella I had hit. The bouncers then kept the group inside while my friend's daughter took me back across the road to the hotel, but I wriggled free and went along the road to another bar to carry on drinking.

My wife, still in the bar, spoke to these lads and said, 'You're all as bad as one another.' One of them replied, 'Trouble was, he got the wrong person.' When I heard this later, I said it didn't matter, the fact that the bloke I had hit was wearing a Liverpool shirt was good enough for me. The missus sent me to Coventry for a day or so and vowed never to go on holiday with me again (she later relented).

I have to say that punch was the best I ever threw and to do that to a Scouser made me proud. I was sixty-five at the time yet I am glad I had still got it in me to do something like that. I even remembered to take my shirt off, so the other bloke had nothing to get hold of. You see – the fire still burns.

The older Cockney Reds live well these days, enjoying each other's company and opting for smart hotels when travelling away. There are no clapped-out, stolen Ford Granadas these days, but Mercedes, Range Rovers, even the odd Bentley.

THE GHOST *When up in Manchester the Cockney Reds' pubs were always Mulligans and Henry's. Mulligans was famous back in the day because the players used to go in there. Roy Keane used to be a regular and wrote about it in his book as it was the only place he was left alone. Other teams also used to come in; Blackburn Rovers had their Christmas party there one year. We would be in there by nine in the morning on match days, drinking, and Gerry, the manager, used to give us a free breakfast. The trouble was it became very popular and started to get so packed it was uncomfortable, as it is only a tiny pub. Stafford Reds started to join us there and added to the crowd. We felt they were encroaching on 'our turf' but they were decent lads and so we let it pass and we started to look elsewhere. Now we tend to favour quieter but posher restaurants, tapas bars and bistros.*

Things move along so fast among supporters now. Apart from CCTV and hand-held cameras, we have videoing by mobile phone, as seen first-hand at Palace in 2016. There is no escaping some sort of filmed coverage and social media will expose anyone if the footage is there. The police might have spotters in any crowd and fans will grass each other up at the drop of a hat. That is not altogether a new thing: back in the late Eighties, when I was held for conspiracy, I know someone grassed me up to get themselves off the hook. I have my suspicions as to who, and even now, if it is ever proven, I'll sort it out.

I have already said that many of us find the football a bit boring now, and look forward more to a day out in good company. We miss the old days when football life had a pattern. Most Saturdays were the same as the one last week and the one next: kick-off at 3pm Saturday afternoon, with always the same train to and from Manchester. The fixture list would be out in July and I would look for the games that mattered, where there were scores to settle or trouble was likely: Liverpool, West Ham, Chelsea, Leeds, Tottenham, Arsenal and, when we occasionally played them, Cardiff, Portsmouth and Millwall. I would even look up when some of these teams played each other and plan a trip there, an advantage for the Cockney Reds in having so many games in the South to choose from.

Nowadays a weekend game could be on any day from Friday to Monday, with about a month's notice to suit TV. And United are always on the box so it is difficult for us to plan far ahead. Away games are a lottery to even get a ticket, such is the demand. There is no chance these days of the Red Army forming up on the hoof like we used to at Euston or Manchester Piccadilly. Perhaps only on a Wembley trip or one like a recent visit to Huddersfield do we see a mass gathering like the old days. You normally have to buy a ticket ahead of the game, having registered to do so or owning a valid season ticket, the police and the club also knowing who has every seat.

I am also disappointed with the youth today. Yes, they turn up for games but not in the numbers we did, and too many bring their girlfriends or wives – what's all that about? They ponce about in overpriced replica shirts and spend their time posing for stadium selfies and happily consuming ridiculously expensive pies, drinks and sausage rolls. The hardened teenager from a sink estate or, like me, a renegade from somewhere a bit more prosperous, will not generally use football as an outlet for their more wayward excesses any more. They can sit at home getting their kicks from watching porn and violent films and playing on their games console. They can't be arsed trying to source tickets, spend all day travelling and being herded like sheep onto coaches, and have to sit or stand still for a couple of hours, when they can follow a game on TV or online without leaving their bedrooms.

Out on the streets perhaps they get into other things now, like gun or knife crime and drug supply. Many are from backgrounds and immigrant cultures where football is not a popular sport. In the Seventies only the toffs took serious drugs – or more likely were the only ones able to afford them. Instead of spending their cash on football, youngsters are also more likely to save up for their two weeks of the high life with their mates in Ibiza, Ayia Napa, Pattaya or even Vegas. You rarely see masses of youths together at football. Away games do put people together in the same part of the ground, but seats allocations then split them up. It has all become too sanitised. Only a few younger Reds are up for it these days, more's the pity.

We remain a group of friends with a shared history, but look back at times past with nostalgia and a feeling that the best times are gone, or nearly so. In December 2017 a small group of hardcore met up at Drake and Morgan, a flash gastro pub next to King's Cross Station and a stone's throw from our old stamping ground of Euston. Once, hordes of football maniacs would gather in this area ahead of the Saturday games, with mayhem the usual result. Not anymore. That swirl of excitement and anticipation around the traditional Saturday fixture list has gone. On this free Saturday, with no United game, me, Joe, The Ghost, BIG K and Brian met over a few lagers to look back over the past fifty-odd years. We invited along our ghostwriter, Steve Little, to capture what was said and to put some questions to us.

STEVE As a football fan older than all those present, I abhorred the violence I had witnessed from afar for more than fifty years. But I have always been interested in what came with the game I love, including the hooliganism. This day in King's Cross was like a reunion of veterans recounting heroic campaigns from bygone days, proud to be bearing their symbolic medals. I looked round the table, in a pub a few hundred yards from their old battleground of Euston Station. Bob and Joe sat together, short, stocky men who I could imagine as wily fighters when provoked, shoulder to shoulder as they often would have been in the past. Bob still up for anything – if only his back and legs would allow it! Joe, now an organiser, a man of some substance these days but who still recalls with glee the tales of old.

The Ghost remained more aloof but has an air of menace even now and still revels in stories of the Cockneys' brutality. He also has outstanding memory, and reminisced about Glasgow, Millwall, St Albans and other pivotal events as if they were yesterday. Big K lived up to this name and had that same eerie menace as The Ghost, recounting in particular that vivid battle on the high seas with West Ham on the way to Holland. Finally, young Brian, an able toughie apprenticed in his early teens to the Cockney Reds to learn the black arts of the hooligan. He was at nearly all the main events from the late Eighties, as the others present confirmed.

My first question was, 'Do you think you've let down Manchester United by what you've done?'

THE GHOST *I'm United through and through. I care about United but don't care about the owners. The St Etienne game back in 1977 was a good example of how the club reacted to its fans. Then more recently the Roma tie and the way the club treated that poor woman who was beaten by the police. I'd like to add something else. I'm still fanatical about the Cockney Reds but the football is crap compared with how it used to be when crunching tackles were allowed and the players were men and not prima donnas. Plus being on the terraces gave us a buzz that's no longer there.*

BRIAN *I don't enjoy it like I used to, what with having a seat and all that – it's never going to be like being in that crowd inside and outside the ground. There is no buzz now. I was hooked from the age of fifteen after helping these bastards out by smashing windows in pubs from outside to distract the opposition inside, whilst they crashed in through the front doors. The rush I got from that was fantastic. There's nothing exciting like that now.*

THE GHOST *Amongst most older United fans, someone like Dobbo has a reputation, but these younger Mancs don't know who he is. Take Banana Bob, some people think he's six feet two, black and whatnot. They have no idea. The* *young Mancs would never recognise him or Dobbo and so never give them respect.*

You have women in your group now but there were never women in the old days?

JOE *It shows how times have changed. Some are mothers or even grandmothers, but many are single. This all makes us one big family and, as we all know, families have their disagreements and fallings out and we're no different.*

BOB *We even had a lord's daughter, Mary Parkinson, whose father was the Tory MP Cecil Parkinson. She had her own colourful life. She died far too young in December 2017 and will be sorely missed. She was good company and fun to be with.*

You now all look for 'five-star' travel these days, a far cry from old?

BOB *It's true. We have some great times travelling as a group and living it up in posh hotels, but I do miss those days when we got up to all sorts.*

THE GHOST *It was an adventure, what with all the scams we got up to, plus the semi-legit travel. Do you remember when we used to get tickets from a mate who worked at British Airways? We could then hide who we were.*

BRIAN *We were the 'Spanish Riding School Association' when we went to Vienna.*

BOB: *And when we went to Madrid.*

JOE *The 'Sandeman Society' when we went to Porto.*

BRIAN *The 'ABBA Society' when it was Gothenburg.*

BIG K *I remember that flight on BA. We got this meal on the plane that was chicken, which I can't eat. Because we were causing trouble on the flight, this stewardess said, 'Take it or leave it.' I had to be held down as I was about to take a swing at her. For the rest of the flight we gave her abuse non-stop. Then outside the ground I picked a fight with some scrawny bloke with a ponytail and swung him around while hanging onto his hair.*

BOB *We used to get some cheap travel tickets too for some games. Do you remember Bertie Rail, as we called him? He used to march into travel agents, nick a wad of tickets for whatever event, then sell them to us for something like a fiver.*

JOE *He lasted a few seasons until we found out he was really a Leeds fan.*

THE GHOST *He had a heart attack at an Arsenal game and after that we didn't see him – probably snuffed it. There were some characters doing the travel for us. Who can forget Teresa, sadly dead now? Brilliant organiser and founder of Red News.*

BRIAN *But there were also some tarts who tagged along back in the eighties who would do a turn for the lads.*

Ange the Flange would give anyone a blowjob on the train, coach, even in the bogs at a ground.

BIG K *Then there was Suck-it-Suzy who would do the same. The joke was that some of the boys would have to explain to their old ladies how they had lipstick on their dicks when they got home.*

JOE *These days the ladies with us are as different as they could possibly be and are given respect throughout the Cockney Reds. It is far more acceptable for them to be seen at games. That has been one massive change. Look at crowd photos from as late as the Fifties and spot the woman.*

After meeting up in London at Euston or wherever, you must have been a nightmare to the police on the Underground or other trains.

BOB *The train journeys were legendary but some of the worst incidents were on the Underground in London.*

THE GHOST *One of my best was at Chelsea in the late Seventies or early Eighties. We had taken over The Shed and they were well and truly pissed off. As we left and were outside the ground, the police segregated us, with us sent to Fulham Broadway Station. Some Chelsea had somehow got there ahead of us but the coppers put United into three carriages and Chelsea in the rest. When we pulled into High Street Kensington, the platform was also packed with Chelsea and so the guard refused to open the train doors. Chelsea charged at the windows and one or two were smashed in. I saw some of them using knives to prise the glass out and a fire bucket was hurled through another window.*

In response, United started yanking the seats from their mountings and hurling these through the glass in the doors, all the while trying to prise open the doors. Once it was clear we were up for retaliating, the Chelsea started to look less confident and more like 'rent boys', as we usually call them. When someone chucked the train's huge battery at them from under a seat, they all took a step back. The acid from it sprayed everywhere and they all toppled backwards like a load of dominoes. We then broke out through the windows and they turned and ran. Some shot down the track to get away, with United going after them – I assume they weren't electrocuted – while others ran up the stairs into the station and onto the street.

There were some real characters in the Cockney Reds some now sadly gone. You all must have great memories of them?

BOB *Some, like Griff, we'd like to forget. I always thought he would be destined for a short life or a long sentence. Now he lives in fear of his life. Then there's 'Prince' Charlie – a right nutter. I wonder where he is now. Tank had a screw loose.*

BRIAN *There was old Peter, or 'Smeller' as we used to call him. Always wore the same clothes, smelt like it and doubtful if he ever changed his underwear.*

BIG K *Remember Cornish? In a train buffet one day this steward wouldn't open up, so Cornish grabs him round the neck and I swear he'd have killed him.*

BOB *I pulled him off and probably saved the bloke.*

BIG K *He had bright red marks on his neck and they were still there when the train stopped at Milton Keynes and the British Transport Police got on, but Cornish somehow got away with it.*

THE GHOST *Cornish did the same thing to a barman in Mulligans. Back in 1974, after a Stoke game, he smashed up the toilets. Another time he lit a bonfire using loads of rubbish from the terraces. He always had that mad look in his eyes. He's probably locked away somewhere, or dead.*

Looking back, should you regret many of the things you've done?

BOB *No. I wish I had been more violent, gone further, evened things up more – like that time when the Scousers threw darts at us. That's not on, and one time when I wished I'd had a weapon.*

JOE *We could have been more organised. If only we'd had mobiles then. Word somehow got around, but our numbers were so huge it was difficult. Yet we managed, up to a point.*

BOB *I don't regret what I did when I was younger, but when much older I stepped back more than I would have liked, as I couldn't see the point of risking getting banged up for five to ten years for some major crime, like armed robbery or doing someone over. But I came close. I was up for anything, often made worse by drink. I would think nothing of threatening to glass someone over nothing much. But I enjoyed life then, free and easy – girls, a few flash cars like a Rolls, a Porsche, Mustang, Daimler and*

*some classics I wish I had kept, cash in the back pocket,
and I'd have been a mug to lose that life.*

JOE *There was crime all around us in South London, it
was difficult to avoid.*

BOB *Too right. We've both moved in circles where crime
was rife. The building trade I have always been in was
full of scams. The clubs and pubs were outlets for drugs
and my muscle was often sought, but I just couldn't get
into something major. We both know those that did and it
ended in tears.*

JOE *Still, you more than made up for it around football.*

BOB *It was like a drug and still is. Nowadays I enjoy our
little firm's outings and still drink plenty, often too much,
plus enjoy talking of old times and wishing football wasn't
as sanitised as it is now.*

Do you think there's further to go with what you call being
sanitised?

BOB *It's probably gone as far as it will, but European
football is less well policed than here and, with so many
of our teams playing in Europe, maybe that's where the
trouble might spread from. Plus the costs of policing,
stewarding and monitoring might become too expensive.*

JOE *Deaths at football still happen around the world, and
we have gone through Heysel, Bradford and Hillsborough,
but I wonder how long before the Manchester Arena
bombing tragedy happens at a football match? We've*

already seen a suspect package at Old Trafford call off a game, which at least proves we're alert to these things, but what if that had been a bomb? It showed how easy it might be to get one into a stadium.

BOB *I'd like to think our security is tight enough, but if you really want to do something that badly, you'll find a way to do so.*

You tell of fights in Luton and St Albans, to name just two, when mums and kids and old people were caught up in what went on, perhaps fearing for their lives. Does that not upset you now?

BOB *We didn't deliberately intend that to happen but it's collateral damage, if you like. It's like in a war when innocents get caught up in it and suffer as a result. It didn't concern me then, when I was a young bloke, but I wish it hadn't happened.*

Do you consider your reputation still exists in the same way as it did over all those years?

JOE *I think it does. It is shown in stories written in books and on social media. Take a recent online post from a Chelsea fan: 'Banana Bob, a decent geezer, got to know him when he was working the doors at The Greyhound in Croydon on Sunday punk nights back in the day – really nice chap.'*

BOB *I've not often been called that over the years. I always went a bit lighter on Chelsea, as so many mates followed them.*

JOE *A QPR fan on their forum: 'Banana, an ace bloke in the 80s and 90s.' Another one is a bit worrying on the Cardiff forum a couple of years back, from some bloke: 'You ain't seen Banana Bob around The Smoke have you? If you do see him tell him I want a word in his ear!'*

BOB *Should I be bothered?*

What was the worst you saw in all the violence, Bob?

BOB *I've mentioned the Scousers and throwing darts but that axeman in Wolverhampton was bloody frightening. If he'd hit anyone it would have killed them, but I only saw him threaten with it. Griff was different – he'd stick the knife up your arse given half a chance.*

JOE *You never went tooled up though.*

BOB *Not really. There were always stones, bricks, pieces of wood to use as a weapon.*

What's the worst then you've looked to do at a game?

BOB *Whatever was needed.*

Changing the subject, I hear the Cockney Reds are now charity fund-raisers. Is it true?

JOE *Who'd have thought it forty years ago? It's true. Bob talks in his story about what we did for Kilburn John's family, but we've had our own gatherings with families raising money for good causes. Up at Old Trafford we paid for a sign to be donated in memory of those who died at*

Munich and after we had won the Champions League in 1999, we clubbed together and bought a replica trophy, which we then took round to fêtes and whatnot. People could pay to have their photos taken with it, with all monies going to charity.

Is it true that when you go to games, even those in Europe, you occasionally don't even bother to watch?

JOE *It has been known, even if we have a ticket. Many did it for the Feyenoord game in Rotterdam, when they stayed in Amsterdam, perhaps watching the game on TV in a bar. Certainly we've done it over here, enjoying each other's company in a bar so much we can't be arsed about the game.*

I eventually left these 'veterans' of many a campaign to carry on reminiscing well into the evening. Although I am totally against what they did in the past, I could see what it had all meant to them. Violent and unacceptable it might have been to people like me, but it nonetheless created a camaraderie of the first order. I'll leave the last word to Status Quo Tony, who I first spoke to not long before this meeting.

TONY *I'm often asked about Bob from those who have admired him from as far back as the Seventies. I saw Bob as one of the few blokes that seemed to bridge that gap between the old Cockney Reds and those that came in the Eighties and later. I also saw Bob, The Ghost and others calling on the younger blokes for support – I suppose that's down to being less nimble on their feet! Bob is very much South London. Watching from the sidelines and avoiding trouble whenever possible, I saw the South London part of* *the Cockney Reds as the more violent and more clinical, with a fair dose of criminals amongst them. North London were noisier and more active but not perhaps with the same cutting edge as their peers from over the river. They will think differently, of course, but to me, Bob and his mates were the tops.*

ACKNOWLEDGEMENTS

Many have joined me on this journey as a Cockney Red from my teenage years and my first game at Arsenal's Highbury in 1965. We were inspired by Manchester United FC, with its traditions built from tragedy in 1958 and its massive support drawn from all quarters of the UK and even around the world. For my part I was South London and proud of it. From there my little firm sprung as a hard core of fanatical Reds sucked into violence, and not just a football.

At first we were few, including Snowy and The Ghost, but soon others joined us, not all from south of the Thames. They became *my* Cockney Reds in those early days that took us into the Seventies: Tooting Steve, St Albans Steve, Doris (who moved to Manchester), Pancho from Stoke, Frank De Silva, Mick the Con, Clarky, Sharpy, Choc, Clunk, Tony C, Dummy, LFM, Mick O'Farrell, Maverick, Mallet, Clive and a host more. These have all, in one way or another, contributed to our story. Later other South Londoners were to join us; hundreds in fact. Some who stood by my side were Joe, Big K, Cornish, Brian, the brothers Robert and Dougie, Micky W, Didi, Rob the Scaffolder, J Stander, Johnny Wynn, Micky K, Mick the Brick, Stoneleigh Mark, Matt, Phillip, and more recently Budgie. Many have form, and not just at football matches.

Also embraced as Cockney Reds were what I call the North Londoners, some equally as violent as us, others less so or not at all, but who were often present at the events described in the book. There have been the duo Wayne and JT, Hayes Bob, Steve the Greek, Kongus, Gurney, Ernie, Black Mick, Bealsy, and a whole mob from St Albans. East of London did not miss out either, from where Groomy, Paki Steve, Ads, Stevie B, East End Mick, Romford Steve emerged through the Seventies and Eighties. A mob from Northampton and Corby were also as tough as they come, with leading lights like Tank and Stutter Bomb. Later others came to join us in a time when the violence had lessened, like Fat Jack and Fulham John

Of course, we owe a debt to the Mancs, who often joined us to make a force of many hundreds, creating havoc wherever United played, home and abroad. Tony O'Neill was often at their head with Little Des, Crookie, Harry H, Dale, Grogan, Gordon, Pubby, Big Si, and of course the formidable early leader, Geoff Lewis. In more recent years we have been joined by those with stories to tell but not of violence, men like the Prof and others. To me they are legends all. Many have kindly contributed to this story and I am truly grateful for their help.

To put all this together into some sort of order I am thankful to our writer, Steve Little, for his patience and diligence in making sense of it, and to Peter Walsh and his team at Milo Books for taking us on the project that completes a missing part of modern hooligan history, that of the Cockney Reds.

Lastly, and sadly, we have lost a large number over the years. So RIP: Tank, Kilburn John, Roy Downes, Black Sam, Mick Barber, Johnny Payne, Manchester Coco, Gibbo, Teresa, Mary Parkinson, Michael O'Donald, Pat Munroe, and of course, the 'Flowers of Manchester'.

Banana Bob